AQA Humanities

Keith Davison

Alan Marchant

Philippa Woodyatt

Nelson Thornes

Published in 2009 by:
Nelson Thornes Ltd
Delta Place
27 Bath Road
CHELTENHAM
GL53 7TH
United Kingdom

13 14 15 16 / 10 9 8 7 6 5 4 3

A catalogue record for this book is available from the British Library

ISBN 978 1 4085 0304 1

Cover photograph by Jupiter Images

Illustrations by Pantek Arts, Oxford Designers and Illustrators and Zanzara Illustration

Page make-up by Pantek Arts, Maidstone

Printed in China by 1010 Printing International Ltd

Contents

Nelson Thornes has worked hard to make sure this book offers you excellent support for your GCSE course.

▇ How to use this book

Learning Objectives

At the beginning of each section or topic you'll find a list of Learning Objectives based on the requirements of the specification, so you can make sure you are covering what you need to know.

Objectives

Objectives

Objectives

Objectives

First objective.

Second objective.

Study Tips

Don't forget to look at the Study tips throughout the book to help you with your study and prepare for your exam.

Study tip

Don't forget to look at the Study Tips throughout the book to help you with your study and prepare for your exam.

Practice Questions

These offer opportunities to practise questions in the style that you may encounter in your exam so that you can be prepared on the day.

Practice questions are reproduced by permission of the Assessment and Qualifications Alliance.

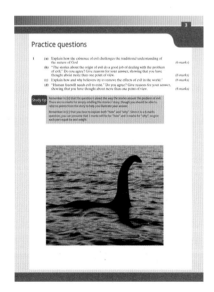

Visit **www.nelsonthornes.com** for more information.

GCSE Humanities

What is Humanities?

Humanities is about what has happened and is happening in the world – the challenges people face in their daily lives. For some, life is about survival from poverty. For others, life involves fighting for their beliefs, perhaps for their freedom. In many countries, people still suffer from prejudice and persecution. Even in developed countries such as Britain, there are many differences in the way people think and live, at home and in the workplace.

Humanities is a subject which makes connections and blends together subjects such as history, geography, religious studies, citizenship, environmental science and the social sciences. By doing this, humanities becomes much more than the sum of its parts.

As a student of humanities, you will be encouraged to be critical and make informed judgements. You will explore issues that really matter and will learn there is not always a right or wrong answer. You will be able to use your direct experience of the world around you and you will extend your knowledge in personal, national or global contexts.

AQA Humanities

The AQA GCSE Humanities course is a challenging programme of study about exciting, relevant issues where you interrogate sources and investigate different viewpoints.

The course focuses on important issues. Depending on which options you follow, you could find yourself learning about such diverse topics as global warming, youth gangs, euthanasia, the war in Iraq and apartheid in South Africa. Some issues affect individuals and communities, others are of national or international concern. Case studies have been included in this book which your teacher may choose to use, or you may investigate other case studies which allow you to go into detail about the topic or issue.

As a student, you will be encouraged to be critical, arguing your own viewpoint and make informed judgements. You will learn to reflect and ask yourself what you would do if faced with the same issue. By considering the rights and responsibilities you have and the contribution you can make to the world, it will help you to become a more knowledgeable and active citizen.

The specification

Content

The course has a Core Unit 1 consisting of Culture and Beliefs and Environmental Issues. The kinds of topics and issues you will investigate include:

- Why do cultures differ and change?
- Is our behaviour a result of genetics or how we have been bought up?
- What are the challenges we face living in a multi-cultural society?
- What are the different arguments for or against the death penalty?
- What are the causes of pollution?
- What is the evidence for climate change?

Unit 2 has five options: Conflict and Co-operation, Prejudice and Persecution, Global Inequality, Family and Socialisation and People and Work. You will study two of these. The kinds of topics and issues you may explore include:

- How could the holocaust happen?
- What can be done about child labour in developing countries?
- What can be done to reduce global inequality?
- How is the role of the family changing?
- What are the causes and consequences of terrorism?
- How has information technology changed working lives?

Assessment

There is an exam for the Core Unit and one for the options which make up Unit 2. Before your written exams, your school or college will receive a sources booklet that you will study with your teacher before the examination. You will be asked questions about these sources in your examination. Questions are made up of a set of sub-questions each requiring a response. Some questions will ask you to use your own case studies to help answer the question.

Chapter 8 in this book gives you guidance on how to approach various types of exam questions. There is also a question at the end of each of chapters 1 to 7 which you can try answering to help prepare you for your exam.

Unit 3 is a Humanities Investigation or Controlled Assessment Task. This is an extended piece of writing of approximately 2000 words about one of seven tasks. The seven tasks are related to each of the seven topics of study. The coursework will be written up under controlled conditions at your school or college, with teacher supervision. The tasks change each year. Some exemplar tasks are:

- Investigate whether religion is in decline in the UK.
- Investigate the experience of one group of immigrants to the UK or the US.
- Choose an international conflict and investigate what caused it.
- Investigate whether tourism is a cost or a benefit to the environment.

Features in this book

This book contains many features to help you learn and revise effectively.

Objectives

You will find these in the margin at the beginning of each topic within a chapter. They are based on the requirements of the specification.

Check your understanding

You will find these questions at the end of each topic within a chapter. When you answer these questions you will immediately find out whether you have understood and can remember what you have read.

Activities

These occur on most pages and are aimed at helping you to learn actively. Many of them refer to textual and visual sources so they help you to develop your analytical skills.

Going further

Many of these activities encourage you to carry out further research on the topic, either in the classroom or at home. In some cases, suggestions are made about websites to use. These research activities will help to broaden your knowledge of the topic and develop useful examples to use when answering exam questions.

Did you know

These provide short sharp snippets of information.

Links

If there is relevant information in a different part of the book you will find a link to it in the margin.

Study tips

The Study tips throughout the book will give you useful insights for making the most of this course.

Practice questions

Guidance as well as practice questions are included at the end of every chapter. Try answering these so you are fully prepared.

1 Culture and beliefs

1.1   What is culture?

Culture is the whole way of life of a community or social group. Look at the case study of the Plains Indians of North America 150 years ago.

Objectives

You will be able to:

understand that there are common and contrasting aspects of culture

explain the similarities and differences between simple and complex cultures

explain the similarities and differences between the culture of two European countries.

Case study

Plains Indians of North America

A   *Native American village*

The Great Plains area of America was inhabited by 31 Native American Indian tribes each with its own name, culture and language. Most lived in small bands and worked closely together. There were few laws as the bad opinion of the tribe was punishment enough. The safety of the whole tribe was more important than individuals. The very old were left to starve if food was short. Each tribe was different and independent from each other. They all however had a great deal in common. They hunted buffalo for their food. They made their dwellings (tepees) of poles and skin and usually set them up in a camp circle.

B   *Native American hunt*

They made clothes from buffalo and deer hides and used the hides for other purpose as well. They created geometric works of art. They organised men into warrior clubs, where they earned prestige through their fighting skills. They practised the sun dance linked to their religious **beliefs**. They worshipped the Great Spirit and believed the land belonged to them all. Plants and animals were as important as people. They had ritual dances each year which they hoped would bring back the buffalo in spring. These ways of behaving constituted Plains Indian culture.

Activity

1 Read the case study and look at Source C. Find an example of the Indians' **values**, the importance of **norms**, their beliefs, and a **tradition**. What was their attitude to animals?

The spider diagram in Source **C** and the definitions in the key terms box in the margin show the many different aspects that make up a culture.

Cultures change and progress, benefiting from what previous generations have discovered. Through the education system, the family and the media, knowledge is passed on and the culture evolves. Each generation adds a little to the culture and loses a little from it. These aspects will be studied over the rest of the chapter.

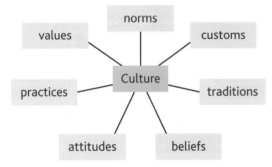

C

Activities

2 Think about your own culture. Try to write a very short description about it using the headings in Source **C**. Make a list of the difficulties you meet when trying to do this task. Don't worry – by the end of this chapter you will find it much easier to do!

3 Can you think of any aspects of your culture that have been lost or are in decline? For example, is maypole dancing still a strong **custom** in some parts of the country? Do people still maintain the tradition of sending birthday cards or is it birthday texts now?

Going further

1 Find out more about the Plains Indians at:

whitewolve.com/native_americans/indexblok.plains.htm and www.answers.com/topic/plains-indian

Key terms

Culture: a shared set of beliefs, values, attitudes, norms, customs, traditions and practices.

Beliefs: a set of ideas about the world that form the basis of a religion or other way of making sense of life.

Values: what a person feels to be important to them. Values are usually shared among members of a culture.

Norms: unwritten rules defining the appropriate pattern of behaviour.

Traditions: the handing down from generation to generation of customs and beliefs.

Attitudes: positive or negative feelings towards objects or people.

Practices: the way culture, beliefs, values and so on are put into action, for example a person with religious beliefs may regularly go to a place of worship.

Customs: the long-established habits of a society.

Study tip

Know your definition of culture well. Remember the key elements of culture: norms, beliefs, customs, traditions, values, **attitudes** and **practices**. These can help you if you are describing cultural differences and similarities.

How is order maintained in a culture?

Social norms

Norms are what is acceptable within a culture. Norms of dress can be very different between cultures, and can change over time. For example, it was unacceptable for women in the UK to show their legs in Victorian times. One hundred years later, in the 1960s, many younger women wore miniskirts. Today on specially selected beaches nudity is acceptable.

D *Social norms can differ widely*

Activity

4 Think about the language people use today. Which words are acceptable and which are not?

Are there words you can think of which are acceptable nowadays but which your parents or grandparents would not have been allowed to use?

Group activities

1 Working with a partner, make a list of as many social norms as you can think of. Decide which are the most serious ones to break. Compare your lists with others.

2 Can you think of any other law that has come into force in a similar way to the one in Source E?

Activity

5 Can you think of groups of people whom society 'labels' as deviant, although their behaviour may not be criminal? Would you categorise children who play truant from school as deviants?

Anything goes. 1980–2000	Some groups of people disagree	Many groups of people disagree	Pressure to create a law limiting such behaviour. In 2003 it becomes illegal to use a phone while driving
Mobile phones are new. A few accidents caused by use of phone because of driver inattention	Public hear about accidents caused by using mobile phone while driving. Hands free kits appear	Research indicates dangers of using phone and 'texting' while driving A number of deaths. Campaign to make use illegal while driving (police, judges, victim's families)	Continued law breaking leads to heavier penalties. By 2008 the same punishment as dangerous driving

E *From a norm to a law: the use of a mobile phone while driving*

  Dangerous driving

People who do not conform to the norms of their culture may be called social deviants. Their behaviour is not criminal, that is, it does not break the law but it is unacceptable because it breaks social norms.

Laws

When an individual breaks social norms, the sanctions may be formal. The UK has criminal and civil laws. The laws are either created by parliament and written down (Acts of Parliament) or they are the result of what has appeared to be just and fair over many generations, that is common law. Common law forms the basis of the modern legal system in the UK. The formal agencies of social control are the government, the judiciary (criminal and civil courts), the penal system (probation, prison, etc.), law enforcement (the police) and the army (a force of last resort to maintain social order).

Morals

Morals provide informal guidance on what is right or wrong. The religions that people follow in the UK all offer guidance on morality and how lives should be led and this becomes generalised guidance in the culture, even to those who are not religious.

Values

Values identify what an individual considers important. Different cultures have different values that are shared by their members. Western societies tend to value individual achievement and the acquisition of material possessions. Plains Indian tribes were very much a 'collective', the group coming before individual success.

> ### Group activity
>
> 4 The sanctity of human life is a value held strongly in the UK. The fact that there is no death penalty fits with this value. However, opinion polls indicate the general public would like to see it return. Hold a class debate about whether the death penalty should be given for very serious crimes or whether this would contradict an important cultural value.

> ### Going further
>
> **2** Find out what law and order in the UK was like in the past:
>
> - Search Today's Citizens, Past Lives at Beverly www.mylearning.org
> - Search Anglo-Saxon law and order page 5 www.bbc.co.uk
> - www.schoolhistory.co.uk/ gcselinks/crimepunishment/ resources/punishment.pdf
>
> ### Going further
>
> **3** To find out about the morality and values of society in southern Italy and Sicily which enabled the Cosa Nostra (mafia) to take hold visit
>
> da_wizeguy.tripod.com/ omerta/

> ### Group activity
>
> **3** Think about your own morals and values. Answer the following questions true or false. Then share your answers with others in your group.
>
> a Parents are right to smack naughty children.
>
> b Lying is always wrong.
>
> c Earning lots of money is the most important thing in life.
>
> d A husband or wife should never cheat on each other.
>
> e Old people should be cared for by their family.

> ### Key terms
>
> **Morals:** provide guidance on what is right and wrong.

> ### Study tip
>
> When revising, ensure you can provide examples of norms, deviance, values and morals.

Why do cultures have belief systems?

The earliest **religion** known to man is shamanism. It was not an organised religion but a set of practices and beliefs which spread across the Asian continent more than 20,000 years ago. The evidence for its existence comes from cave paintings. The shaman was a man who would enter into a trance to communicate with the spirit world. As with today's religions, in shamanism there were two worlds – 'this world' and another 'spirit world'.

Why did these early religions come into existence?

From studies of simple societies across the world it would appear that religions are likely to have been a response to the problems humans encounter. These problems include bad weather, disease, shortage of food and fear that the sun may not return. Explanations were also sought for the mysteries of the physical world such as: How was the world created? How did life begin? Is there a greater power that makes the world work?

G   *A shaman*

Religions and beliefs

A religion is a system of beliefs about life and death and the mysteries of the physical and spiritual worlds. Beliefs are the foundation of any religion and they differ between religions. Sometimes people within the same religion hold slightly different beliefs.

Key terms

Religion: a system of beliefs about life and death and the mysteries of the physical and spiritual worlds, usually involving the idea of a supreme being.

Ritual: an event that expresses some religious meaning.

Rites of passage: a ceremony or event that marks an important stage in a person's life.

Facts about world religions

	Christianity	Islam	Judaism	Sikhism
Leader/founder	Jesus	Muhammad	Abraham	Guru Nanak
Supreme being	God	Allah	Yahweh	Reheguru
No. of followers	2 billion	1.25 billion	13 million	23 million
Place of origin	Palestine/Israel	Saudi Arabia	Palestine/Israel	Punjab
Religion began	30 CE	600 CE	2000 BCE	1500 CE
Sacred writings	Bible	Qur'an	Tenakh	Guru Granth Sahib
Place of worship	Church	Mosque	Synagogue	Gurdwara

H

The functions of religions

Today's religions in developed societies provide a number of functions.

- provides an identity
- individual help in times of crisis
- group cohesion
- role in charity and voluntary work
- functions of religion
- role in conflict creation
- control stress & tension
- maintain behaviour

I

Activity

6   Redraw the spider diagram in Source I. Then attach the correct example to each of the branches.

- Clear guidance on moral issues
- Praying together
- Missionary work after a disaster
- Religious wars
- Help coping with the death of someone
- Calm and the promise of better times
- An involvement that provides an identity

Beliefs and rituals

Ceremonies and **rituals** came into existence to please 'a great power' and to celebrate the disappearance of problems. As religions developed, certain key events for individuals and their families came to be celebrated, for example birth, coming of age (transfer to adulthood), marriage unions, and death. Such ceremonies and rituals are still with us and are sometimes referred to as the **rites of passage**.

Jewish rites of passage

Jewish male babies are circumcised and given a special Hebrew name at a ceremony a few weeks after circumcision. Bar Mitzvah is a coming of age celebration for boys at 13. The boy reads from the Torah in Hebrew (see Source **J**). Girls come of age at the Bat Mitzvah at 12. Jews are expected to marry Jews. Weddings are conducted by a rabbi (a Jewish priest) in the synagogue. Jewish sacred books say little about life after death. Religion is primarily involved with living your life. They believe people should be buried, not cremated, as soon as possible after death.

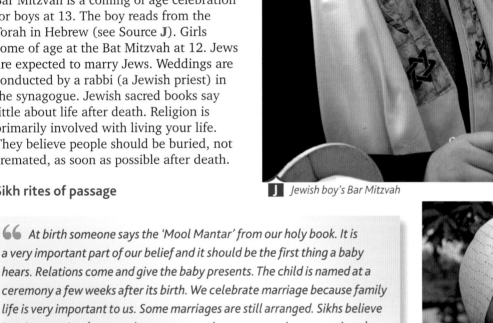

J   *Jewish boy's Bar Mitzvah*

Sikh rites of passage

66 *At birth someone says the 'Mool Mantar' from our holy book. It is a very important part of our belief and it should be the first thing a baby hears. Relations come and give the baby presents. The child is named at a ceremony a few weeks after its birth. We celebrate marriage because family life is very important to us. Some marriages are still arranged. Sikhs believe in reincarnation (your soul moves to another person and you are reborn). You do not die – it is just like going to sleep. We cremate our dead and no headstones or plaques remember them because they return.* 99

K   *Sikh man*

Activity

7   Compare Christian rites or Muslim rites of passage with those in Sources J and K. Point out the similarities and differences.

Going further

4   Find out about religion today at
www.guardian.co.uk/uk/2006/dec/23/religion.topstories3

A contrasting culture

Bushmen

The Bushmen (sometimes now called the 'San') are the oldest inhabitants of Southern Africa and one of the oldest cultures in the world. They have been in existence there for at least 20,000 years. The map shows the location of the Kalahari Desert which is their homeland.

The lifestyle of the Bushmen is a simple one. Knowing about a simple rather than developed society will help you understand the basic elements of a culture. The Bushmen are a **primitive tribe** of nomadic hunter gatherers who live in small bands but with kinship (family) links to other groups which creates a unity among them. There is a clear division of labour in the family with men hunting mainly antelope with poisoned arrows and women gathering fruits, nuts and roots. The traditional nomadic (wandering) existence means they rely on temporary homes.

L *Map of Southern Africa*

Each of the groups has a chief but he has limited powers and, because the group is small, it can meet as a whole to make decisions. Men and women have different responsibilities and their own expertise but are broadly equal and both sexes are involved in decision-making. Children spend most of their time playing in a mixed-gender group. There is no formal education. The children learn by 'doing' the survival skills taught by their parents. A boy becomes an adult when he kills his first antelope. Leisure time is spent in talking, playing music and dancing around the central campfire.

For many thousands of years, the Bushmen have given each other gifts on a regular basis rather than trading using money. A gift economy relies on goodwill. If you receive a gift, you feel obliged to give the person one in return.

Bushmen believe in a supreme being called Kaang. They believe that they used to live underground with the animals until Kaang brought them all above ground and that is how life for them began. Shamans are at the centre of the Bushman's religion. The shaman enters into a trance to communicate with the spirits to ask for their help. The people engage in dancing which they believe releases healing energy and use different dances for different problems. When they are happy, they do their traditional 'dance of the giraffe'.

This account of the Bushmen's lifestyle is now true only for about 3,000 people split into 25 groups. Around 1000 CE another tribe, the Bantu, invaded the Bushman's territory pushing them into less hospitable areas such as the Kalahari Desert. Later, as the white man began to explore and **colonise** Africa, they suffered even worse treatment, which some people have seen as genocide. From a population of several million, there are today only 100,000. Most have been forced onto settlements, their hunting and gathering lifestyle replaced by crop agriculture and raising livestock.

M *Bushmen setting a trap*

Group activity

5   Working with a partner, find the place in the description of the Bushmen where each of the following is described:

a   the social norms of the group
b   the roles of men and women
c   the place of children
d   their beliefs
e   their customs and traditions
f   their values and attitudes.

⚭links

Also see Topic 4.3 for information on Australian resettlement.

The current situation

The central Kalahari Game Reserve was founded in 1961. The Botswana Government argued that the Bushmen's lifestyle was not compatible with preserving wildlife resources there. They said it was therefore sensible to relocate them (many went) and help them to learn to grow crops and raise livestock.

The Bushmen and their supporters like Survival International argue that this is a cover story for the Government's desire to develop tourism and diamond mining on the Reserve land. The Bushmen say they want to preserve animals and would not overhunt the Reserve.

In 2006 the Bushmen won a partial victory in the long-running court case over access to the Reserve land. The court decided that Bushmen 'had been forcibly and wrongly deprived of their possessions and that they should be allowed special hunting licences for the Reserve'. What they did not win was the battle to access water there.

Key terms

Primitive tribe: one with a simple culture that has survived for a very long time. It is likely to be characterised by a hunting and gathering existence.

Colonisation: when one country goes to another country and takes over important aspects of its culture.

Did you know ❓❓❓❓❓❓

The Bushmen are not the only simple culture in the world. There is a charity called Survival International which tries to support simple societies. Its website monitors the monthly progress and problems of 11 different groups similar to the Bushmen.

Study tip

You may be given an example in the Sources Booklet of a different simple/primitive culture to the Bushmen. You will have to take your examples from that society rather than the Bushmen. Use the activity above to help you analyse the culture in the Sources Booklet.

 Diamond industry protest

Group activity

6   Discuss whether you think there is any place for the Bushmen's simple lifestyle in today's world. Is it time for them to move on?

A contrasting culture

Spain

Spain, is a member of the European Union, as is the UK, and is only a couple of hours away by plane. It is one of the favourite destinations for holiday makers and more than one million UK citizens now live there. A short holiday visit, however, will only give you a glimpse of the distinctiveness of its culture.

Spain covers a much greater area than the UK but has a smaller population at 40 million. It has a monarchy and a democratic government like Britain. Roman Catholicism is the main religion in Spain whereas in the UK it is the Church of England which is Protestant. Spain and Britain both had empires in the past, ruling countries and taking them their language.

Both countries have been subject to various invasions and subsequent settlements that have left a heritage of internal divisions in each country. The people in the northern part of Spain (Basque area) have a different cultural heritage to those in southern Spain. Some of the Basques want self-government. In Britain there are now separate government assemblies for Scotland, Wales and Northern Ireland.

O *Flamenco*

P *Bullfighting*

Q *Spain and surrounding countries*

Folk traditions

Spain's main folk traditions include Flamenco and bullfighting. Flamenco is a popular musical tradition in the south of one country in Andalusia province. It involves three elements: song, dance and guitar playing. Bullfights are found throughout the country each year the "Running of Bulls" event in Pamplona makes the Europen news as the bulls run wild through the streets and have an opportunity to get their own back. Bullfights are a blood sport as was, the now outlawed, fox-hunting in the UK.

Hi Jayne,

I'm having a wonderful time with Maria. Her family is very friendly. Her grandmother and older brother live with them. They live in a villa outside Granada in southern Spain (but they haven't got a pool!). The family are Roman Catholic and grace is spoken at each mealtime and there are religious pictures everywhere. Maria says that many of her friends at school are not so religious. Her school sounds like ours but they have longer summer holidays and start earlier in the morning. After 16 they get jobs or do something called the baccalaureate. Most nights, at about 9.30 pm, the whole family walk into the village centre and go to a bar. It seems going out and being seen as part of the community is important. The men and women tend to split up and talk among themselves and then we return to the villa about an hour later and watch TV which is just like at home except in Spanish! Her dad Fernando works in Granada and is a business man. He is taking us to see a Spanish castle tomorrow. He seems very much in charge. I asked Maria if men and women were equal in Spain and she said they were but the men tend to leave the responsibility of the home to the women. I certainly haven't seen her dad in the kitchen cooking or cleaning the floor!

By the way you were wrong about the food. Spanish omelettes are really good and even the paella we had on Sunday was okay. On Sunday after Church we are going to see a bullfight. Next week there is a festival for some saint and we will go to the coast where we will meet another part of the family. That will mean another round of kissing and hugging. Maria says they have a lot of festivals and it means time off school and she says they are fun. It's so laid back here and hot!

See you soon

Lisa

Spanish invaders

These invasions and the settlements that followed covered many different parts of Spain. They have left a varied cultural and architectural legacy.

35,000 BCE	Iberians
1100 BCE	Phoenicians
600 BCE	Celts
228 BCE	Carthaginians
74 CE	Romans
409 CE	Visigoths
711 CE	Arabs and Berbers
1212 CE	Christians

Activity

8 Make a list of similarities and differences about the cultures of Spain and the UK.

Did you know ??????

- In Spain, children cannot be written out of a will.
- The age of consent is 13, the lowest in the EU.
- The male/female ratio for who does the housework ratio is 1 to 11.
- In 2004, half the cabinet of the Government were women.
- The Muslim religion was the religion of Spain for 400 years.
- The Spanish Inquisition tried to ensure the Roman Catholic religion was supreme.
- Spain was one of the first countries in Europe to sanction same sex marriage.
- In Spanish hospitals there is a chair by each bed which is expected to be occupied 24 hours a day by a relative as a 'no cost nurse'.

Going further

5 Find out about the weather in Spain at

gospain.about.com/od/
spanishclimate/ss/weather.htm

It may surprise you.

Find out about the Spanish Civil War at

www.users.dircon.co.uk/
~warden.scw/scwindex.htm

Subcultures

Within a culture there can be subdivisions. These are called **subcultures**. A subculture has many similarities to the dominant culture but there are also important differences. The subculture may be focused around certain activities, values, beliefs or material objects which significantly differ from the main culture. This was true of 1960s hippy culture in the US. The hippies had some different values and ideas from mainstream American culture, including believing that the use of drugs was acceptable. In other ways they shared much of the main culture.

Key terms

Subculture: a culture that exists within the dominant culture and has many similarities to the dominant culture, but also significant differences.

Case study

Gang subculture in Glasgow

For gangs in certain parts of the city of Glasgow, violence is a matter of conforming to the norms of their subculture. The young people 'hang out' in their territory, have an established folklore, and a set of values which is different from the mainstream culture. The street is their world. Their identity involves being a member of the local gang.

Gang warfare is virtually a tradition – it can be traced back for almost 100 years and for 50 years serious violence at weekends in particular has come to be considered normal. At first there was a religious element but today gangs fight over territory with named gangs being present on most housing estates. 50 years ago the gangs mainly consisted of 18 to 30 year olds, now they are 10 to 18 year olds. Gang members carry cleavers, hatchets, pickaxes and knives. Many fights are now organised using the internet. The focus is not on street crime but recreational violence. The aggression is fuelled by illegal drugs and alcohol.

R   *Members of a gang*

Many say they feel safer in a gang. Once inside the gang they follow the gang's rules. Young people may go to schools in different neighbourhoods and play together in the same school football team and share an identity with the school but when they return home it is only their territory that counts.

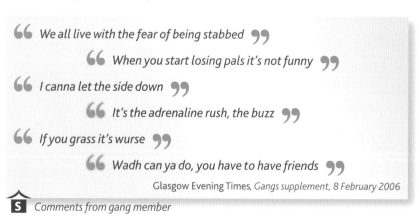

66 *We all live with the fear of being stabbed* 99

66 *When you start losing pals it's not funny* 99

66 *I canna let the side down* 99

66 *It's the adrenaline rush, the buzz* 99

66 *If you grass it's wurse* 99

66 *Wadh can ya do, you have to have friends* 99

Glasgow Evening Times, *Gangs supplement, 8 February 2006*

S   *Comments from gang member*

There have been many attempts to solve the problem. Operation Reclaim is an attempt to provide the boys with activities – free swimming, 5-a-side football and youth facilities. The stumbling block remains on which gang's territory the activities take place. Operation Blade was a knife amnesty and led to 4,500 weapons being surrendered but a couple of years later little has changed. It's not just the boys either:

 Girl gang member

 When the boys are fighting we go down to watch. Sometimes we start fighting ourselves. If the boys are fighting, we'll throw bricks and bottles. Girls rarely carry knives unless the boys want them to carry them so the polis don't find them. 99

Glasgow Evening Times, *Gangs supplement, 8 February 2006*

U *Comments from a girl gang member*

Activities

9 Read the case study and look at the sources. Write down the main reasons that these young people want to be in gangs.

10 Identify two values that they hold to be important.

11 Identify two ways in which this gang culture differs from mainstream culture in Britain.

Group activity

7 Is it bad kids who are drawn to gangs or gangs that create bad kids? Discuss.

Going further

6 In the 1950s there was a period of 'gang panic' in the press. Teddy boys went around with knuckle-dusters, flick knives and some with guns. Eventually the spate of gang fighting settled down. Find out more about the teddy boy gangs. Ask yourself if they formed a subculture like the Glasgow gangs.

■ Watch a video clip on Glasgow gangs at:
current.com/items/88245211_deadly_glasgow_teens

■ Read more about Glasgow gangs at:
www.gangland.net/glasgow.htm

Check your understanding

1 Define 'culture'.

2 What headings would you use to investigate the similarities and differences between cultures?

3 Make a list of some of the differences between a simple society such as the Bushmen and a complex society such as your own.

4 Make a list of five similarities and five differences between the culture in Spain and that in the UK.

What is socialisation?

Primary **socialisation** is the first stage of socialisation when a child learns to eat, walk and talk, and interact with their parents and other family members. These people who influence the child's early perceptions are called **significant others**. As the child becomes older, they compare themselves with these others. They act as a frame of reference in shaping behaviour – children will model some of their behaviour on them. They are their **role models**.

A   *A father reads to his son*

B   *A mother and daughter knitting*

The family is the main agency of socialisation but it does not work alone. There are other agents that combine with the family in the process. In simple societies, the family educates individuals in the skills needed for survival but in complex societies there are schools and other educational institutions.

Secondary socialisation is a stage that now starts earlier as increasingly children find themselves in the care of others at play school or nursery school. They learn to interact with other children before the start of formal education in primary school.

C   *Children at nursery school*

Objectives

You will be able to:

explain the process of cultural transmission from one generation to another

understand that there are a wide variety of factors that influence an individual's culture and identity

explain the process of identity formation

explain the contrasting evidence in the nature and nurture debate.

Key terms

Socialisation: the process by which a child learns the ways of its culture. It can be seen as a process of stages.

Significant other: a person who is of great importance to you in your life.

Role model: someone whom you use as a reference point for your behaviour. You want to be like them.

Peer group: people of the same age who associate regularly.

⚭ links

Also see Topic 6.2 for information on the socialisation function.

Activity

1.   Which members of your family had the most influence on you at the primary socialisation stage of your life? Did anyone outside of your family influence you significantly?

Schools have a formal curriculum to ensure certain things are learned. The content of the curriculum is approved by the government. In secondary schools, citizenship is a new subject which schools are expected to teach. There is also a hidden curriculum where norms and values are transmitted via other aspects of school life.

D   *Girls cooking at school*

At school and in your leisure time you are also influenced by your peer group. **Peer groups** are people of the same age as yourself with whom you associate regularly. To remain a member of the group you are expected to conform – another skill expected of you in a work group. The actual norms of your school peer group are, however, unlikely to be the same as those at work! When you go to work you will join another group of peers, this time linked with the common purpose of work.

E   *Children playing hopscotch*

4 a   Do you agree with the government about the curriculum? What do you think you should be taught and why?

   b   What skills do you learn by being a member of a school team?

   c   What do you learn by wearing a uniform?

   d   What do you learn in preparation for work by following a school timetable?

Activity

2   Look at Sources **A** and **B**.

a   Fathers do not read to their children as much as mothers. Boys do less well in English and read less. Explain how these two patterns of behaviour could be linked.

b   What aspect of socialisation is taking place in Source **B**?

⚭ links

See Topic 1.1 for the Bushmen case study.

Activity

3   Look back at the Bushmen case study. What are the main agencies of socialisation for their children?

Discussion activity

1   Some research says that the home, which is a real-life environment, presents a child with more challenges than a nursery school. Debate your views in a small group.

Study tip

Do *not* define socialisation as mixing with others, for example socialising at a weekend. This is not socialisation. Use the definition in the key terms box.

Activity

5   a   Sources **B** and **D** are from the 1950s. What do these photographs tell you about the socialisation of girls in the 1950s?

   b   In Source **E** you see children playing in the street with their peers. Have things changed?

Other agencies of socialisation

Religion

Religious groups have norms and values that may influence your behaviour. Religion used to play a greater part in young people's lives in the 19th century when there was no formal education. The only schooling many children received was at Sunday school. By making this provision, churches gained new members. Children learned to read by reading extracts from the Bible. Moral guidance was also provided. When schools first opened for the children of ordinary families many were Church schools. Today there are few Sunday schools but there are still Church youth clubs. The increasing weakness of the Christian Church in the UK means that it now has less ability as an agency to mould the ideas of young people. However other ethnic groups often have religion more strongly integrated into their daily life.

> 66 'An estimated 100,000 school-age Muslim children attend religious classes held at mosques in Britain daily, generally after regular school hours', said Jane Houghton, a spokeswoman for the Department of Communities and Local Government. 'The impact this teaching could have is quite considerable', she said. 99

Going further

1 To read about a Muslim religious school visit:
news.bbc.co.uk/cbbcnews/ hi/newsid_4730000/ newsid_4735400/4735449.stm

The mass media

The mass media, especially television and the press, help us make sense of what is happening in the world and influence our attitudes. However, some people would argue that the values and attitudes which it puts forward are creating a culture which is obsessed by money and fame rather than less selfish values and beliefs.

X Factor generation
Talent shop feeds belief in instant success to replace hard work and Christian values, says schools leader

NO RESPECT
Five years of citizenship lessons have bred a generation of 16-year-olds with even less time for authority than before

The media contribute to the behaviour of children in other ways:

- Children may imitate the behaviour of people they see on television. Their new role models may not always be positive ones.
- Children see many acts of violence on television. They may lose their sensitivity to upsetting ideas and images as they see more of them.

■ Children may still see women continuing to be portrayed in the media in a limited number of roles in comparison to men.

Children now spend hours surfing the internet and communicating with each other. This means that the web is now an agency of socialisation under the banner of the mass media.

Activity

6 **a** In pairs consider each of the bullet points about the influence of the media on the behaviour of children. How might they influence the socialisation of the child?

b Think of some soap opera characters and create a list of names. Then put alongside each character your view as to whether their image is positive or negative. What conclusions did you come to?

Resocialisation

Socialisation is a life-long process. When you change jobs, enter a new phase of life (such as being a parent) or when you retire, you encounter new social situations and need to **resocialise** to adapt to them. People who go to a residential care home very late on in their life have to learn its routines and ways.

Activity

7 You may have changed schools or had a week of work experience. What did it feel like the first time you went there?

What norms and rules did you have to learn?

Mechanisms of social control

To make the socialisation process work, there are **social control mechanisms** that make us conform to certain standards of behaviour. They involve rewards and punishments.

Activity

8 Copy and complete the table below.

Individual	rewards	punishments
Child at home	smiles ⟷ presents	
School child	stars ⟷ prize	
Worker	pay rise ⟷ promotion	

Choose from suspension, dismissal, official warning, frown, sent to bed, detention

Use ⟷ to distinguish between low level punishment and high level.

Going further

2 Split into two groups and hold a debate. The motion is: 'The family and other socialisation agencies do not work together effectively to bring up children.' One group must find evidence to agree with this statement and the other group must find evidence to disagree.

Study tip

To revise this topic, make lists of what each agency does for you. Use the following headings: family, education system, religion, peer group, mass media.

Socialisation in Nazi Germany

Hitler wanted to change and control the upbringing of children in Nazi Germany. He did this with his Hitler Youth programme and with a policy of **indoctrination** in schools. His aim was to create a new German nation, a unified community based on blood and race, sharing the same norms and values.

Schools

Periods	Monday	Tuesday	Wednesday	Thursday	Friday	Saturday
8:00–8:45	German	German	German	German	German	German
8:50–9:35	Geography	History	Singing	Geography	History	Singing
9:40–10:25	Race study	Race study	Race study	Ideology	Ideology	Ideology
10:25–11:00	Break, with sports and special anouncements					
11:00–12:05	Domestic science with maths	Domestic science with maths	Domestic science with maths	Domestic science with maths	Domestic science with maths	Domestic science with maths
12:10–12:55	Eugenics	Health Biology	Eugenics	Health Biology	Eugenics	Health Biology
14:00–16:00	Sport and PE					

H *A typical Nazi school timetable*

The Nazi Party monitored what was taught in schools very closely as they thought it was extremely important. These German children would be Germany's future and they must be taught the correct values according to the Nazi ideals.

Most teachers were happy to teach this curriculum. By 1936, 97 per cent of teachers were members of the Nationalist Socialist Teachers' Association. The Nazis thought character-building and physical education were more important than knowledge and intellect. They believed the purpose of education was to make children realise the importance of discipline, duty, courage and serving the German nation.

> 66 *The weak must be chiselled away. I want young men and women who can suffer pain. A young German must be as swift as a greyhound, as tough as leather, and as hard as steel.* 99
>
> *Hitler, 1939*

Books which were seen as unsuitable for children to read were taken from the schools and sometimes burned. School history books were altered to promote the Nazis. Biology and **eugenics** were taught to fit Hitler's ideas of a 'Master race' where Jews were racially 'inferior'. Physical education was extremely important as the Nazis wanted the young men to be fit so they would be good soldiers and win battles for Germany in their quest to become a 'great nation' again.

> 66 *Sport means we will have men fit enough for the army.* 99
>
> *From a newspaper for German teachers, 1938*

Youth groups

The youth groups which were set up by the Nazi Party had a great impact. There were separate groups for boys and girls and they were moulded for their roles in society. Boys were taught many physical skills and military activities and were encouraged to be strong fighters. The girls, in contrast, were prepared for domestic tasks such as cooking and cleaning and their future role as mothers. There was a great emphasis on teamwork in these groups. By 1938 most of the young Germans were members of the Hitler Youth.

K *Camp life for boys in the Hitler Youth*

L *Children saluting Hitler*

Activity

9 Using the text and Sources H, I and J, list the subjects that were taught in Nazi schools. Then write down beside each subject as many reasons as you can why the Nazis thought they were important.

Is there anything in your timetable that you feel is there to enforce discipline rather than knowledge?

Key terms

Indoctrination: when someone attempts to make you accept certain facts and ideas without question.

Eugenics: the study of ways to improve human inheritance.

Activity

10 a What is happening in Source K? Explain how the tents would help to create a unified community.

b What does Source L tell you about childhood in Nazi Germany? Why do you think the photo was taken?

Going further

3 Find more information on the Hitler Youth at:

www.ngfl-cymru.org.uk/vtc/ ngfl/history/hitler_youth/ index.html

What is identity?

M

When you are born, the process of **identity-giving** begins immediately, although you are too young to know what is happening. A tag with your surname on is attached to your wrist or leg if you are born in hospital. Soon you will be given a first name and these facts will be registered on your birth certificate. People many years later may want to see it to establish your identity. In no time at all your clothes will show others your **gender identity**, whether you are a boy or a girl, and relatives will purchase gifts accordingly. Your **ethnic group** will be evident from your facial features or your colour. Where you are born gives you your national identity.

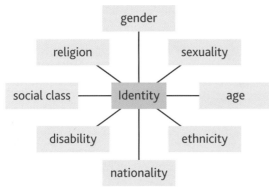

N *The components of identity*

This process of developing your identity continues through the socialisation process. As you grow older you have a choice of who to identify with, and this forms your **social identity**. Perhaps there is someone you admire or a group you would like to join.

O *Football fans*

Key terms

Identity-giving: an act or process that defines part of a person's identity.

Gender identity: all of the attributes and characteristics that are associated with belonging to one or the other of the sexes.

Ethnic group: a group with a distinct culture that can be traced through history to a specific location.

Social identity: when a person is identified or labelled as a specific type of person.

Multiple identities: when a person has a number of identities in different parts of their life.

Activity

11 Imagine it is you waking to find you have lost your memory like the woman in Source **M**. What do you think you would need to know to establish your identity?

Activity

12 Copy out the spider diagram in Source **N** and add some branches. What aspects of identity can change? Make a list of what cannot be changed.

I enjoy Saturdays. Off to the match with my friends. We have all the gear. Scarves, tee-shirts, roll-out banners and honking horns. We go together and share our sandwiches. Sometimes there's a bit of bother but that's because they are different to us.

People can identify with others by the team they support, the clothes they wear, the paper they read, their accent and so on. Culture provides us with a range of identities from which we can choose, including the job we do. In simple societies far fewer identities are available. Some identities used to be fixed, for example, a nurse was a woman. Some identities were restricted, for example, a woman could not be a doctor. Today occupational identities are blurred and people are likely to identify themselves in different ways. They also have **multiple identities**. A woman may regard herself as a mother at home, a doctor at work and a football fan in her leisure time.

P *A woman can have multiple identities*

Some identities are given to you by others that you may not like. This may involve a label being associated with you whether it is justified or not. Would you be happy being called a ladette or a lout? Identities define how you see yourself and how others see you.

Activity

13 Do you or many members of your family have multiple identities? Write your answers down with the main identity first.

⚭ links

Also see Topic 1.3 for information on multiculturalism in the UK.

Q *National identity and the EU: passport*   *National identity and the EU: EU flag*

National identities are important. There are many different countries in the EU and the people in these countries think of themselves as French or German or British rather than European. When people immigrate, there are pressures to conform to the rules of the host society. This can cause potential identity conflicts that are not always understood.

Study tip

This topic is one of the more difficult ones and questions are likely to be worth 2 or 4 marks. This means you will be expected to write a definition or explanation about how someone gains an identity.

What is the influence of nature?

There has been a debate about nature versus **nurture** for over a hundred years. Researchers want to discover why you become who you are. Is it the **genes** you are born with – your **genetic inheritance** (nature) – that has the most influence? Or is it the way you have been nurtured – the environment you have lived in and your social background?

> ❝ *The first message from genetic research is that genes play an important role for almost all complex characteristics, both behavioural or medical.*
>
> *The second message is just as important: individual differences in complex characteristics are due at least as much to environmental influences as to genetic influences.* ❞
>
> Professor Robert Plomin, Institute of Psychiatry, London, 2000

Research that has taken place

One of the ways to research this is to study identical twins as they have the same genetic makeup. While most are brought up together and share the same sort of environment, there are examples of identical twins who are brought up apart and may have a very different up-bringing.

The Jim twins

The identical Jim twins were studied first in 1979. They had been brought up apart in adoptive families since they were a few weeks old. At the age of 40, they were reunited. There were many similarities and coincidences. They had the same medical histories and sounded the same when they spoke. Both had the same main interests (stock-car racing and basketball), both had carpentry workshops, both went to the same place for their holidays and so on. There were many more similarities than differences. The coincidences were that both had wives called Betty, both had divorced from a woman named Linda, and both named their first child James Allen (although the spelling of Alan was different).

When identical twins are brought up together, most studies suggest they are very similar in weight, perform similarly in education, are likely to share the same chances of becoming mentally ill, share similar interests, and have the same chance of being gay. The likelihood for many other individual characteristics has not yet been studied. Identical twins reared apart are not quite as similar. The Jim twins were perhaps an extreme example.

Going further

4 ■ Read more about the Jim twins at
science.howstuffworks.com/twin1.htm

■ Find out about other identical twins at:
current.com/topics/75906602_identical_twins

Key terms

Nurture: the effect of personal experiences from the womb to adulthood. It is how you have been brought up.

Gene: the basic unit of heredity.

Genetic inheritance: the result of a transfer of genes from parent to offspring.

IQ test: a means of measuring intelligence.

Activity

14 a Why do you think the nature versus nurture debate is worth researching?

b How might the findings from research help individuals and society?

Twin study – intelligence test performance

In 1979 Thomas Bouchard started testing twins' intelligence using **IQ** tests. He also used information from other twin comparison studies around the world. He found the following pattern:

Information	
Identical twins reared together	86%
Identical twins reared apart	76%
Non-identical twins reared together	55%
Brother reared together	40%
Unrelated people living apart	0%

The higher the percentage, the closer the twins' test results were.

From Thomas Buchard's research, 1979

Brain study research

Brain scans of identical twins show great similarity (95 per cent) in the frontal lobes of the brain which are responsible for communication and understanding. Non-identical twins have approximately 68 per cent similarity.

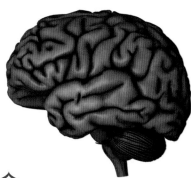

U   *The human brain*

V   *I think they're identical twins. But I'm not sure*

Activity

15 **a** What conclusions do you think can be drawn from these figures? Write them down as statements.

b What problems do you think might occur when doing twin study research?

Did you know ???????

IQ stands for 'intelligence quotient' which is calculated as mental age over chronological age multiplied by 100. So if you are 12 and you perform on a test as a 12 year old should you would have a score of 100. If you scored like a 15 year old then your score would be 125. You need to be in the top 2 percent to join Mensa.

Going further

5 Find out about nature and nurture and obesity. Is it all in the genes?

Look at:
news.bbc.co.uk/1/hi/health/7230065.stm

Activity

16 Some twins look alike but may not be identical. How do you know that twins are identical?

Use this link to help you:

multiples.about.com/od/funfacts/a/differenttwins.htm

What is the influence of nurture?

Research suggests that what is important is that a child is brought up in a family or with a family substitute where there is communication. Without this environmental framework normal personality development and speech suffer.

> 66 Genie is a 'wild child' discovered at 13 years old. She had been kept in isolation strapped to a potty for some time and was not taught to speak. When she was 15 she was returned to her mother but it did not work out successfully and she was fostered. A series of foster parents tried to help her but without success. In 2006 she was living in an adult home for the mentally retarded. 99

Description of Genie Wiley of Los Angeles, California

The identical twins Paula and Elyse were reared apart by adoptive parents and were united again after 35 years. When they met, Paula commented on their meeting. 'We looked similar but we were both unique. Elyse is an alternative version of me. We have our own distinctive style.'

X   *Identical twins Paula and Elyse*

Education and achievement

Schools in the same local authority often have very different GCSE results. One school in an affluent suburb obtains 90 per cent A to C grades and one serving a council estate near the inner city obtains 15 per cent A to C grades. What is the cause?

What we do know is that there is underachievement by boys and some ethnic groups and that social background appears to influence achievement.

Activity

17   a   Read Source W. Why do you think communicating in a family environment is so important for the development of a child's personality? Write down as many ideas as you can think of.

    b   Do you think Source X supports the nature or nurture side of the debate? ·

Going further

6   Look at these websites for more information on **feral children:**

- www.bbc.co.uk/dna/h2g2/alabaster/A269840/

- www.feralchildren.com/en/index.php

7   Read the BBC website report and find out the twins' favourite book and film:

news.bbc.co.uk/1/hi/world/americas/7152762.stm

Activity

18   Discuss the following questions with a partner:

a   Do you think one school is full of genetically clever children and the other is not?

b   Is the difference to do with the pupils' different social backgrounds?

c   Is it a result of better or poorer teaching?

Are sporting superstars born or made?

In the 2008 Olympic Games Britain had their best medal tally for over 100 years. When the results were analysed, 40 per cent of the medal winners had been educated privately. In Britain 10 per cent of children are educated in private schools.

Recently a television series tried to establish if the world championship gold medallist hurdler, Colin Jackson, had been born to run or whether it was the result of training. The outcome was that he had some potential physical characteristics in his favour. However, it was very much more to do with the opportunities he had, the supportive home environment that encouraged competition, his own drive to succeed and the fact that he lived near an athletics facility that had good coaches.

Y Colin Jackson – nature or nurture?

How much is down to lifestyle?

People are becoming fatter. In the Western world the average weight of people is increasing. While genes play a considerable part in children's physical characteristics (and there is even a 'fatness gene' that has been isolated), the general weight gain can be explained by environmental factors. People eat more than they did and exercise less. This is a case of the interaction of genes and the environment.

Check your understanding

1 Define 'socialisation'.

2 List the agents of socialisation.

3 What makes up a person's identity?

4 How does nurture impact on an individual?

Activity

19 Write a few sentences saying whether you think nature or nurture are more important or whether they are both equally important. Try to use some of the evidence on this page and the previous three pages.

Study tip

Avoid taking an extreme view on nature and nurture. Research now accepts the greater role in some things of nature and in others of nurture and sometimes the interaction of both are responsible.

What are the causes of cultural change?

Cultures are subject to both internal and external forces which either encourage or resist change. Some of these forces are introduced below and many involve interaction between cultures.

Inventions and new technology

No one knows who invented the first mechanical clock but it appeared in Britain in the late 13th century. The clock brought order to life. It determined when people would wake, go to work, open and close markets and go to sleep. With the measurement of time, human productivity could be measured. Muslims initially only used clocks to signal prayer time.

A   *Why is it important to know what time it is?*

Objectives

You will be able to:

understand some of the causes of cultural change

understand that interaction between cultures can bring benefits and can cause conflict and change

explain the causes and effects of immigration into the UK

explain the challenges of living in the UK's multicultural, democratic society

explain the causes and effects of migration to the US in the 19th century.

B   *How do ideas spread?*

Diffusion of ideas

Some ideas spread out gradually in a process called **diffusion**. The feminist movement began in the US in the 1870s and arrived in the UK in the 1880s. Both these societies have embraced the ideas of female equality but at different rates and the aims are yet to be fully realised. In Spain, the movement towards female equality and cultural change was 'put on hold' for 30 years during General Franco's dictatorship.

C   *Why can war change culture?*

Wars and revolutions

Wars can be the source of many changes. At the end of Second World War, people wanted more than peace for all their endeavours. The foundation of the National Health Service was one of the results of the new Welfare State. The Russian Revolution of 1917 saw the removal of the monarchy and completely altered the structure of Russian Society.

Monarchy and governments

Roman Catholicism might have been the dominant religion in the UK had Henry VIII not closed all the monasteries and fallen out with the Pope. In this case it was a monarch who forced changes on the people. Dictators in the 20th century did the same, enforcing their political ideologies. Religious leaders often want to prevent change. In Iran, however, in 1979 the monarch was overthrown by a quiet Islamic

D   *Henry VIII: those in power can force change*

revolution spearheaded by Ayatollah Khomeni who was in exile. In 2003, the Chinese Government decided that all elementary school children should learn English. The French Government, on the other hand, has banned the commercial use of English words.

Globalisation

Globalisation has accelerated the movement of goods and ideas from one culture to another. Worldwide television coverage has introduced new sports, fashions and celebrity cults around the world. Football is now played virtually everywhere. Kentucky Fried Chicken is now a

E   *How do different cultures influence each other?*

food choice in hundreds of countries. The adventures of James Bond are known across the world. The Chinese Government limits access to foreign media and the worldwide web in an attempt to stop the people finding out about more democratic political systems and ideas in other countries.

F   *How does assimilation happen?*

Acculturation

Acculturation happens when an invader brings new ideas to a society to replace existing cultural patterns. The Plains Indians have been assimilated into American culture, living and working like everyone else, or living on reservations. The same is true of other indigenous groups such as the Aborigines of Australia. The traditional Bushmen lifestyle seems about to die out.

Migrants

Migrants move to and from countries taking their culture with them. Immigrants to the UK over the last 50 years have certainly changed the food eaten here (curry, pizzas, paella, fried rice). Resistance to immigration can prevent external ideas entering the country.

G   *How do the movement of people affect culture?*

Environment

Changes to the environment can force change on people. For example, in the UK we have to recycle our rubbish more and also change how we use energy. Global warming may make some South Pacific Islands disappear altogether and their peoples will be forced to migrate.

H   *How does the environment influence you?*

⚭ links

Also see Topic 1.2 for information on Nazi socialisation.

Key terms

Diffusion: the idea of something spreading out gradually.

Globalisation: where activities in one part of the world have consequences for people in other parts of the world.

Acculturation: where members of one cultural group adopt the culture and beliefs of another group.

⚭ links

Also see Topic 1.3 for information on the Bushmen of Southern Africa.

⚭ links

Also see Chapter 2 Environmental Issues.

Study tip

Remember that change can be small or great. Change can be positive or negative to some members of a culture. Change can be resisted, stopped or overturned.

Activity

1   a   Think of another example of each of the causes of cultural change.

   b   Create your own spider diagram to help you remember the causes of cultural change.

   c   Identify from the influences above examples of resistance to change.

Who has migrated to the UK and why?

Who has migrated here?

The Celts were the first recorded people in Britain, but were conquered by the Romans and adopted much of Roman culture. The Romans settled here, built roads, Hadrian's Wall and the country's first cities. They also introduced black people to the country. As the Roman Empire began to fail, there were invasions and settlement from Europe by the Angles and Saxons, then the Norse and Danes. This pushed Celtic culture to the edges of Britain in West and North Wales, North West Scotland, Cornwall and western Ireland. Jewish settlers started to arrive along with the French, after the invasion of 1066 by William the Conqueror.

As Britain began to explore the world, this brought a trickle of immigrants from across the world. Gypsies arrived from Europe in the 16th century and as Britain became involved with the slave trade more black people arrived. Britain was seen as a safe place for refugees, and Huguenots and other Protestants arrived here from Europe, to escape religious persecution.

In the 19th century many Irish people settled in Britain to escape poverty, particularly the Irish potato famine and because there was work here building railways, sewers and roads. More Jews came here fleeing persecution in Poland and Russia. With the Empire at its height, and much trade with India and Africa, there was a stream of new arrivals on returning boats seeking new opportunities in Britain.

After the Second World War

Britain needed **immigrant** workers to rebuild the economy and take up jobs where there were vacancies that could not be filled.

- London public transport paid for workers from the West Indies to come to the UK by boat. In later years they also came to work in the NHS.
- Indians, Pakistanis and Bangladeshis came to work in the textile and other industries.
- A steady stream of Chinese came to work in the catering and restaurant industries. They were joined by Hong Kong Chinese and Vietnamese refugees in the catering and beauty industries.
- African Asians from Kenya, Tanzania and Uganda came to escape racial discrimination and persecution. Many were highly skilled.
- Eastern Europeans came following the expansion of the EU, benefitting from freedom of movement legislation and higher wages in Britain.

Key terms

Migration: the movement from one place to another on a permanent or semi-permanent basis.

Immigration: the movement of people into an area across a national boundary.

Culture shock: when newly arrived immigrants find the host country's culture very different.

○○links

Also see Topic 7.3 for more information on economic **migration**.

Activity

2 a What were the reasons for people settling here? Were people pushed here or pulled?

   b Put the names of the migrating groups under one of the following headings: persecution, new opportunities, invasion, improved standard of living and work.

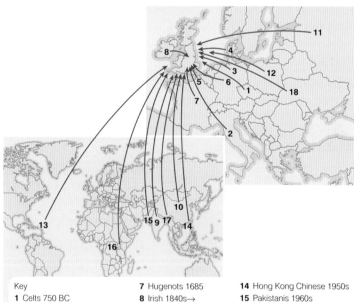

Key
1 Celts 750 BC
2 Romans 43 AD
3 Angles and Saxons 400s
4 Danes 865
5 Normans 1066
6 Germans 1500s–1800s
7 Hugenots 1685
8 Irish 1840s→
9 Indians 1850s→
10 Chinese 1850s→
11 Jews 1880s
12 Poles 1946
13 West Indians 1948
14 Hong Kong Chinese 1950s
15 Pakistanis 1960s
16 Ugandan Asians 1972
17 Bangladeshis 1980s
18 Eastern Europeans 2000→
→ Continuing

I *Immigration to the UK*

J *West Indian immigrants at Southampton, 1951*

K *Eastern European immigrants queue at the British Embassy for entry visas*

What happens when migrants arrive here?

Find accommodation to rent. Contact relatives if any here. Look for work. May settle where others have the same culture. → Establish and settle down. Culture shock. Acclimatisation phase. → Integration process begins. Influenced by host culture. → Assimilation Take on some aspects of Britishness: language, share values, traditions – leaving some of previous culture behind.

 Immigration to the UK

Activity

3
a   Name the ethnic groups who live in your own village, town or city.

b   How long have they lived in the area?

c   Which ethnic group is the largest?

Going further

1 Find out more about the West Indian immigrants to the UK in the early 1950s at:

- www.connections-exhibition.org/index.php?xml=histories/black/ww2after.xml

- my.telegraph.co.uk/andy_panda/blog/2007/06/08/why_those_of_west_indian_descent_are_societies_losers_

2 Find out about the Romanian Gypsies experience in other EU countries in the new millennium.

- www.timesonline.co.uk/tol/news/world/europe/article2788922.ece

- news.bbc.co.uk/1/hi/world/europe/2293421.stm

- news.bbc.co.uk/1/hi/world/europe/2052298.stm

3 What were the reasons for each group choosing to go to the countries that they did?

4 How were each group treated on their arrival?

Activity

4
a   Give examples of what you think is meant by the term **'culture shock'**?

b   What aspects of British culture (the host culture) do you think it might be difficult for West Indians, Africans and Chinese to take on?

Going further

5 These are excellent website links with personal accounts:

- www.movinghere.org.uk/

- www.connections-exhibition.org/index.php?xml=welcome/_/welcome.xml

Study tip

Remember to use phrases such as 'host country' and 'culture shock'.

What is multiculturalism in the UK?

The UK is made up of England, Wales, Scotland and Northern Ireland. Each of these countries has some of their own cultural traditions. For example, the Welsh have their own language which they want to preserve as well as speaking English. The Scottish have their hogmanay celebration at New Year. The Northern Irish have St Patrick's Day and the English have St George's Day and fish and chips!

Citizens in all parts of the UK are able to share in a democratic political society. The UK has an excellent reputation for justice and protecting human rights. Everyone over the age of 18 can vote for a political party in the general election and can vote for local councillors. Some British freedoms are shown in Source **M**. These are a huge attraction for **asylum seekers** from other countries where there are dictatorships or religious intolerance.

British freedoms

- Freedom to vote
- Freedom of speech
- Freedom of assembly
- Freedom of thought and conscience
- Freedom from slavery and torture

M

Immigrants from other **ethnic groups** have brought different religions and different ways of life to the UK.

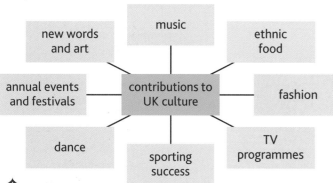

N *The contribution of immigrant groups*

Some ethnic groups have tended to settle in particular areas of the UK. Source **O** shows what ideally happens when immigrants settle. However, some immigrants have **integrated** or **assimilated** more successfully than others. This has made immigration a public and political issue over the last 50 years.

The term **multiculturalism** emerged in the 1970s. Source **P** gives two different interpretations of the word.

O *Notting Hill carnival*

> 66 *Multiculturalism is where every culture has the right to exist and there is no overarching thread that holds them together.*
>
> *Multiculturalism is where people have their own cultural beliefs and they happily co-exist – but there is a common thread of Britishness to hold the society together.* 99
>
> Ruth Lea, Director of the Centre for Policy Studies, April 2004

P

Key terms

Asylum seeker: a person classed as a refugee fleeing persecution. He or she is not an economic migrant.

Ethnic group: a group with a distinct culture that can be traced through history to a specific location.

Integration: when two cultures combine and live alongside each other in harmony.

Assimilation: when an ethnic group adopts the host culture as their own.

Multicultural: a society which consists of the culture of several different races.

Going further

6 Find a guide to UK human rights at:
www.yourrights.org.uk

Activity

5 Look at Source **N**.

Provide an example that will extend each branch on the spider diagram. Add any other main branches that you can think of.

Activity

6 Read the two interpretations of multiculturalism in Source **P**. Which view do you think best describes the UK today? Why?

Some issues produced by immigration

- Immigrants work and therefore contribute to the economy, often doing jobs that others do not want to do. There are, however, costs for the country's social services, the NHS and education.

- There can be conflicts of culture which can cause divisions between people. Examples include religious symbols, arranged marriages, women's unequality and terrorism fears. The concentration of immigrant populations in particular areas has sometimes led to tensions and in certain towns there have been riots.

- Some people are concerned that migrants take jobs from the host country's citizens.

Going further

7   Find out more about racial tensions and riots at:

- news.bbc.co.uk/1/hi/ uk/1355718.stm
- www.independent.co.uk/ news/uk/this-britain/ multicultural-britain- an-unlikely-success- story-509634.html

Q   *The Bradford riots, 2001*

Going further

8   For more background on the development of UK race law go to:

news.bbc.co.uk/1/hi/ uk/4510062.stm

Legislation and control

The UK has, over the years, introduced laws to help reduce any problems caused by living in a multicultural society. In 1965 a law was passed to prevent people refusing access to anyone on racial grounds. It also made incitement to racial hatred a criminal offence. In 1976 a new law made it an offence to discriminate against a person on racial grounds. The law was strengthened in 2000 and 2003.

Because immigrant numbers have been increasing, a points system was introduced in 2008 based on entrants' skills. An annual ceiling on numbers may be introduced. In 2005 the Government introduced a British citizenship test. The aim of this was to help people integrate, *share in British values* and traditions and recognise that alongside UK *rights* there are *responsibilities*.

Activity

7   Divide into groups and look at Source **R**.

a   How many of the questions can you answer?

b   Then discuss what you think it means to be British?

Some clues for your discussion: equality, tolerance of others, democracy, freedom of expression.

Questions from Life in the UK test

Where are the Geordie, Cockney, and Scouse dialects spoken?

What are MPs?

Do women have equal rights in voting, education and work, and has this always been the case?

What is the Church of England and who is its head?

What are the minimum ages for buying alcohol and tobacco? What drugs are illegal?

The whole test is at: www.lifeintheuktest.gov.uk

Did you know ??????

Tony Blair (Prime Minister 1997–2007) said immigrants have a duty to integrate. 'That is what being British means, the right to be different. If outsiders are not prepared to conform to values such as tolerance then they should not stay.'

Immigration to the US

The Statue of Liberty was the symbol of liberty that greeted new immigrants to the US who were trying to escape famine, hardship and poverty or just seeking a new beginning. The American economy needed both unskilled and skilled workers. The country in its pioneering phase needed migrants willing to take risks and explore and open up the rural west. Then, towards the end of the 19th century, the country needed unskilled workers for factory jobs.

In Europe there was a dramatic population increase as child mortality fell. This led to an increase in the need for food which encouraged farmers to expand. Land costs then increased because of the demand for it. Farmers with small holdings did not have the money to expand and were squeezed out – a reason to seek their fortune in the US.

S *Welcome to the promised land*

Immigrants moved to both rural America and the cities. Cities were for those who had nothing because those wanting to farm needed money to purchase land and equipment. The cities were regarded as melting pots consisting of many varied people together each with their own cultures. The assumption was that each group would gradually integrate into American culture and be assimilated. When this did not happen, there was sometimes hostility. Many immigrants were disappointed in how things turned out. They found boring jobs, low wages and poor living conditions. Those who benefited were often the next generation.

Activity

8 **a** What do you think it must have felt like after crossing the Atlantic Ocean and seeing the Statue of Liberty? Write a short paragraph telling of your hopes and dreams.

b Make a list of the push factors and pull factors that took the Chinese and Italians to the US.

c Was immigration a successful experience for the migrants?

T *Italian immigrants waiting to be processed*

The experience of migration was different for each person but there were some general patterns. More Italians migrated to America than any other group. Many came from southern Italy. Here there was poverty, too many trying to live off too little land and taxes were crippling. Most of the Italians who arrived were men who saw migration as only temporary. They came to make money. They would work long hours for low wages. Some Italians who turned to crime made a lot of money but most Italians were law-abiding and hard workers. Not everyone liked the Italian immigrants and so they looked to their own community and family for help. This encouraged them to keep their own culture. Parts of some American cities had a quarter which was called 'Little Italy.'

Chinese immigrants arrived in California from across the Pacific. Most were single men, planning to return home after making money. They turned towards America because of civil unrest and poverty in China.

The Central Pacific Railroad was trying to build a railroad across America but had a shortage of labourers. The head of construction argued that the company should try Chinese workers because if they could build the Great Wall of China then a railroad must be easy in comparison. Two years later there were 12,000 Chinese building the railroad at a low wage rate and with a reputation for working hard. Despite this contribution, they suffered prejudice and discrimination.

U   *Chinese building the railroad*

Going further

9   Find out about some of the pioneer settler groups from Germany, Sweden and Britain who opened up the west of the USA. This website allows you to navigate to different nationalities.

http://lcweb2.loc.gov/learn/features/immig/alt/introduction.html

Going further

10   The following are useful links to find out more about other groups who immigrated to the US. In 1894 a pressure group to limit immigration was formed, the Immigration Restriction League. Eventually in 1921 a quota system was introduced to control immigration.

■   www.spartacus.schoolnet.co.uk/USAEitaly.htm

■   www.casahistoria.net/usa_immigration.htm#2._The_immigrants

Study tip

This case study is about the US. If a question specified a national example instead of an international example then you would have to use the UK. Watch question wording as some questions expect response on the UK only.

Check your understanding

1   Make a list of factors that can influence cultural change and give a short example of each.

2   Name two push and two pull factors contributing to migration to the UK.

3   What does 'multiculturalism' mean?

4   Give three examples of successful assimilation.

What are issues?

This topic will help give you a framework for examining any cultural, moral, political, religious or social **issue**. Sometimes an issue has all these dimensions.

The number of groups of people with different **perspectives** about an issue will vary depending on the issue, as the following examples illustrate.

The capital punishment debate

Perspective	View
Christians	Christian principles would promote forgiveness, reconciliation and rehabilitation as the most important things to consider, rather than punishing a murderer with death.
Muslims	Islamic law accepts capital punishment for murder and for threatening Islam.
Jews	Jewish law allows capital punishment for murder provided the person was of sound mind and knew the consequences of the act and their act can be supported by witnesses.
Humanists	They see the death penalty as revenge and believe this is destructive and uncivilised.
UK political parties	They originally took different positions over the death penalty in the 1950s but, by the time the vote to ban capital punishment took place, there was support from all parties.
The US	In 2007 in the US there were 42 executions, with 60% of these in Texas. Of the 42 executions, 41 were by lethal injection. Many people are kept on death row for years. 38 US states have capital punishment.
Others	The views of ordinary men and women differ on whether capital punishment should be reinstated in the UK.

A

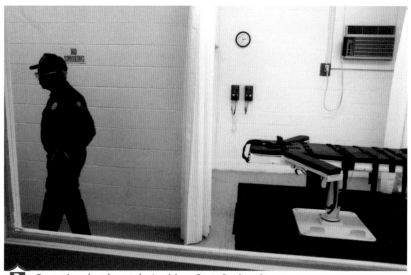

B *Execution chamber at the Louisiana State Penitentiary*

Objectives

You will be able to:

understand some of the perspectives held by individuals and groups on some important issues

explore a cultural, moral, political, religious or a social issue

provide reasons why individuals and groups hold their views.

Key terms

Issue: something about which people have different views.

Perspective: a viewpoint that a person or group has about an issue.

Group activity

1 Working with a partner, write down your own views on capital punishment.

◼ The abortion debate

Perspective	View
United Nations	According to the Declaration of the Rights of the Child, children are important even before birth and their rights should be considered.
Feminists	They think women should have the right to an 'abortion on demand'.
Church of England	The life of the mother is more important and if endangered an abortion is an acceptable necessity.
Roman Catholic Church	The abortion of a foetus is a sin in all circumstances. Life begins at conception and human life is sacred.
Doctors and medical experts	They hold differing views about the number of months' gestation when a baby's life is viable.
Pressure groups	In favour: Pro-choice and the Abortion Rights Action League. Against: Life, the Society for the Protection of the Unborn Child.
UK Political Parties	They have in the past had different views about aspects of abortion. When debates occur, it is generally a matter of conscience for MPs, i.e. their party does not force them to vote in a particular way.
Others	The views of ordinary men and women differ on whether abortion should be permitted and up until what stage in a pregnancy.

C

D   *Anti-abortion protestors*

◼ Medical ethics debates

There have been a number of issues about medicines and medical care that have arisen in the last 40 years as medical technology has advanced.

- If a new drug is available to prolong life, should it be prescribed regardless of cost?
- Who should be given priority for transplant operations?
- When someone dies, should their organs be available for transplants unless they have opted out?
- Should genetic engineering be permitted?
- There are a number of different views about artificial insemination, surrogate mothers and in vitro fertilisation (IVF).

To investigate any issue, you need to research and summarise the views of different groups of people such as political parties, scientists, doctors, religions and pressure groups. There will almost certainly be views for and against the issue.

Voluntary euthanasia

Euthanasia was once not even discussed but now it is a major issue. A 2007 social attitudes poll found that 8 out of 10 people in the UK were in favour of **voluntary euthanasia** but current laws in the UK prohibit it. In Holland, euthanasia is still illegal but doctors are unlikely to be prosecuted for their involvement. In the state of Oregon in the US, assisted suicides are not illegal. UK citizens sometimes go abroad to countries where it is allowed, subject to certain safeguards. The organisation Dignatas has medical facilities in Switzerland and helps people travel there to end their own life.

> *Hugo Claus, a writer, had been suffering from Alzheimer's disease and had 'picked the moment of his death' in consultation with his doctors. After he died, the ex-Prime Minister of Belgium, Guy Verhofstadt, said 'You cannot imagine the inevitable and unbearable torture for him of Alzheimer's disease. He could no longer write. I can live with the fact that he decided to die, because he left us as a great glowing star, right on time, just before he would have collapsed into a black hole.'*

 E

The Voluntary Euthanasia Society argues that doctors should be allowed to help patients who want to die to do so. They say the law should be changed to allow euthanasia for people who have indicated their wish for such a death in advance. This would ensure that the decision is thought out and not done on the 'spur of the moment'.

The Roman Catholic Church sees voluntary euthanasia as being similar to suicide – a grievous sin – because it is against the Church's teachings. To take an innocent person's life is opposing God's love for that person.

> *I'm a Roman Catholic and I cannot agree with euthanasia. Human life is a gift from God and humans have a responsibility to use God's gifts to the full. The Ten Commandments say, 'Thou shalt not kill.' God is the creator and the taking of life is overstepping human responsibilities. The Hospice Movement and Macmillan nurses have done much to alleviate suffering and pain. It enables those dying to spend their last days in a loving and caring environment. It allows 'death with dignity'.*

 F

Humanists believe people should be in charge of their own life and its quality; it is therefore up to each person whether to live or die. It is the natural order of things that people will die. They should have the right to euthanasia after discussing it with doctors and relatives and signing a declaration asking for it.

> *I knew someone who tried to commit suicide because the pain was getting so bad. Do you know what? They found her in time and she had her stomach pumped and she was resuscitated. Can you imagine that? If she could have only asked to die she would not have had to go through all that. She died three days later.*

 G

Key terms

Voluntary euthanasia: where someone is helped to die with their consent.

Going further

2 At http://news.bbc.co.uk/1/hi/health/4761143.stm you will find an article 'We were there when she died.'

Group activity

3 a   Using the information you have read in the case study, make a list of arguments for and against voluntary euthanasia. List key phrases that summarise the views of the Roman Catholic Church and humanists.

   b   What moral dilemmas do you think doctors face over voluntary euthanasia?

   c   Hold a class debate on the topic: 'Voluntary euthanasia should be made legal in the UK'.

There are many occasions now when doctors withhold treatment during the last stages of a terminal illness because it will not cure or prolong life. This is sometimes seen as passive euthanasia.

> ❝ *I'm a doctor and there are drugs that can help people with the pain. Each situation for a patient approaching death is different. There are some in a coma or with dementia who couldn't tell you if they wanted to die such is their condition. Others would say they wanted to die because they think they are a burden on others and the truth is they want to live. If euthanasia was legalised some people might push their relative into signing their life away. I worry that the trust between patients and doctors will be destroyed. The Hippocratic Oath, to preserve life, must be preserved or we might find people being slipped a pill to free up a hospital bed. What we need are better facilities, but unfortunately there are too few hospice beds and with an ageing population it's going to become worse.* ❞

 H

I   *Hugo Claus*

Going further

3   Find out about the laws on voluntary euthanasia in Australia.

Go to **news.bbc.co.uk/** and use the search terms 'Australia voluntary euthanasia'

4   Some people worry that if there is voluntary euthanasia for the elderly it will soon be made available to others.

Follow up the issues at **www.timesonline.co.uk/tol/news/world/article737519.ece**

Check your understanding

1   Identify a range of perspectives you might investigate in the issue you are going to study.

2   Explain why the issue you are going to study may have moral, social or political consequences.

3   Identify religious issues involved in the issue you intend to study.

Did you know ??????

- The Romans accepted that suicide was an honourable death for someone who was in terrible pain.
- Approximately 4,000 patients a year die through active euthanasia in the form of a lethal injection that kills in minutes.

Going further

5   The BBC website provides comprehensive coverage including the views of other religions at:

www.bbc.co.uk/ethics/euthanasia/

6   Listen to someone explain about killing her aunt 30 years ago. Go to

www.bbc.co.uk and use the search term **4678180.stm**

1

Culture and beliefs

The Yanomami culture

The Yanomami are one of the largest indigenous tribes in the Amazon. Today their total population stands at around 32,000. They live in an isolated area of northern Brazil in a rainforest. Their culture has remained relatively unchanged until recently.

They live in villages in large, circular, communal houses called yanos. Some can house up to 400 people. Each family has its own hearth where food is prepared and cooked during the day. They sleep in hammocks near the central fire at night. The Yanomami believe strongly in equality among people. Each community is independent from others and they do not recognise 'chiefs'. Decisions are made by consensus.

They depend on the resources of the rainforest for their survival. The culture is polygamous with one man generally having multiple wives. Tasks are divided between the sexes. Men hunt for game like deer. Women tend the gardens, growing crops which provide 80 per cent of their food. Both men and women catch fish. They move their village every few years after resources are depleted.

A

The Yanomami and outsiders

- In the 1940s, contact with 'outsiders' led to epidemics. Flu and measles killed many.
- In the 1970s, villages were destroyed. The Government built roads in their forest area.
- In the 1980s, gold-miners invaded their land destroying villages, killing Yanomami who stood in their way (estimated at 2,000 deaths). The gold-mining industry uses mercury to separate gold from rock. This pollutes rivers and damages the ecosystem. The miners also brought alcohol and this has had negative effects on the Yanomami.
- Stagnant water has attracted mosquitoes and they have spread malaria. There has been an increase in children born with defects.
- Yanomami do not have land ownership rights. The Government wants to open up the forest for mining and farming.
- Government initiatives have meant the Yanomami have been taught to read and write. Yanomami now receive medicine and health services. However, corruption has meant that medicines, drugs and equipment have often failed to reach them.

B

Practice questions

1   **a)**   Using Source **A**, what is a yano?   *(1 mark)*

   b)   Using Source **A**, what is women's work in the Yanomami culture?   *(1 mark)*

   c)   Using Source **A**, describe and explain the social organisation of the Yanomami.   *(4 marks)*

   d)   Is it true to say, 'the future looks poor for the continuing existence of simple/primitive cultures'? Explain your views using Sources **A** and **B** and your own studies of simple cultures.   *(12 marks)*

2   **a)**   What is meant by 'nurture'? Briefly explain using your own studies.   *(2 marks)*

   b)   Explain how nurture can influence an individual's development. Use your own studies to answer.   *(4 marks)*

   c)   Choose a cultural, moral, political or social issue you have studied. Put forward the different views that people hold about the issue. Conclude by stating which view you support and why.   *(12 marks)*

2 Environmental issues

2.1 How do individuals and groups use the environment?

Natural resources

The natural environment has been used by humans for thousands of years. The Stone Age, Iron Age and Bronze Age were cultures that used **natural resources** in the past. Some cultures like the native Indians use the natural resources in the rainforest such as trees and water.

Today many of the things you use come from natural resources. Natural resources can be grown on the land, caught in the sea, reared by farmers, mined or harnessed from the air or water.

A *Natural resources*

Renewable resources are those which can be used again. The UK is fortunate in that it has many renewable resources. It is said to be the windiest country in Europe. We are surrounded by fish in the sea which are renewable, provided they are not over-fished. Fertile soil provides land for crops and cattle that provide 60 per cent of our food needs. Water needs to be managed so it is kept free from pollution and stored in reservoirs so that it is available in times of drought.

Non-renewable resources cannot be used again. The UK has many deposits of **minerals** which are non-renewable resources. The Industrial Revolution was based on coal deposits in Yorkshire and Wales. In the 19th century the UK was the greatest producer of copper in the world. As non-renewable resources begin to run out, and the demand for them

Activity

2 Copy these words and match the natural resource with the correct manufactured item.

Cod	Wooden table
Oil	House brick
Gold	Plastic bottle
Wool	Fish finger
Timber	Sweater
Clay	Wedding ring

Study tip

Understand the difference between renewable and non-renewable resources.

Did you know ? ? ? ? ? ?

Unsuccessful attempts have been made to extract the small amount of gold from sea water.

increases, they become more valuable. Demand for copper in India and China increased the price to £4,000 per tonne. This led to thieves stealing copper from railway lines, causing rail travellers in the UK to be delayed by 240,000 minutes in 2007. In 2008 as the price of gold increased, it became economic to re-open old gold mines in Scotland. However, during the financial downturn of 2008–2009, the price of non-renewable resources like copper halved.

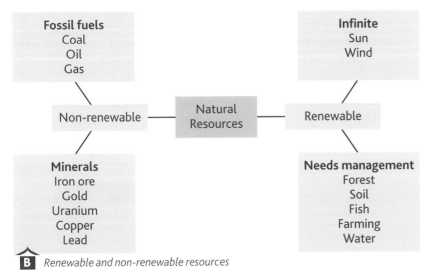

B   *Renewable and non-renewable resources*

The rate that non-renewable resources are used up depends on how developed a country is and how much demand there is for a resource. As the population of the world increases and countries become more developed, demand will only increase. In the UK, there is a 'throw away' culture, which gives little thought to where resources have come from. Resources and people are not spread evenly across the world and problems occur when there are too few resources, or they are misused. New supplies are being found, but there are still not enough to meet the demand.

Activity

3 Using Source B, are the following natural resources renewable or non-renewable?

Coal, wheat, oil, fish, cotton, timber, iron ore, diamonds.

Going further

1 a Choose a natural resource and investigate where it comes from, how it is used and any environmental or cultural issues associated with it.

b Write a short story about what the world will be like when all the non-renewable resources have been used up.

Energy in the UK today

Fossil fuels

Modern homes require energy in the form of electricity or gas. Electricity can be generated in many ways including from **fossil fuels, nuclear power** and renewable sources. Many homes have gas central heating and gas cookers. Fuel for cars, planes and other vehicles comes from oil.

Coal, oil and gas are all fossil fuels. They were formed millions of years ago from dead plants and animals. They are non-renewable and can not be replaced. In **power stations**, the coal, oil or gas is burned to heat water. The water produces steam. The steam is used to drive turbines which then turn an electrical generator, producing electricity. As fossil fuels are burned in power stations or vehicles, they release carbon dioxide into the atmosphere. This is a major cause of global warming and acid rain.

Group activity

1. List the products you use, or the activities you do, that require electricity.

links

Also see Topic 2.2 for more information on global warming and acid rain.

New LNG terminal costs £500 million

167 die in Piper Alpha disaster

Closed coal mine to reopen

44 years of oil left in North Sea

Gas bills increase by 35%

Oil spill from Sea Empress covers 200 miles of beach

Petrol prices up again

 C *Newspaper headlines on fossil fuels*

The UK is fortunate in having its own supply of fossil fuels. Coal deposits are found throughout the UK, but only a handful of mines are open today. Natural gas was found off the Norfolk coast in 1965 and North Sea oil was discovered in 1970. As these non-renewable resources are used up, the UK has to import more fossil fuels from other countries. There is enough coal in the world to last another 300 years. Gas is difficult to transport so it is often converted to Liquefied Natural Gas (LNG) and transported by tanker. Oil is subject to political and pricing issues which can affect supply.

 Did you know

The energy in fossil fuels originally came from the sun.

Study tip

Remember fossil fuels and nuclear power provide most of your energy needs.

Activity

4. Using Sources C and D, what are the problems of using fossil fuels?

 **D** *Piper Alpha oil and gas rig on fire, 1988*

Nuclear power

In 2007 nuclear power provided 18 per cent of the UK's electricity generation and 7.5 per cent of total UK energy supplies. In 1956 the first nuclear power station was built at Calder Hall, Cumbria, and in 2008 there were 23 reactors generating electricity at nine sites. The fuel is a mineral called uranium, which is mined and therefore non-renewable. However only 50 tonnes a year of uranium are needed at a nuclear power station compared to 540 tonnes of coal an hour at a coal-fired power station.

Nuclear power is seen as a possible replacement for fossil fuels as it does not produce carbon dioxide and only small amounts of uranium are needed. However there are problems associated with it. It is difficult and expensive to dispose of the radioactive waste. Nuclear power carries the risk of nuclear explosion similar to the one that occurred at Chernobyl in 1986. A radioactive cloud spread over Europe causing many environmental problems affecting people, animals and soil. Sheep farmers in Wales lost business due to their sheep eating contaminated grass and becoming unfit to eat.

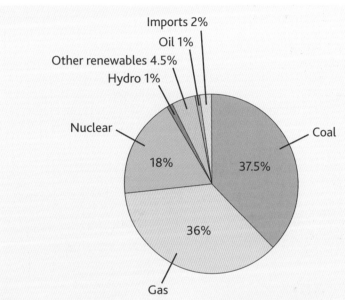

E *UK electricity production*

By 2023 only 4 per cent of UK electricity will come from nuclear power as most of the power stations will have closed down because they are too old. Calder Hall was closed down in 2003 and it will take over 100 years to make the site safe. To increase the percentage of electricity from nuclear power, new stations will have to be built. In 2008 the UK government put forward plans to build new ones, but they did not say where or when.

Activity

5 Using Source **E**, describe how most electricity is produced in the UK today. How do you think this chart will look 50 years from now?

Activity

6   Use the text and Sources **C**, **D** and **E** to complete this table.

Energy source	Advantages	Disadvantages
Coal		
Oil		
Gas		
Nuclear		

Going further

2 a Find out more about the Piper Alpha disaster on 7 July 1988 at:

www.bbc.co.uk/onthisday

   b Find out about the effects of the Sea Empress oil spill at:

www.georesources.co.uk/empress.htm

   c Find out more about the effects of the Chernobyl nuclear disaster 20 years on at:

news.bbc.co.uk/1/hi/in_depth/europe/2006/chernobyl/default.stm

Group activity   ▪▪▪▪

2   Have a debate on whether nuclear power could be a fuel of the future in the UK.

Future energy in the UK

Non-renewable energy resources are limited and will eventually run out. The UK government has set a Renewables Obligation target to produce 15 per cent of UK electricity from **renewable energy** and **alternative energy** sources by 2015. Most alternative energy sources cause less pollution than fossil fuels and carry less risk than nuclear power.

Wind power

Wind power is the fastest growing alternative energy source in the UK. A wind farm is a collection of wind turbines that generate electricity as the wind turns them. They need to be situated in areas with regular high wind speeds. Although wind is free, the turbines are expensive to build and noisy. They take up land and some people do not like the visual impact on the landscape. The pressure of the turning blades can also affect bats. The world's largest wind farm will be built by 2011 off the Kent coast.

F *Offshore wind farm, Liverpool*

Solar power

Solar power is best suited to small scale use for individual homes or remote buildings. Sunlight is a free, infinite, pollution-free resource, but the photovoltaic cells needed to convert sunlight to electricity are expensive to produce. Even on a cloudy day in the UK there is enough sunlight for solar power. In the future, solar panels may be used on car roofs or even aeroplanes.

Geothermal

Geothermal energy uses heat from the earth. It can only be used where the earth's crust is thinnest, but there are low running costs. Offices in Southampton are heated by 700°C water that is pumped from 1,800 m below ground.

Hydro-electric power

The UK is ideally suited to **hydro-electric power (HEP)** as it has a high annual rainfall. It is very efficient as 90% of the water's energy is converted to electricity. It requires steep-sided valleys to build a dam. Large areas of land need to be flooded to create the reservoirs and the dams are expensive to build. Fish and ecosystems are disrupted.

G *Dinorwig HEP station, Wales*

Wave and tidal power

Fixed wave generators, as found around Scottish islands, use **wave power** to force air up a column to turn a turbine. They are relatively easy to build and their small size does not impact on the landscape. Floating wave generators use the motion of the waves. The world's largest wave farm is planned for Scotland. A **tidal power** station requires river estuaries with a large tidal range. The River Severn would be ideal, but the ecosystem would be badly affected. Submerged turbines that use the tide to generate electricity have been put in the sea off the coast of Devon.

Biofuels

The most common form of **biofuel** is wood. This is renewable provided the wood is grown faster than it is used up. Biofuels such as bio-ethanol, sold as E85 for use in cars, are produced from crops such as sugar beet and corn. Problems with biofuels include the amount of land needed to grow the crops and the amount of energy used in transporting the crops. Landfill waste or animal dung can also provide biofuels in the form of a biogas, methane, which can be burned.

Going further

3 a   Find out more about renewable energy at:
www.therenewableenergycentre.co.uk

  b   Find out more about thermal energy at:
www.southampton.gov.uk/building-planning/sustainability/chp.asp

  c   Produce a poster to inform motorists about bio-fuels.
Find information at:
www.biomassenergycentre.org.uk and www.britishbioethanol.co.uk

---

Key terms

Hydro-electric power (HEP): energy generated by water spinning a turbine.

Wave power: energy generated by waves in the sea.

Tidal power: energy generated as the tide goes in or out of a coastal area or estuary.

Biofuels: energy generated from organic matter (biomass), including wood and crops.

Activity

8   Using Source G, explain how reservoirs can be used by humans for other uses.

Study tip

Not all renewable energy is alternative. For example, HEP causes damage to the environment.

Activity

9   Explain which type of renewable energy you would recommend to:

a   a cattle farmer who has spare animal dung

b   a small island facing the Atlantic Ocean

c   a small village in a mountain valley, with fast flowing streams.

Group activity

3   Design a house or small village to use only alternative types of energy.

Tropical rainforests

Tropical rainforests are large **ecosystems** found along the Equator. The largest is the Amazon rainforest in South America. They contain many natural resources, including trees, animals, plants, water and soil. The trees grow quickly in the warm, wet climate. Insects and fungi help break down dead plants and return them to the soil as nutrients. These are quickly absorbed by the shallow roots. The rainforests have been called the 'lungs of the earth' as they control the amount of carbon dioxide in the atmosphere.

Kayapo

Indigenous peoples such as the Kayapo, have used the Amazon rainforest in a **sustainable** way for thousands of years. Seven thousand Kayapo live in nine villages. They use the forest for shelter, medicines, hunting animals and collecting Brazil nuts. In return they only take what they need without causing damage. Their beliefs are linked to the environment. Traditional ceremonies mark the start and end of the seasons. The Kayapo believe in animism which teaches that all the plants and animals contain spirits that must be treated with respect. They have at least one use for 90 per cent of the plants, including medicines and dye for body painting. They use the River Xingu for transport, water and catching fish. Crops like manioc and yams are grown in small areas using shifting cultivation which allows the forest to recover.

H *Kayapo man, shelling Brazil nuts for the Body Shop*

Key terms

Ecosystem: all living and non-living things in a particular environment and the way they work together.

Sustainable: methods that preserve and maintain, rather than destroy.

Deforestation: loss of forest due to climate change or the use of trees without replacing them.

Extinct: the total disappearance of a particular type of living organism.

Did you know ???????

Over half the known plants and animals in the world live in tropical rainforests.

Activity

10 Copy out these sentences in the correct order to describe the process for shifting cultivation:

Manioc and yams are planted.

Ash is put on the soil as fertiliser.

People shift to a new clearing.

Trees are cut down and burned.

Crop yields fall.

Activity

11 Using Source H and the case study, explain how the Kayapo use the forest in a sustainable way.

Study tip

Make sure that you are able to write about at least three different viewpoints on the use of rainforest resources.

Deforestation

Other groups entering the rainforest have been more interested in its economic value. Twenty per cent of the Amazon rainforest has already been destroyed. These are the main causes of **deforestation**:

- **Logging**: Trees such as mahogany and ebony are felled and sold as timber to be made into furniture.
- **Farming**: Large sections of forest are used for cattle ranching (Source I) and growing crops like soya beans for biofuels.
- The Brazilian government is also keen for people from the crowded cities to move into the forest and start farming.
- **Mining**: Gold mining destroys forest as trees are cut down for the mine and the roads that lead to it.
- **HEP**: In 2008, 1,000 Kayapo protested against new plans to build the Belo Monte Dam on the River Xingu. It would involve five dams and flood 18,000 sq km.

I   *Cattle ranching causes deforestation in the Amazon rainforest*

The main effects of deforestation are as follows.

- Lifestyle of the indigenous people is lost as they are forced to move onto reserves.
- The soil is made infertile once the trees are removed.
- Soil is eroded by the heavy rain.
- Wildlife and plants become **extinct**.
- Changes to the climate, including reduced rainfall and global warming.

Activity

12   Using Source I and the case study, describe three causes of deforestation.

Environmental groups and the indigenous people would like to stop the destruction of the rainforest. Scientists have identified 2,000 plants that could be used to tackle cancer. Ecotourism is one way the forest could be used in a sustainable way.

Activity

13   Design an advert for a product that uses the rainforest in a sustainable way. Products include Brazil nut cosmetics, ecotourism, sustainable wood furniture, ice cream made from Cupuacu fruit.

Group activity   ▪▪▪▪

4   Have a debate on which is more important, economic development or rainforest conservation.

Going further

4   a   Find out more about the Kayapo tribe at:
        www.survival-international.org
    b   Find out more about the destruction of the Amazon rainforest at:
        kids.mongabay.com
    c   Take the quiz at:
        www.savetherainforest.org
    d   See if you can run your own eco-tourism resort in the rainforest at:
        www.eduweb.com/amazon.html

Coral reefs

Coral reefs are a marine **ecosystem**. They grow in the tropical waters of the Atlantic and Indo-Pacific Oceans. Coral polyps are small tube-like animals that leave limestone skeletons when they die. To grow they require:

- clear water, which allows sunlight to reach the coral
- warm water
- strong waves to carry nutrients and wash away sediment
- salt water.

Coral grows very slowly at 1 cm per year. Some of the world's coral reefs are over 6,000 years old. Coral reefs support many different species, including fish, dolphins, sharks, seaweed, turtles, birds and humans.

Ahus, Papua New Guinea

Case study

The inhabitants of Ahus have used the coral reef for generations. They use it in a **sustainable** way. Line fishing is allowed, but net and spear fishing is restricted. This allows fish to grow larger and healthier. There is a cultural tradition to restrict fishing in six areas. An area is restricted after the death of an individual. After a mourning period of a few years, the inhabitants can fish that area again. There is enough fish for a feast! Fish are traded for agricultural products from the mainland that cannot be grown on Ahus. In 2008 a plan was put forward to relocate villages on Ahus island due to rising sea levels making it difficult for them to build or fish.

Activity

14 Using Source J and the case study, explain why coral reefs are important.

Study tip

Make sure that you are able to write about different uses of coral reef resources.

J *Coral reef in the Pacific Ocean*

Case study

Threats to coral reefs

Coral reefs provide $30 billion to the economy each year and 1 billion people rely on them worldwide. Twenty per cent of coral reefs have already been destroyed. The main threats are as follows:

- **Fishing**: Over-fishing using methods such as dynamite and cyanide fishing causes species to become **extinct** and damages coral. Live fish are taken for the pet and restaurant trade.

- **Pollution**: Sediment washed out to sea cuts off the sunlight and causes increased growth of algae. Invasive species such as the crown-of-thorns starfish destroys the coral by eating the coral polyp flesh.

- **Tourism**: Damage from building, boats and sewage in tourist areas.

- **Mining**: Coral limestone is mined for use in road and building construction.

- **Global warming**: Increased carbon dioxide makes the water more acidic, so the coral cannot make their skeletons and they are more prone to diseases. Increased temperatures lead to 'coral bleaching'.

- **Nuclear testing**: Coral reefs in the Pacific have been used by the French for testing nuclear weapons.

K *Coral is unloaded from a boat for use in hotel construction and tourist development*

Activity

15 Using Source K and the case study, describe three causes of coral reef destruction.

Environmental groups and local communities would like to stop the destruction of coral reefs. They protect shores from the impact of waves and storms. They provide nurseries for a quarter of the world's ocean fish and are a source of medicine. The drug AZT, made from reef sponge, is used to treat HIV patients. Ecotourism is one way the coral reefs could be used in a sustainable way.

Did you know ??????

The anchor from a cruise ship can destroy coral over an area equivalent to half the size of a football pitch.

Going further

5 a Find out more about life in coral reefs at:
www.coralfilm.com/fun.html
b Find out more about the destruction of coral reefs at:
oceanworld.tamu.edu/students/coral/coral5.htm
c Take the quiz and web of life challenge at:
www.bbc.co.uk/nature/blueplanet/challenge.shtml
d See how you can help coral reefs at:
www.coralreef.noaa.gov/outreach/thingsyoucando.html

Group activity ■■■■

5 Have a debate on which is more important: economic development or coral reef conservation.

Check your understanding

1 Name two non-renewable resources.

2 Describe two problems associated with nuclear power.

3 Explain how the UK will meet the Renewables Obligations target by 2015.

4 Explain how human activity affects a large scale ecosystem.

Activity

16 Design a poster or leaflet giving ecotourist 'tips for divers'. Tips may include going on a diving course, not touching or feeding any aquatic life, taking only photos and reporting any disturbances.

Pollution

As the world population increases, it is causing many global environmental problems. When countries develop, **urbanisation** and **industrialisation** occurs. People consume more energy and demand more consumer goods. This leads to increased **pollution** of the air, water and land. Pollution can damage human health and the environment.

Land pollution

Radioactive nuclear waste is stored above the ground. The village of Drigg in Cumbria will be paid £75 million to store low level radioactive waste. Industrial and household waste from cities is dumped in large landfill sites. Britain sends more household waste (22.6 million tonnes) to landfill than any other country in the EU. Landfill releases toxins into the soil and water. Rotting rubbish releases methane gas. Landfill attracts pests and causes a nuisance from traffic, noise, smells, dust and litter. In many less economically developed countries (LEDCs), children living on waste dumps suffer lead poisoning and asthma.

Activity

1. Using Source A, how many sources of pollution can you identify?

Objectives

You will be able to:

explain how urbanisation and industrialisation cause pollution

describe the causes and effects of global warming

explain how human activity leads to loss of biodiversity

explain how tourism causes environmental problems.

Key terms

Urbanisation: the movement of people from the countryside, to live in towns and cities.

Industrialisation: the change from a farming society to a society based around production of goods in factories.

Pollution: something that poisons or damages air, water or land.

Acid rain: rain, snow, fog or dust with a pH below 5.

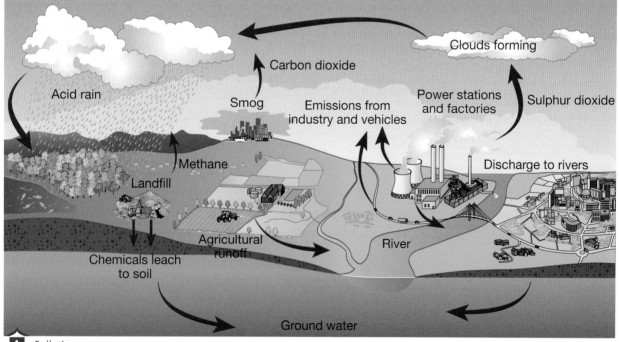

Acid rain · Smog · Carbon dioxide · Clouds forming · Emissions from industry and vehicles · Power stations and factories · Sulphur dioxide · Methane · Landfill · Discharge to rivers · Chemicals leach to soil · Agricultural runoff · River · Ground water

A Pollution

Water pollution

Many rivers, seas and coral reefs are being destroyed by pollution. Rubbish and sewage are dumped at sea. The pesticides farmers use on their land often runs into rivers causing algal blooms. Factories dump over four billion tonnes of waste water into the Yellow River in China each year. This has turned the Shandong province into the 'cancer capital of the world'. Oil spills from ships such as the *Sea Empress*, which released 72,000 tonnes of crude oil into the sea around the coast of South-West Wales in February 1996, are costly and difficult to clean up.

Did you know ? ? ? ? ? ?

750,000 people die in China every year as a result of pollution related diseases.

B *Pollution in Lanzhou, China, one of the world's most polluted cities*

Air pollution

The main cause of air pollution is the burning of fossil fuels. As power stations and vehicles release gases and smoke into the atmosphere, smog can develop. In Mexico City smog can last for days and cause lung irritation and chest pains. Sulphur dioxide causes **acid rain** which kills trees, dissolves stone on buildings and kills fish in rivers and lakes. CFCs released from fridges and aerosols are responsible for destroying the ozone layer. This allows harmful UV radiation to reach earth causing skin cancer and cataracts in humans. Radioactive particles from the Chernobyl nuclear explosion were carried across Europe affecting soil and water supplies and causing health problems in the immediate blast area.

Activity

2   Using Source B, write a letter explaining what it is like to live in Lanzhou, and what action you would like to be taken.

∞ links

Look back at topic 2.1 for more information on Chernobyl.

Activity

3   Using the text and Sources A and B, explain why pollution is a global problem.

Going further

1   a   Find out the top 10 most polluted cities and The Dirty Thirty at: www.worstpolluted.org
    b   Watch an acid rain animation at: www.epa.gov/acidrain/education/site_students
    c   Search in 'facts' and 'science' for more about the Ozone hole at: www.coolantarctica.com

Study tip

Remember some pollution such as nuclear waste can affect land, water and air.

Global warming

Since industrialisation more fossil fuels have been burned. This has released more carbon dioxide into the atmosphere. With more people to feed in the world, there are more cattle and more rice fields. These produce methane gas. Fluorinated gases (F-gases) including HFCs, PFCs and CFCs are now banned, but were found in fridges and aerosols. These produce a small percentage of the total **greenhouse gases**, but their effect can be a thousand times more damaging than the same amount of carbon dioxide.

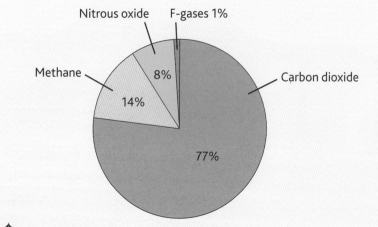

C *Greenhouse gases*

Carbon dioxide and methane are greenhouse gases because they act like glass in a greenhouse, trapping heat in the earth's atmosphere. The amount of carbon dioxide has increased from 313 parts per million (ppm) in 1960 to 386ppm in 2008. As the amount of greenhouse gases in the atmosphere increases, more heat is trapped. As more heat is trapped, the earth becomes warmer. This is called **global warming**. The average world temperature has increased by 0.5°C since 1900. Scientists predict it will increase between 1°C and 6°C during the 21st century.

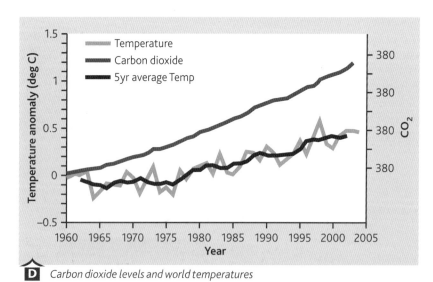

D *Carbon dioxide levels and world temperatures*

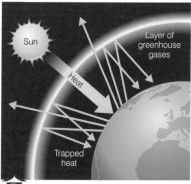

E *The greenhouse effect*

There are some scientists who dispute the link between rising carbon dioxide levels and global warming. They point to the 'Roman warming' and the 'Medieval warming' when temperatures were as warm as today. However the challenges posed by global warming remain the same.

Effects of global warming

Global warming can cause the following problems:

- Global changes in climate causing some places to become wetter and other places to become drier.
- An increase in droughts.
- An increase risk of forest fires.
- An increase in the amount and severity of storms.
- Melting ice caps and glaciers retreating, leading to global rise in sea level.
- Flooding and loss of land in coastal areas.
- Changes to plant and animal life, leading to the extinction of some species.
- An increase in mosquitoes leading to the spread of diseases like malaria.

Study tip

Make sure that you know at least three effects of global warming.

Case study

Tuvalu

Tuvalu is a collection of nine coral reef atolls in the Pacific Ocean. It is home to over 10,000 people and is the first country in the world expected to disappear due to global warming. The low lying islands are increasingly threatened by the rise in sea level and more frequent storms. Scientists predict it will be uninhabitable within 50 years. The inhabitants will become **environmental refugees**, moving to New Zealand, Australia or a futuristic floating island.

F Tuvalu. The highest point is only 4.5 metres above sea level

Group activity

1 Using Source F and the case study, have a debate on whether humans should try to stop global warming or adapt to it. Groups could represent residents of Tuvalu, politicians and environmentalists.

Activity

6 Draw two columns, labelled advantages and disadvantages.

Put each of the following effects of global warming in the UK in the correct column.

Scottish ski resorts close

Higher crop yields

More pest and diseases

Plants grow further north

Valuable farmland lost

High cost of sea defences

Mediterranean summers

Vines and oranges grown

Going further

2 a Play 'I'm alright Jack' at:
www.bbc.co.uk/climate

b Watch the climate animations and do the quiz at:
www.epa.gov/climate/kids

c View pictures showing evidence of global warming at:
www.effectofglobalwarming.com/global-warming-pictures.html

d Find out more about Tuvalu at:
www.tuvaluislands.com

Loss of biodiversity

Rainforests and coral reefs are home to many different species. This **biodiversity** is important because even small insects play vital roles within an ecosystem. The loss of one species can affect an entire ecosystem. Many of the 7,000 **endangered** species of plants and animals could be potential cures for diseases such as cancer or HIV/AIDS.

There are over 5 million species in the world today, of which 1.75 million have been identified. It is estimated that 100 to 200 species are lost everyday. There are five main causes leading to the loss of biodiversity.

Habitat destruction

Habitat is lost to agriculture, housing and industry.

Climate change:

Species are not able to adapt to changes in climate due to global warming and the destruction of the ozone layer. Increased sea temperature causes coral bleaching.

Pollution

Pesticides, sewage, nuclear waste and rubbish all affect habitats. Acid rain kills fish in lakes and rivers.

Exploitation

Deforestation destroys habitat. Over-fishing and whaling causes species to become endangered. **Poaching** for the illegal wildlife trade is the second biggest threat after habitat destruction.

Invasive alien species

Alien species can harm the existing ecosystem. The Harlequin ladybird arrived in the UK from Asia in 2004. It competes with native species, eating their food and even other ladybirds.

G *A stall in Burma selling clouded leopard skin and horns, teeth and bones for traditional medicines*

⚭ links

See Topic 2.1 for more about biodiversity in rainforests and coral reefs.

Key terms

Biodiversity: the variety of species found in a particular area.

Endangered: when the numbers of a species are so low or it is facing such severe threats it may become extinct.

Habitat: the natural environment of an animal or plant.

Poaching: catching or killing animals illegally.

Alien species: a plant or animal that moves from its original habitat into a new area.

Did you know ??????

90 per cent of species on earth are insects.

Going further

3 **a** Research one of 34 biodiversity hotspots at: www.biodiversityhotspots.org

   b Find out more about endangered species and invasive alien species at: www.panda.org

   c Play 'to the rescue' and other games at: www.wwf.org.uk/gowild

   d Report sightings of the Harlequin ladybird at: www.harlequin-survey.org

Activity

7 Using Source G and the text, explain how the illegal wildlife trade leads to loss of biodiversity.

Tourism

Tourism causes environmental problems in more economically developed countries (MEDCs) and LEDCs. Negative impacts occur when the visitor numbers are greater than the environments ability to cope. In the UK, '**honey pots**' such as Malham in the Yorkshire Dales have suffered from traffic congestion, footpath erosion and trampling of vegetation. Over half a million tourists visit Kenya each year. On the beaches near Mombasa, sewage from the hotels is pumped out to sea polluting coral reefs. Coral reefs are also damaged by **leisure** activities such as boating and snorkelling. Off-road driving on safari causes erosion and affects the behaviour of animals. Some animals neglect their young or fail to mate, due to intrusive tourists.

H *Rubbish on Mount Everest*

Tourism causes environmental damage from building bigger airports, hotels, roads and marinas. Pressure is put on local resources especially water for use in hotels, swimming pools and golf courses.

Fragile environments are also being affected as tourists travel further. Antarctica has over 30,000 visitors a year. Mount Everest is called 'the highest junkyard in the world' due to the 120 tonnes of rubbish left on the mountain since 1953. Rubbish includes oxygen tanks, tents, ropes and 120 frozen bodies! Trekkers cause deforestation and erosion by burning wood for cooking and hot showers.

Activity

9 Write a postcard from a tourist destination. Describe the damage caused to the environment.

Check your understanding

1 Name two causes of loss of biodiversity.

2 Describe two effects of global warming.

3 Explain how industrialisation and urbanisation cause pollution.

4 Explain how tourism affects the environment.

Key terms

Tourism: a trip made for pleasure, usually including at least one night away.

Honey pot: an area of attractive scenery or historic interest visited by large numbers of tourists.

Leisure: free time to do whatever you want subject to finance and ability.

Study tip

Use named tourist resorts or honey pots in your answers.

Activity

8 Using Source **H** and the text, give two ways that tourists cause environmental damage on Mount Everest.

Did you know ??????

A golf course in a tropical country uses the same amount of water as 60,000 locals.

Going further

4 a Find out more about the environmental impact of tourism by searching the 'sustainable tourism' section at: www.gdrc.org

b List the activities of tourists by clicking on 'facts' and 'tourism' in the human impacts and threats science section at: www.coolantarctica.com

c Find out more about rubbish on Mount Everest at: www.theuiaa.org/waste_management.html

d Play the Mount Everest game and find out how much an expedition costs at: www.nationalgeographic.com/everest

How do individuals and groups respond to environmental issues?

Different responses

The response of individuals and groups is determined by their beliefs and values. Some have a sense of **global responsibility** and see protecting the environment as important for the future of the planet and humankind. Others seek the short term economic benefits natural resources can bring. MEDCs are concerned about global warming, loss of forests and biodiversity. LEDCs are concerned that environmental pressure will prevent their development. They point to the fact that the UK cut down most of its trees 1,000 years ago. If everyone in the UK has a car and a TV, why can't everyone in China?

Political groups

The Green Party see environmental issues as the main political issue. They campaign for 'green' issues such as more public transport and restricting air travel. They seek to educate and exert political power.

Pressure groups

Environmental pressure groups such as Greenpeace take **direct action** on a wide range of environmental issues such as climate change and pollution.

Businesses

Many businesses are concerned about their profits before the environment. The chemical industry, mining and coal-fired power stations cause pollution, but they also employ large numbers of people. Trade unions have a duty to protect people's jobs.

A *Fuel protest*

Government

The government may respond to environmental issues by passing new laws, for example stopping the sale of leaded petrol in 2000. It can set up initiatives such as Agenda 21. It may introduce 'pay as you throw' schemes for waste collection. It can make environment issues part of compulsory education.

Scientists

Scientists sometimes known as 'bright green environmentalists' respond by using science and technology to improve efficiency of motor vehicles and power stations and research solutions to environmental problems.

Key terms

Global responsibility: individuals and businesses making choices that affect the world in a positive way.

Direct action: the use of violent or non-violent methods to influence a political decision.

Stewardship: looking after something so it can be passed on to the next generation.

Did you know ???????

Over one billion people will celebrate the 40th Earth Day in 2010.

Activity

1 Imagine you are a trucker taking part in the protest shown in Source A. Explain how you could have conflicting views on environmental issues.

∞links

Also see Topic 2.4 for more information on Agenda 21.

Study tip

Be prepared to write about viewpoints different to your own.

Sceptics

There are still a minority of scientists and others who deny that global warming exists. Even when global warming has been shown to exist, some sceptics dispute the causes, saying it is natural rather than man-made. Some people do not want to believe that global warming exists as it means they will have to take action and that will change their lifestyle.

> I'm not going to stop driving just because of global warming

B

Religion

Many religions have the idea of **stewardship**. They believe the world was created and humans are responsible for looking after it. Hindus have the concept of Ahimsa, meaning non-violence and respect for life. This prevents Hindus from harming creatures and most are vegetarian. In Islam, Prophet Muhammad taught about caring for animals 1,400 years before it was a political issue. The Christian Ecology Link was set up in 1982. It has given out certificates to churches which carried out 10 environmentally positive activities. Source **D** shows its current food campaign.

A Message from Christian Ecology Link
Use your LOAF to make a difference!

The importance of food as an environmental issue is increasingly apparent.
As you eat your meal today, Christian Ecology Link invites you to reflect on the LOAF principles:

Locally produced
Organically grown
Animal friendly
Fairly traded

Enjoy your meal!

Food matters. The kind of food we choose should demonstrate our care for God's creation. What food is provided in our church? At home? How far did it travel?

Bread has symbolic meaning. Jesus blessed and broke bread and gave it to his disciples saying 'Do this in remembrance of me'.

Do photocopy and use this 'placemat' at communal meals to prompt reflection on the environmental impact of our choice of food. **Christian Ecology Link**, Britain's leading church-based environmental charity, can be contacted at 3 Bond Street, Lancaster LA1 3ER, or by phone on 01524 36241, email info@christian-ecology.org.uk, website **www.christian-ecology.org.uk**

D *Christian food campaign*

C *"Treat the earth well. It was not given to you by your parent, it was loaned to you by your children"*

Activity

2 Using Sources **B** and **C**, explain why people respond differently to environmental issues.

Activity

3 Using Source D, evaluate the effectiveness of LOAF on environmental issues.

Going further

1 **a** Find out the latest campaigns and policies of the Green Party at: **www.greenparty.org.uk**

b Read the stories 'The two scholars' and 'The challenge' in the Kids Stuff section at: **www.biggreenjewish.org**

c Take the 'How earth-friendly are you?' quiz at **www.reep.org/resources/secondary/ecoquiz/**

Pressure groups

Pressure groups have been involved in environmental issues since the 19th century. The RSPB was formed in response to a single environmental issue. The fashion in the 1860s for feathers in hats led to the near extinction of the great crested grebe. Protests eventually led to the 1921 law banning the sale of the feathers. There are now over 1,000 pairs of grebe in the UK.

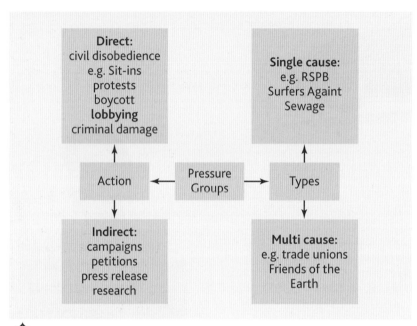

Direct:
civil disobedience
e.g. Sit-ins
protests
boycott
lobbying
criminal damage

Single cause:
e.g. RSPB
Surfers Againt
Sewage

Action ← Pressure Groups → Types

Indirect:
campaigns
petitions
press release
research

Multi cause:
e.g. trade unions
Friends of the
Earth

E *Pressure groups*

Some environmental issues such as road building have pressure groups on both sides of the issue. The Independent Bypass Group is a single issue party campaigning for a bypass to be built around Boston, Lincolnshire, to reduce congestion. In 2007 it took control of the local council with the aim of moving the bypass plans forward. In 1996 Earth First! set up camps along the site of the proposed Newbury bypass. It was the largest road protest in Europe with over 7,000 protestors, some of whom lived in tree houses called 'twigloos'. Although the Newbury bypass was built, these camps did result in other road schemes being cancelled. In 2008 Earth First! joined Camp for Climate Action which included a one-day event at Heathrow airport in protest at runway expansion followed by a march to a camp at Kingsnorth power station.

Greenpeace

Greenpeace is one the most high profile environmental pressure groups in the world today. It acts to change attitudes and behaviour, to protect and conserve the environment and to promote peace. Its first campaign in 1971, involved taking a small boat into Alaskan waters to witness underground nuclear tests. The action was successful and the US government banned nuclear testing later that year and declared the area a bird sanctuary.

In 2008 Greenpeace campaigns included climate change, conserving forests and oceans and the elimination of toxic chemicals. They use direct action in unusual ways that attract media attention to get their message across.

F   *Greenpeace dumping coal outside Downing Street in protest against climate change*

In October 2007 six protestors against climate change spent nine hours climbing up a 200 m smokestack at a proposed coal-fired power station at Kingsnorth in Kent. They planned to write 'Gordon, bin it' down the smokestack. They managed to write 'Gordon' in white paint causing over £30,000 damage. In September 2008 the 'Kingsnorth six' were found not guilty of causing criminal damage, because they had a lawful excuse of protecting property around the world from climate change.

Greenpeace have succeeded in stopping commercial whaling and the mineral exploitation of Antarctica for 50 years. They have also been successful in securing a ban on dumping radioactive waste at sea.

As the earth's non-renewable resources are used up and land, air and water become polluted, individuals, local councils, national governments and global organisations are looking for solutions to these environmental problems.

Activity

5   Using Source F, explain what 'direct action' is.

66 *We respect Greenpeace and their right to protest, but what they have done was irresponsible. It caused a lot of damage and put people's lives at risk. One power station will not make a difference to climate change.* 99

Quotation from power station supporter

G

Activity

6   Write a newspaper report about a Greenpeace protest.

Going further

2   a   Find out where the next Climate Camp gathering will be at:
www.climatecamp.org.uk

   b   Save endangered species or block a discharge pipe at:
www.greenpeace.org/international/fungames

   c   Find out about the latest Greenpeace campaigns at:
www.greenpeace.org.uk

   d   Research a pressure group in your local area.

Check your understanding

1   Name two pressure groups.

2   Describe two ways the government can respond to environmental issues.

3   Explain why business is often reluctant to act on environmental issues.

4   'Kingsnorth six found not guilty.' Using Sources F and G explain why you agree or disagree with the decision.

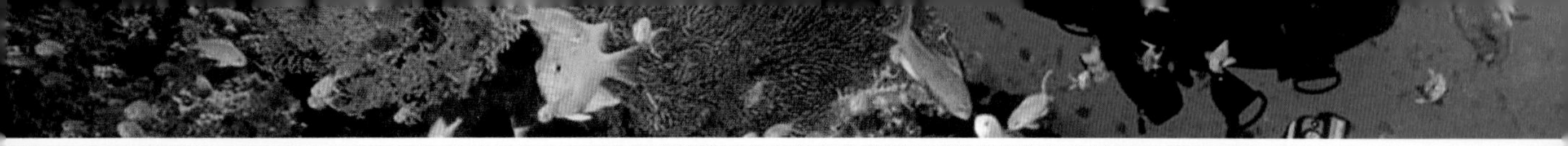

2.4 What are the solutions to environmental problems?

Land pollution

The disposal of nuclear waste remains a problem that new technologies may solve. Options include burying it 1 km underground or sending it into space. The amount of household waste going into landfill can be reduced by following the 'Reduce, Reuse, Recycle' advice. Many supermarkets are trying to reduce packaging and many local authorities now offer **recycling** services.

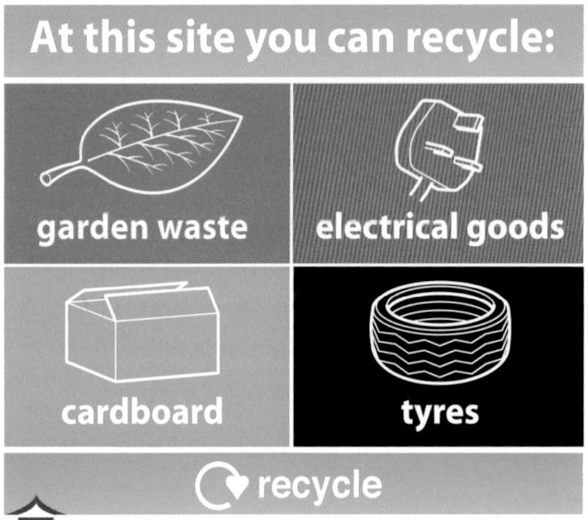

At this site you can recycle:
garden waste
electrical goods
cardboard
tyres
recycle

A *Recycling*

Water pollution

Dumping nuclear waste at sea has been banned since 1983. In 1998 the Milford Haven Port Authority was fined £4 million for the oil spill from the *Sea Empress*.

Air pollution

Smog in cities can be reduced by using public transport or by taking part in a car share scheme. Cars can be made cleaner with catalytic converters and by removing lead from petrol.

Reducing acid rain requires cutting sulphur emissions. To repair the damage already caused, lime can be added to lakes to reduce the acidity.

The Montreal **protocol** on the depletion of the ozone layer (1987) is claimed to be one of the most successful **international agreements**. It is hoped the ozone layer could recover by 2050 due to the reduction in CFCs. However the replacements for CFCs are known to increase global warming.

Objectives

You will be able to:

- understand the term 'sustainable development'
- describe a range of methods for reducing or solving environmental problems
- evaluate the effectiveness of the methods.

Key terms

Recycling: turning used products into new products in order to prevent waste, reduce pollution and lower greenhouse gases.

Protocol: a written record of an agreement between two or more countries.

International agreements: agreements between two or more countries.

Activity

1. Using Source A, make a list of items that can be recycled.

Did you know ??????

25 recycled plastic bottles can be used to make a fleece jacket.

Study tip

Use your own experience of recycling when answering questions in your exam.

Sustainable development

The term **sustainable development** was first used by the Brundtland Commission in 1987. This report led to the Rio Earth Summit in 1992, attended by 108 world leaders. It produced three main outcomes:

- Climate change convention
- Convention on biological diversity
- **Agenda 21** (21 refers to the 21st century).

These are represented by 3 E's in Source **B**, and the solutions by 3 R's.

Agenda 21 is the environmental action that is taken by individuals as **global citizens**, by local councils and by central government. The issue of climate change is tackled by reducing energy use and greenhouse gas emissions. Ecology covers the issue of biodiversity and forest conservation. It involves respecting the plants and animals that are contained in ecosystems such as tropical rainforests and coral reefs.

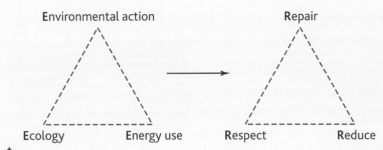

B　*Sustainable development*

The Environmental Sustainability Index is designed to measure a country's progress towards a sustainable environment. It uses 68 different indicators including air quality in cities, water management and the strength of environment laws in the country to give a score out of 100. In 2008, Switzerland came top with an index of 95.5. The UK was 14th with 86.3.

3　Carry out a survey to see how environmentally friendly people are. Create a table like the one below listing 10 everyday items and ask people if they would reuse or recycle each item or if they would bin it.

Item	Reuse/recycle	Bin
Mobile phone		
Old t-shirt		
Glass bottle		
TOTAL		

Sustainable development: economic and social development that meets the needs of current and future generations.

Agenda 21: a commitment to move towards sustainable development at government and local level.

Global citizen: thinks about their effect on the world by preserving the environment and keeping natural resources for others to use in the future.

∞ links

Also see Topic 2.2 for more information on climate change and global warming.

2　Design a poster using the slogan:

'Global citizens: Think global, act local!'

1　a　Find out what young people around the world are doing by reading the Ecotimes at:

www.grida.no/geo2000/pacha/

　b　Find out how different items can be recycled at:

www.recycling-guide.org.uk

　c　Design a leaflet about recycling facilities for households in your area.

Solutions to global warming

The Intergovernmental Panel on Climate Change (IPCC) was set up by the UN in 1988. It produced a report showing the link between rising carbon dioxide levels and global warming. Any solution to global warming involves reducing the amount of carbon dioxide produced and **government action** will be needed to achieve this.

Carbon dioxide produced by burning fossil fuels in power stations could be reduced by using more renewable or sustainable energy. Stopping the burning of tropical rainforests would reduce the amount of carbon dioxide released. The remaining trees would also absorb carbon dioxide from the atmosphere. The government would like all new homes to be 'zero carbon' by 2016. It is also proposing to build 10 new eco-towns, but opponents say there should be more city-centre flats rather than new houses in the countryside.

It's OK. I'll plant a tree later.

C *Carbon offsetting*

Many companies have been set up to offer **carbon offsetting**. They calculate the carbon emissions generated by an activity such as flying or driving and then use an initiative such as tree planting or funding renewable energy to reduce carbon dioxide in the atmosphere by an equivalent amount. Some people argue it delays putting laws in place and looking for alternatives. It even encourages people to continue their carbon-fuelled lifestyles.

∞ links

See Topic 2.1 for more information on renewable and sustainable energy.

Case study

Kyoto Protocol

World leaders met in 1997 in Kyoto, Japan to adjust their 1992 agreement on climate change made at the Earth Summit. This was seen as a global solution to the issue of global warming. The new agreement promised to reduce greenhouse gas emissions by an average of 5 per cent by 2012. The protocol offered funding to LEDCs for new technologies. It allowed countries to buy emission credits from other countries and for heavily forested countries to use their trees to offset carbon emissions.

LEDCs say the protocol threatens their development. In 2001, the USA withdrew from Kyoto. George W. Bush, the American president, felt the agreement was unfair. He thought it would damage the economy and would cost the USA more as they use more fossil fuels.

D *Protesting against the Kyoto Protocol*

Other ways to cut greenhouse gases include eating a vegetarian diet. There are 1.5 billion cattle on the planet producing 500 litres of methane each per day. It also takes less energy to produce vegetarian food. Another radical idea is to have fewer children. Each UK child born today uses 750 tonnes of carbon dioxide over a lifetime. Many solutions require not only money but a change in people's attitudes. Sometimes these are linked, for example as the price of petrol goes up it has been shown that people drive more carefully to conserve fuel.

Activity

5   Using using the Case Study and Source **D**, write a letter to the White House, explaining why the US should or should not sign the Kyoto protocol.

Activity

6   Match these individuals or companies with the appropriate action to reduce global warming.

Industry	Choose electrical appliances that use less energy. Insulate roofs, walls and windows.
Electricity companies	Choose small efficient cars or use public transport.
Homeowners	Use renewable energy sources. Clean up waste gases before releasing.
Drivers	Become more efficient and use more recycled materials.

Going further

2   a   Calculate your carbon and ecological footprint at:
www.footprint.org.uk

b   Take a tour of an eco-house at:
www.channel4.com/lifestyle/green/tour-eco-home/

c   List 35 ways individuals can stop global warming at:
www.stopglobalwarming.org/sgw_actionitems.asp

National parks

National parks help reduce the impact of tourism and increase biodiversity. There are 14 National Parks in the UK, containing some of most spectacular scenery in the UK. These parks are the result of an Act of Parliament (1949), and the first was set up in 1951. There are strict planning regulations that aim to limit the environmental impact of new developments. At 'honeypot' sites like Malham in the Yorkshire Dales National Park there are solutions to some of the problems as shown in Activity 7.

Activity

7 Match these problems with solutions:

Congestion on narrow roads	Artificial surfaces laid
Birds disturbed by climbers	Parking restrictions
Destruction of vegetation	Litter bins removed so people take litter home
Footpath erosion	Climbing restrictions during nesting season
Litter	Improved signs to keep people on paths

Land ownership in the Yorkshire Dales National Park.

Land owner	%
Private (farmers etc)	96.2
Ministry of Defence	0.3
Water companies	0.3
National Trust/English Nature	2.5
National Park Authority	0.1
Other	0.6

E

Activity

8 Look at Source E. Who owns most land in the Yorkshire Dales? Explain why this could cause a problem when trying to implement solutions.

Sagarmatha National Park, which includes Mount Everest, is the highest in the world. It was set up in 1976 and the Nepal Army protects the park by enforcing the laws. It contains many endangered species such as the snow leopard and Himalayan bear. Park officials weigh the incoming and outgoing waste of climbers and charge a fee accordingly. Bottles, cans and batteries are transported to Kathmandu for disposal and human waste is carted to Gorak Shep, where it is buried in bundles at $1 per kilo. From 2009, China may decide to limit the number of permits for climbing Mount Everest from the Tibet side, in an attempt to reduce the environmental impact of tourism.

Did you know ??????

6,555 National Parks cover 12% of the Earth's land surface (1 million sq km).

The World Conservation Union IUCN

Study tip

Use a named national park in the exam.

National parks in Kenya

Kenya is keen to increase **ecotourism** and **sustainable tourism** as a way to develop the country. The Kenya Wildlife Service (KWS) runs 24 National Parks. Amboseli National Park is the second most visited in Kenya and contains Mount Kilimanjaro. Tourists pay $40 to enter the park, but KWS workers are poorly paid and sometimes take no action against drivers who go off road.

Tourists can stay at eco-lodges such as Ol Tukai, which uses solar power, employs local people and participates in tree planting programmes.

F   *Tourists photographing elephants in Amboseli National Park*

National Parks can play a part in **conservation**. Elephants have been placed on Convention on International Trade in Endangered Species (CITES) since 1989. The sale of ivory is illegal. In Kenya, elephants can become isolated if they are unable to move between parks safely. They can be shot by farmers they come into conflict with, or illegal poachers, but their overall numbers have increased.

The Mombasa Marine National Park and Reserve opened in the 1980s to protect the coral reef. The coral had suffered from over-fishing and trophy collecting. Today fishermen are not allowed to fish within the National Park and this can cause conflict. Some fishermen have converted their boats to take tourists into the Marine National Park.

Going further

3 a Follow the countryside code in the Dartmoor National Park at: **www.dartmoor-npa.gov.uk/fz-interactives**

    b List Kenya's Big Five at: **www.kws.org**

    c Explore an eco-lodge at: **www.oltukailodge.com**

    d Track elephants in Kenya at: **www.savetheelephants.org**

Check your understanding

1 What does the term 'sustainable development' mean?

2 Describe two ways that global warming can be reduced.

3 Evaluate the effectiveness of international agreements in reducing environmental problems.

4 Explain how national parks can reduce the environmental impact of tourism.

Activity

9 Using the case study and Source **F**, explain the advantages and disadvantages of National Parks in protecting elephants.

Activity

10 Design an eco-resort in a country of your choice.

- What materials will you use?
- What type of power will you use?
- Who will run it?
- Where will the food come from?
- How will it increase biodiversity?

2

Environmental issues

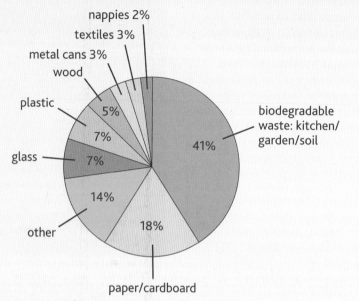

nappies 2%
textiles 3%
metal cans 3%
wood
plastic
5%
7%
glass
7%
biodegradable waste: kitchen/garden/soil
41%
14%
18%
other
paper/cardboard

A *Composition of UK household waste*

Despite the increase in recycling, 72 per cent of household waste goes to landfill sites. Biodegradable waste releases methane, a greenhouse gas. Batteries contain hazardous chemicals that can leach into water supplies. People living near landfill sites are concerned about the health risk, especially from vermin, noise, dust and smell. Councils in England face multi-million pound fines if they miss EU targets to reduce waste sent to landfill by 50 per cent by 2013. The government would like to build thirty new incinerators to burn waste, but these can cause air pollution.

B *The effects of landfill*

Practice questions

2 **a)** Using Source **A**, what are the two main components in household waste? *(2 marks)*

   b) Using Source **B**, briefly explain two effects of landfill on the environment. *(4 marks)*

   c) How important is recycling in reducing landfill? Explain your views using
   Sources **A** and **B** and your own studies. *(12 marks)*

> **Study tip**
> - Make sure you use both sources for this question. You should aim to write about one side A4.
> - How does recycling reduce landfill? Are there other ways such as reducing or reusing that are more important? What about government policies? How effective are policies at changing people's attitudes to recycling?
> - Try to link the sources together. Which of the items in Source A are recyclable?
> - Use your own studies if you are asked.

   d) What is meant by 'natural resources'? Use your own studies to answer. *(2 marks)*

   e) Explain two methods used by environmental pressure groups.
   Use your own studies to answer. *(4 marks)*

> **Study tip**
> - In this question, state the method used, then explain using a named example from your studies.

   f) Explain how tourism can affect a large scale ecosystem.
   Use your own studies to answer. *(12 marks)*

> **Study tip**
> - This question will assess your written communication. You should state your ecosystem, for example, tropical rain forest or coral reef and aim to write one side of A4. You should structure your answer into two parts: the advantages of tourism and the disadvantages of tourism.

> **Study tip**
> - Make sure you use good English and clear presentation in your answers.

3.1 What are basic rights, freedoms and responsibilities?

■ Rights

The idea that people should have certain rights has existed for over 2,000 years. Between 1200 BCE and 300 BCE the scriptures of the ancient Israelites were formed and eventually become the basis of Christian and Muslim thinking. Both the Bible and the Qur'an refer to rights. The right to be seen as innocent until proven guilty originates in Jewish law. The Greek states and later the Roman Empire gave free male citizens certain political rights.

In the past, in many countries, people tended to have rights according to the group they belonged to. In Britain the rich had more rights than the poor; Protestants had more rights than Catholics; men had more rights than women. In the US and South Africa, whites had more rights than blacks.

Three historical documents containing human rights

 The Magna Carta

English Bill of Rights 1689	French Declaration of the Rights of Man 1789	The American Bill of Rights 1791
Right not to be cruelly punished	Right of liberty and property	Right to freedom of religion and free speech

B

In the Second World War over 72 million people died in the world's largest conflict. The idea that *everyone*, no matter what group they belonged to, should be guaranteed **human rights** followed on from this. The United Nations Organisation (UNO) was formed, with the main goal of keeping international peace and preventing future conflict. According to the Universal Declaration of Human Rights (UDHR) never again should anyone be unjustly denied life, freedom, food and shelter. It was to be the **responsibility** of everyone, governments and citizens, to ensure these rights existed everywhere.

Did you know ???????

The Magna Carta or 'Great Charter' of 1215 was England's first document containing commitments by a king to respect certain rights. It included the right of appeal against unlawful imprisonment.

Key terms

Human right: a legal or moral entitlement to do something or to be protected from something, for example, the right to freedom of expression or the right not to be tortured.

Responsibility: a duty which binds you to a course of action demanded by a human right.

Violation: an act which disregards someone's rights.

∞links

Also see the abortion spider diagram in Topic 8.1.

Human rights fall into five categories which all depend on each other if they are to be respected. Without civil and political rights people cannot make use of their economic, social and cultural rights.

Some people argue that it is not possible for rights to be universal. They say it depends on the culture and beliefs of a society as to which rights should exist in that society. For example, the right to have an abortion is considered by some to be a **violation** of the rights of the unborn child, while others see it as the right of the pregnant mother to choose. Some argue that certain economic rights are not possible to respect if there is not enough money. It is argued that workers' rights are only possible if there is a sufficiently strong economy to protect them. Some say that UDHR is a product of western ideas and does not respect the diversity of societies in the world.

The Universal Declaration of Human Rights (UDHR) says people should have different categories of rights

Category of rights	Right to:
Civil	free expression, education
Political	vote, protest
Cultural	choose a religion
Social	maternity pay, family
Economic	work, shelter, health care

C

> This is a free country so I have the right to say anything I want to anyone. If they don't like it that's their problem.

> I want to go wherever I want. Tough if it happens to be somewhere which is owned by someone else.

> When I leave school I have the right to a job so the government had better make sure I get one.

> If I want to have children I'll have them and nobody can stop me.

D   *With rights come responsibilities*

Activity

1   Look at Source **C**.

a   Match each right with the category which it best fits into. You may decide that some rights fit more than one of the categories.

b   Think of other rights which fit into each of the five categories in Source **C**.

c   Can you think of any rights which may be acceptable in one country but not in another?

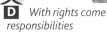
■ Responsibilities

The UDHR says we all have the right to a home. Of course we then need to look after it. It says we have the right to learn but we must make sure we do not prevent others from learning. In other words, with human rights come responsibilities.

Activity

2   Use Source **D**.

a   In each case, the person expresses their right but not the responsibility which goes with it. Copy and complete this table.

Right to	Responsibility
a. freedom of expression	not to insult or offend others
b.	
c.	
d.	

b   Think of other rights to add to the table and add the responsibility each right carries.

c   Explain what society would be like if people exercised their rights but not their responsibilities.

Going further

1   Research one of the following: Magna Carta, English Bill of Rights, French Declaration of the Rights of Man or the American Bill of Rights. Find out which other rights they included.

Did you know ??????

The UDHR principles have been incorporated into the constitutions of most of the more than 185 nations now in the UN. The Rights are set out in 30 sections, known as 'Articles'.

What is life like when human rights are violated?

Countries are generally governed by one of two types of political systems.

A **democracy** is where adult citizens have the opportunity to vote for other people to represent them. These representatives make new laws on behalf of the citizens who have voted for them. This means that if the citizens don't like the people who govern them, they can vote for different people or parties at the next election. In Britain these representatives are called Members of Parliament (MPs) because they make their decisions in the Houses of Parliament in London.

The second type of political system is a **dictatorship**. Dictators usually don't allow the people to vote and, if they do, they often 'rig' the election and intimidate the voters to make sure there is only one winner. Some dictators remain in power until they die. Some of them, such as Hitler, are voted in as part of a democracy and, once they have a taste for power, they don't want to give it up. There are many dictatorships around the world, such as Kim Jong-Il in North Korea.

∞ links

Also see the Mugabe cartoon in Topic 8.4.

Case study

Three of the world's dictators who have violated human rights

Omar al-Bashir, Sudan (in power since 1989)
In western Sudan's Darfur region, over 300,000 people have died and 2 million more have been displaced since February 2003. al-Bashir's Government is responsible for backing the ethnic-Arab militia which has committed many atrocities against non-Arab groups in the region. In southern Sudan, al-Bashir has tried to impose Islamic law on the Christian population. Nearly 2 million civilians have been killed, 4 million displaced and 200,000 women and children taken into slavery.

Kim Jong-Il, North Korea (in power since 1994)
Kim Jong-Il violates many rights and freedoms. Spies inform on anyone who criticises the regime, even in their own homes, and they are then tortured, imprisoned or killed. All radios and TV sets are fixed to receive only government stations. It is a crime to allow pictures of Jong to gather dust or be torn or folded.

General Than Shwe, Burma (in power since 1992)
General Than Shwe has imprisoned more than 1,000 people for their political views. These prisoners are known as **prisoners of conscience**. They include Aung San Suu Kyi, the Nobel Peace Prize-winner. Her party won 80 per cent of the vote in the last open election (1990). Freedom of expression is not allowed. Unlicensed possession of a fax machine or modem is punishable by 15 years in prison.

A prisoner of conscience – Aung San Suu Kyi

E *A violator of human rights – General Than Shwe*

Activity

3 Use the case study and Source **E** to answer the following questions.

a Which human rights have been abused in each of the three examples?

b Why do you think these dictators have abused human rights?

Other examples where human rights are violated

India and Pakistan

Children work a 12- hour-day in sweatshops for virtually no money.

Iraq

A hotel receptionist, Baha Mousa, died in 2003 after being tortured over a period of 36 hours while being detained by British troops. He had 93 separate injuries on his body.

Afghanistan

Under the Taliban during the 1990s, women had to cover themselves entirely. If they left their eyes showing they risked a public beating. Men had to grow their beards and music was banned.

Activity

4   Using the case study and Source **F**, decide which human rights have been abused in each example.

F   *Indian sweatshop*

Life under the Taliban

Going further

2   Research further the dictatorships in Sudan, North Korea and Burma. Other dictators who have been well-known for human rights violations are Pinochet in Chile, Castro in Cuba and Mugabe in Zimbabwe. Find out which rights they have violated.

Human rights violations in China

Non-government organisations (NGOs) such as Amnesty International, the Antislavery Society and Human Rights Watch monitor the actions of all governments in democracies and dictatorships. They pressure them to act according to the UDHR. They work on behalf of people all over the world whose rights have been violated.

China is run by the Communist Party. While economic rights in China have increased under the Communist Party, other rights have been repressed. Some 250,000 Chinese are serving sentences in 're-education and labour camps'. China executes more people than all other nations combined. The death penalty can be given for burglary, bribery or writing slogans on walls. China has no independent judiciary.

Tiananmen Square

In 1989, protesters gathered in Tiananmen Square in Beijing to protest against the Chinese Government. The leaders spent a short time negotiating with the protesters but eventually the army was ordered to disperse and imprison the protesters who were mainly students. The confrontation resulted in killings, injuries and arrests.

Shi Tao

Since 1989, Amnesty International has documented the Chinese Government's abuses of all rights set out in the UDHR. For example, it has brought to the world's attention the case of Shi Tao, one of many who have their rights violated. In 2004, at the age of 37, Shi Tao was working for a magazine. The Government asked all journalists not to report anything about the 15-year anniversary of Tiananmen Square. Shi used his Yahoo email account to send a copy of the Government request to a website called the Asia Democracy Foundation.

G *Imprisoned Chinese journalist Shi Tao*

The Government searched Tao's home and confiscated his computer and documents. His family were told to say nothing. He was charged with leaking state secrets. Tao's lawyer was also arrested. In March 2005, Shi Tao's case was heard in a secret court and he was sentenced to prison for ten years. He was not allowed to appeal the decision.

Activity

5 Write a persuasive letter to China's leader Hu Jintao urging him to release Shi Tao along with many others who have been imprisoned for exercising their right to freedom of expression. Encourage him to respect the UDHR.

Key terms

Non-governmental organisation (NGO): an organisation that is not run by, or associated with, any particular government. It may operate at local, national or international level, for example, Amnesty International, Oxfam.

Study tip

This is a topic which is constantly in the news. Wherever there is a report of a conflict, it is likely that someone's human rights are being violated. You may well be able to refer to the previous day's news in your exam.

Did you know ???????

According to Amnesty International (**www.amnesty.org.uk/education**) there are:

- 132 countries where people are tortured or ill-treated.
- 28 countries where people disappear without trace.
- 44 countries where there are prisoners of conscience.
- 58 countries where people are detained without trial.
- 34 countries where armed groups commit violent acts and killings.

'Free Tibet' protests and the Beijing Olympics

In China, all media is strictly controlled. This was even the case during the 2008 Beijing Olympics. Protesters were arrested after protesting against China's policy on Tibet near the main Olympics venue. At least a dozen 'Free Tibet' and Christian activists were deported for demonstrating around Tiananmen Square.

China's foreign ministry spokesman, Qin Gang, said assemblies or demonstrations could only be carried out after they had been approved. He said this was the Chinese Government's policy and the principle would be strictly followed during the Olympics. Chinese authorities said those wishing to complain during the Olympics could use three selected 'protest parks'. That is, if the Government approved.

H   *The flag of China and the flag of Tibet, which is not allowed to be displayed in China*

Human Rights Watch said a Chinese activist who applied for permission to protest against the Government had been taken into custody just for applying. China's public security officials did not respond to repeated requests for information on how many applications they received and how many, if any, were approved. The parks were a long way from the Olympic venues and were constantly watched by plain-clothed security guards. Not surprisingly, during the Beijing games there were no protests or demonstrations in any of these parks.

During the Olympics, police continued to detain and harass foreign journalists despite Beijing's promise of media freedom. They roughed up and briefly detained a British journalist who tried to report on illegal protests. They also confiscated his equipment.

What it means to live in a dictatorship

For a dictatorship, such as that of Hu Jintao the President of China since 2002, protests are a huge threat to their existence. A dictatorship rules because it thinks it knows best. The people have to accept what the dictatorship decides. However, when the people protest it causes the dictators to worry that they are losing control and they often use force. The people are starved of their influence on how the country is run while the dictators, like big bullies, listen only to themselves.

Did you know ? ? ? ? ? ? ?

Capital punishment divides people all over the world. Is it a right to take away another person's right to life even if they have done the same to someone else?

Figures for capital punishment executions for 2007:

- China 470*
- Iran 317*
- Pakistan 82
- Saudi Arabia 143
- Iraq 65*
- Sudan 65*
- USA 42

(* These figures are approximate)

Going further

3   Amnesty International fights for the release of prisoners of conscience such as Shi Tao, all over the world. Research other prisoners of conscience to find out the circumstances of their arrest and imprisonment.

Check your understanding

1   Name three human rights.

2   Explain why the UDHR exists.

3   Explain why rights and responsibilities have to exist side by side.

4   Describe what an NGO like Amnesty International does for human rights.

5   Explain why more human rights are likely to be violated in a dictatorship rather than in a democracy.

Conflict at a community level: what are the causes, effects and resolutions?

■ Community conflict – bullying

What are the causes of bullying?

Bullying occurs when someone is intentionally and persistently hurt, either physically or verbally. Bullying is a very common form of **conflict** which many people experience as the **aggressor**, **victim** or as observer. Bullies often act with others, in a pack, like animals hunt their prey. This gives them greater strength because they are usually weak when acting alone.

Bullying can have social, economic, religious or political causes. People can be bullied because of their skin colour, nationality, religion, sexuality, views or economic position. These differences are often seen as a threat by potential bullies.

Case study

What bullying can lead to

Caroline Stillman was singled out because she looked different, a common social cause of bullying. She is taller than most children her age because she has a medical condition called Marfan Syndrome, a genetic condition which can cause excessive height. She was 6' 4" at the age of 13.

'At first I was just left out when teachers put us into groups. I gained a reputation for having no mates even though I hung around with people from other classes. Pens from my bag were stolen. Smaller kids were pushed into me from behind as I walked around the school. I got poked with scissors and chewing gum was put in my hair. The bullies never actually show themselves. '

Eventually Caroline had to be taken out of school as she became ill with worry, but the bullying continued. 'People sent me horrible text messages, emails, instant messages like "go kill yourself".'

Key terms

Bullying: the act of intentionally causing harm to others, through verbal harassment or physical assault.

Conflict: a verbal or physical clash.

Aggressor: someone who attacks another person.

Victim: someone who is attacked by an aggressor.

Third party: a person who attempts to find a resolution between those involved in a conflict but is not involved in the conflict itself.

66 *I get called raghead and terrorist* 99

66 *Just because I live in a big house I get called a snob* 99

66 *Others pick on me because I am short and wear glasses.* 99

A *Comments from bullied students*

Activity

1   Match each comment in Source **B** to one of these causes of bullying: social, religious, economic.

Activity

2   Use Sources **A** and **B**.

a   Which of Caroline's human rights have been violated?

b   From your experience of being in school, what are other causes of bullying apart from looking different?

c   Explain the effects on Caroline as a victim of bullying?

B   *The family and friends of Sophie Lancaster*

Preventing and resolving bullying

Online campaigns

Teachers are being advised how to stop students from being bullied through mobile phones and computers. Experts want pupils to understand that passing on videos or images can make the bullying worse. Online campaigns such as 'Laugh at it, and you're a part of it' are now regularly posted on popular websites.

Restorative justice

Restorative justice aims to restore relationships which have broken down through conflict. Both aggressor and victim are encouraged to get together in a safe environment and talk. The aggressor is encouraged to see the causes and effects of their actions. At the same time, the victim is helped to see if they contributed to the conflict in any way by their own behaviour. Both participants are then able to agree their own joint contract of how they are going to treat each other in the future. This gives them a personal stake in the success of the contract. Respect, responsibility, repair and re-integration are the key words.

Peer mediation

Peer mediation is another way of helping to resolve conflict. It involves both parties, aggressor and victim, and also a **third party**, another person around the same age. The third party is a peer mediator who is trained in the skills of conflict resolution. They encourage the aggressor and victim to discuss all issues in dispute, not only the most recent incidents. Even in cases where a written agreement is not drawn up, the aggressor and victim often learn enough about the situation to reduce the tension between them. As a result the social effects of bullying are reduced greatly.

Activity

3   a   Explain why the three ways of resolving conflict identified above might work to stop bullying.

   b   Describe the methods your own school uses to resolve bullying.

   c   Suggest some other ways you think bullying could be prevented and resolved.

Community conflict – gang violence in cities

A new report reveals that children as young as eight are carrying knives. They arm themselves because they fear attacks. The report says a third of young people in London, Manchester and Bristol think it is acceptable to carry a knife in self-defence. Twenty per cent of schools admit to having a problem with **gangs**.

Case study

What gang violence can lead to

In 2000, 11-year-old Damilola Taylor's death shocked the nation. He bled to death on the stairs of the block where he lived in south London having been attacked on his way home.

In 2007, a 16-year-old A-level student, Kodjo Yenga, was left dying in the arms of his girlfriend after an organised gang, who had just killed him, ran away laughing. Five teenage members of the gang were given lengthy sentences. Judge Christopher Moss told them Kodjo's death was an example of the 'needless loss of another young life on the streets of our cities by youngsters like you. You were all part of a gang culture. All of you come from decent and caring backgrounds which makes the situation all the more worrying.'

C The funeral procession for Kodjo Yenga

Young people join gangs for several social reasons such as peer pressure, to gain status and for a sense of belonging. Some believe there is a 'copycat' culture in some areas where young people believe gangs can provide excitement and glory. According to government research, gangs are based more on territory than ethnicity although White British and Afro-Caribbean males are more likely to be in gangs than Black African and Asian males.

Did you know ??????

It is estimated that there are over 1,000 criminal gangs in England and Wales with over 170 in London alone.

Types of gangs

According to the police, there are four types of gang:

- Close friendships
- Associates who share estates
- 'Crews' who control local drug markets
- Crime networks involved in drug markets in clubs.

D Types of gangs

What measures have been taken to try to resolve Britain's gang culture?

In 2008, in Deptford, London, a bus was taken over by police to prevent a planned gang fight that would almost certainly have resulted in death. Officers arrested 24 teenagers aged 14 to 18 and seized six knives, a claw hammer, a metal bar, a mallet, two wrench handles, a metal baseball bat, two screwdrivers, a corkscrew and a golf club.

Adapted from Sean O'Neill, The Times, 20 May 2008

Activity

4 a   Explain why a 'gang culture' exists on some of Britain's streets.

    b   Describe some effects of this 'gang culture'.

Source **F** is an example of Operation Blunt Two. This is the Metropolitan Police's effort to try to combat the rise in stabbings among young people in London.

Information

Ways of preventing and reducing the violent gang culture

- Tackling Gangs Action Programme
- Witnesses who give evidence to be guaranteed anonymity
- Court orders to restrict movement of gang members
- Government advice to teachers to check on Facebook and Bibo to identify whether their pupils are gang members
- Schools should be alert to signs of gangland activity including graffiti 'tags'
- Government advertising campaign to challenge the fear, glamour and peer pressure that can cause young people to join gangs.

Going further

2 Research the Tackling Gangs Action Programme, a six-month government initiative set up in 2007. Find out if it was successful and, if so, why.

www.crimereduction. homeoffice.gov.uk/violentstreet/ violentstreet011.htm

66 *I remember wanting to fit in, and it did mean that sometimes you end up hanging out with people you don't really like that much. I think it is really important that young people have interesting stuff to do, new things to try out. I am working with some friends to set up a space where young people can come and feel safe and get involved in sports and arts.* 99

Hester Lilley, aged 29, London

Activity

5 Use Sources F, G and H.

a State three ways in which gang conflict can be tackled.

b Explain why 'gang culture' is difficult for the government and the police to change.

c Produce a poster giving some reasons for not joining a gang.

Check your understanding

1 Name three causes of bullying.

2 Describe what effects bullying can have on a victim.

3 Explain why gang violence is a serious form of conflict in the community in Britain.

4 Explain how community-based conflict (bullying or gang violence) can be prevented or resolved.

Conflict at a national level: what are the causes, effects and resolutions?

In all the countries in Source A, people have had to become accustomed to conflict. In these countries, armed soldiers or bands of armed individuals roaming the streets or the countryside are a common sight. In all these places there are groups fighting over who should be in control. In Britain we assume a government changes when it is voted out at an election, usually every four or five years. However, there are a number of countries where governments change because they are forced out by violence. This is a common political cause of conflict.

Objectives

You will be able to:

understand why conflict happens at a national level

understand the effects of conflict on the people involved

understand the variety of ways conflict at this level can be resolved.

Palestine (Fatah/Hamas)
Conflict started: 1967
Death toll: unknown

Chechnya in Russia
Conflict started: 1999
Death toll: 100,000

Darfur in Sudan
Conflict started: 2003
Death toll: 400,000

Sri Lanka
Conflict started: 1983
Death toll: 70,000

Democratic Republic of the Congo
Conflict started: 1998
Death toll: 5,400,000

Somalia
Conflict started: 2006
Death toll: 10,000

A

Key terms

Civil war: a war between sections of the same country or different groups within a country.

Going further

1 Research one of the civil wars named in Source A. Find out which groups are fighting for political power. What are the effects on the country and what attempts are being made to resolve the conflict?

Activity

1 Use Source A.

a Why do you think the death toll in each national conflict is difficult to know exactly?

b Discuss why some of the national conflicts may not always be in the news.

c Discuss why the countries where there are national conflicts are generally in the poorer parts of the world.

d Many of the soldiers fighting in these countries are teenage boys. Why do you think they are so young and what impact do you think this has on their lives and on the future of the countries they live in?

Study tip

A common reason for losing marks is not being specific. It is not good enough to merely refer to 'Africa' or 'countries in Africa'. Say exactly which countries have conflicts such as DR Congo or Somalia.

War in the Democratic Republic of Congo – a tragedy of modern times

In the Democratic Republic of Congo over five million people have died in what has been described as the worst war since the Second World War. Over two million have been made homeless in a bloody civil war involving Government troops, militia groups and rebel forces. This war began when soldiers invaded from the bordering countries of Rwanda and Uganda. Their justification was to prevent attacks from armed groups based over their borders in DR Congo. Other countries then sent their soldiers to support DR Congo, and so it has continued for several years. Control of territory, revenge and political power are all reasons for the continuation of the war.

In the middle of the conflict are the innocent Congolese people. They have suffered terrible losses as their country becomes a bigger and bigger battleground in this escalating war. All sides are accused of carrying out horrific atrocities against civilians, in particular mass rape. The variety of tribes, with different cultures and languages are further reasons why the war is so difficult to control. These social causes of the war cause it to grow continually.

B   *Congo boy soldier*

The DR Congo has a vast wealth of natural resources which include zinc, tin, lead, copper and gold. Whoever controls the country can make a lot of money. In fact, DR Congo should be one of the world's richest countries. Instead it is one of the poorest.

It is one of the few places on earth where coltan is to be found. Refined coltan produces a highly heat-resistant metal powder called tantalum. This is a key component in the electronic equipment that is now essential to modern life. If you are carrying a mobile phone as you read this, you most certainly have a bit of DR Congo in your pocket. So, tantalum and other such valuable resources are economic reasons for war in Congo.

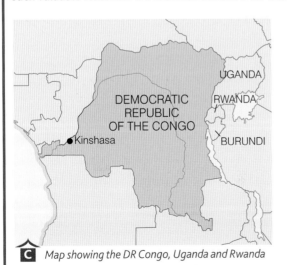

C   *Map showing the DR Congo, Uganda and Rwanda*

Did you know ??????

The mountains that span the DR Congo, Rwanda and Uganda are home to an endangered population of silverback gorillas. In 2007, the alpha male of one family group was killed by rebels as a demonstration of power in the war-torn region.

Activity

2   Explain the various causes of war in DR Congo. Use these terms to help you: political, social, economic.

National conflict – apartheid in South Africa

South Africa experienced over forty years of national conflict under the **apartheid** system. This was a racial system which affected all of the people.

Short-term causes of the Soweto protest, 16 June 1976

On the morning of 16 June 1976, hundreds of black secondary students in Soweto, near Johannesburg, walked out of classes. They took to the streets to protest against a law which forced them to learn in Afrikaans, the language of the ruling Nationalist party. With the freedom of choice taken away, tensions increased as students had watched their parents and teachers fail in attempts to reverse the Afrikaans rule.

Tension had been growing since 17 May when students from Phefeni School had refused to attend classes given in Afrikaans. The students demanded to see the area inspector of schools. When he refused to meet with them, some students damaged school property. The students were threatened with expulsion but they continued their protest with the support of four other schools in Soweto. The students were educating themselves in politics.

On 9 June, two policemen arrested a student at Naledi High School even though the head teacher warned them it would provoke the other students. An angry mob of students surrounded the policemen who locked themselves in the head teacher's office. Meanwhile their police car was set alight in the school car park.

Some of the black students knew they would never be allowed to be socially equal to white students and being made to learn what they saw as the 'whites' language' made them angry. Older black students such as Steve Biko urged them to protest so they would one day have a chance to vote. This protest was both social and political.

Key terms

Apartheid: 'separateness' – a system of segregation or discrimination on the basis of race.

Short-term cause: immediate cause which triggers an incident.

> 66 *I am writing to you, Sir, because I have a growing nightmarish fear that unless something drastic is done very soon then bloodshed and violence are going to happen in South Africa almost inevitably. A people can take only so much and no more. A people made desperate by despair and injustice and oppression will use desperate means.* 99
>
> Letter from Bishop Desmond Tutu to Prime Minister John Vorster, 8 May 1976

Activity

3 Use Source D.

a Explain what the **short-term causes** of the student protest were.

b Why do you think the Government wanted black students to learn subjects in the Afrikaans language?

c What do you think Desmond Tutu meant by 'desperate means'?

The effects of the Soweto protest

The protest of secondary school students on 16 June 1976 was meant to be peaceful but the mood deteriorated as confrontations grew between the students and the police. Eventually the police opened fire with tear gas and live bullets, resulting in the deaths of 15-year-old Hastings Ndlovu and 12-year-old Hector Peterson. Chaos ensued as student leaders were unable to disperse their followers. Streets were barricaded, cars burned and two white officials were killed. By midday, students were looting and burning government buildings across much of Soweto. The police shot dead another 11 people before the evening. By the end of 16 June, 23 people had been killed. For the following three days, protests by school students continued as rioting, stand-offs with the police and burning of property did little to reduce the tension. By the end of the third day of conflict, all schools in Soweto had been officially closed. Rioting then spread to other towns.

Events in Soweto had sparked off protests across the country and within days South Africa suffered approximately another 500 deaths. The number of wounded was estimated to be over a thousand men, women, and children.

A new generation had made their voice of opposition to apartheid heard. Many left South Africa to join the armies of the exiled political movements now based in bordering countries. Many who remained in South Africa became active, often risking their lives, to ensure the struggle against apartheid continued; 16 June would never be forgotten.

16 June is commemorated today by a South African national holiday. This is called Youth Day. It remembers those who lost their lives in the struggle against apartheid.

Activity

4 **a** Why do you think the South African police found it so difficult to put down a protest by young people who were not armed with guns and tear gas?

b Explain how 16 June 1976 had such a big impact on many young people's lives in South Africa.

Did you know ??????

Unbeknown to Nelson Mandela there was a plot to help him escape from Robben Island Prison which was organised by the South African Government. The Government wanted Mandela to escape so they could shoot him during recapture. The plot was foiled by British intelligence.

Inside BOSS Gordon Winter, 1981

E *Students protesting in Soweto, 16 June 1976*

Going further

2 Around the world, various countries have named buildings and streets and hold national holidays to commemorate those who have given their lives in the cause of freedom. Try to find the details of places, dates of holidays and names of those remembered.

Long-term causes of the Soweto Protest

The Afrikaans issue provided the spark for the explosion of 16 June 1976 but to understand the **long-term causes** of the conflict it is necessary to go much further back in South Africa's history.

South Africa was colonised by the English and Dutch at the end of the 18th century. The Dutch descendents, Afrikaaners, eventually came to dominate the country but they were in a small minority compared to the original black Africans who made up over 75 per cent of the population.

The purpose of apartheid, which began in 1948, was the separation of the races. Those who were considered neither White nor Black (**Bantu**) were officially called Coloured and Asian. Everyone had to be in a racial category and they had different rights and freedoms according to their racial group. Apartheid meant that South Africa was in conflict because people were placed in separate social, political and economic categories because of their racial background.

A forerunner to the Soweto shootings occurred on 21 March 1960, when South African police fired on a crowd

F *A segregated beach under apartheid*

of black protesters in the township of Sharpeville. The police continued firing even when the crowd had turned to run, and the majority of those killed and wounded were shot in the back. There was no evidence that any of the crowd were armed. Sixty-nine people were killed including eight women and ten children. Over 180 were injured.

> 66 *Our aim is to restore feelings of pride and dignity to Blacks after centuries of racist oppression.* 99
>
> Steve Biko, 1976

G

The apartheid system

The apartheid system was a combination of over 300 separate laws which covered all areas of life: political, social, moral, religious and economic.

The Group Areas Act (see Source I) removed 1.5 million Blacks from cities to rural reservations. Separateness was an important part of apartheid to ensure there was no mixing. Schools, parks, cities, beaches and public toilets were among the many places where people were racially segregated.

> **Key terms**
>
> **Long-term cause:** cause which takes many years to develop.
>
> **Bantu:** the name given to Black South Africans.
>
> **Inter-racial:** between different races.

> **Did you know** ??????
>
> The creation of separate living areas groups is not unique to South Africa. Reservations exist for native people in the USA and in Australia.

H *Aftermath of the Sharpeville massacre*

The various types of conflict under Apartheid

Reasons for conflict	Minority White Afrikaaner-led Government	Majority Black Africans
Political	▪ Wanted to hold on to power and not allow political parties or trade unions which could threaten this ▪ Acts passed (among others): – Unlawful Organisations Act – Separate Representation of Voters Act – Population Registration Act	▪ Wanted to have the right to vote ▪ Wanted other constitutional rights
Social	▪ Wanted to keep racial groups apart in order to protect the White way of life. Education, sport and living areas were segregated by race ▪ Acts passed (among others): – Group Areas Act – New Passes Law – Bantu Education Act	▪ Wanted basic human rights such as: – freedom of expression – freedom of movement – the right to decent housing, health, education and employment
Moral and religious	▪ Wanted to protect their way of life from what they saw as an inferior culture. Wanted to keep the Afrikaans bloodline 'pure' ▪ Passed laws banning **inter-racial** marriage	▪ Wanted to be treated equally in the eyes of the law and to be free to inter-marry
Economic	▪ Wanted to keep hold of the great natural resources such as gold mines ▪ Wanted to ensure the 'Bantus' remained in the lowest paid jobs ▪ Acts passed (among others): – Mines and Work Act – Separate Development Policy	▪ Wanted the return and redistribution of land taken from them ▪ Wanted equality of opportunity in employment

I

Case study

Black South Africans were even called a separate name – Bantus. Under the Separate Development Policy (see Source I) they had to be citizens of a Bantustan or 'homeland' which was about 14 per cent of South Africa's poorest land. Basic human rights such as freedom of movement, voting and expression were not permitted to Blacks. They had to carry pass books to travel and work. Many Black men had to work in mines which were outside the Bantustan. Many lived in townships on the borders of the big cities where they faced curfews, arrests and poverty. The biggest of these townships was Johannesburg's SOuth WEst TOwnship – SOWETO.

J Soweto

Resolution of the apartheid conflict

There were various attempts to bring the apartheid system conflict to an end.

Shortly after the Sharpville Massacre of 1960, the African National Congress, a black political organisation, was banned. These two events finally convinced Nelson Mandela that **force** needed to be met with force. His group, called Spear of the Nation, coordinated a campaign to bomb government-owned properties and made plans for a possible armed struggle. Mandela saw such force as a last resort because all other peaceful protests had failed. In 1962, he was imprisoned for trying to cause a strike. While in prison, in 1963, he was convicted of sabotage and sentenced to life imprisonment. He spent 18 years of his 27 years in prison on Robben Island performing hard labour. In the years after the Soweto Uprising in 1976, the Spear of the Nation continued with force and carried out many attacks on government targets.

K *Nelson Mandela revisits his confinement cell in 1994*

> The time comes in the life of any nation when there remain only two choices - submit or fight. That time has now come to South Africa. We shall not submit and we have no choice but to hit back by all means in our power in defence of our people, our future, and our freedom.

Nelson Mandela speaking in 1962

Did you know ? ? ? ? ? ?

When President Nelson Mandela launched the new constitution for South Africa in 1996, he chose to do so at Sharpeville.

The United Nations

The United Nations (UN) was set up after the Second World War to help ensure that no government was allowed to persecute people. The Sharpeville massacre caused the UN to get tough on apartheid but not by using force. The UN employed a number of strategies which eventually led to the end of apartheid. The UN called on its members to stop selling arms to South Africa and **sanctions** began to hurt the South African economy. UN members were also told to end political, cultural and sporting links so South Africa became increasingly isolated from the rest of the world. This pressure from sanctions and the international condemnation, together with increasing protests in the 1980s and 90s within South Africa, led to the abolition of some apartheid laws.

Archbishop Desmond Tutu put pressure on the South African Government through his passionate speeches which emphasised the power of non-violence. Tutu's pacifism inspired many people to protest. This was like the **pacifism** practised by Gandhi in India and Martin Luther King in the US.

In 1991, President de Klerk called for a new constitution as he realised apartheid had to change. **Negotiations** began in 1990, when Mandela was released from prison. Elections were held in 1994. Twenty-two million people could now vote compared to three million in the previous election under apartheid.

The African National Congress led the new democratically elected Government with Nelson Mandela as President. He shared the Nobel Peace Prize along with former president de Klerk for laying the foundations for a new democratic South Africa.

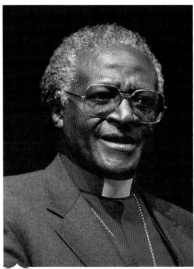

M   *Archbishop Desmond Tutu, 1986*

Desmond Tutu continued in his efforts to resolve the 50-year apartheid conflict with the Truth and Reconciliation Commission. Tutu believed that 'goodness is powerful'. He convinced former aggressors and victims of apartheid to listen to each other in an effort to heal the wounds. Tutu was presented with the Gandhi Peace Prize in 2007 for his non-violent approach to resisting injustice under apartheid.

N   *President Mandela and Deputy President de Klerk receive the Nobel Peace Prize, 1993*

Going further

4   Research one or both of the pacifists Mahatma Gandhi and Martin Luther King. Find out why they chose pacifism to fight against social, religious, economic and political violations of human rights. What protests did they organise and how successful were they?

Activity

6   **a**   Which methods of resolving the conflict were used by Nelson Mandela? Which were used by Desmond Tutu?

b   Explain how the conflict of apartheid was eventually resolved.

c   How easy do you think it is for countries to solve conflict within another nation? What methods can they use?

Check your understanding

1   Describe the short-term causes of the Soweto incidents in 1976. Try to identify whether they were political, economic, social or religious or a combination.

2   Describe some of the effects that the apartheid system had on people's lives.

3   Explain which methods were successful in resolving conflict in South Africa.

Going further

5   Reconciliation was also used following the troubles which paralysed life in Northern Ireland for over 30 years. Find out how truth and reconciliation works by researching how it worked in South Africa or Northern Ireland.

3.4 Conflict at an international level: what are the causes, effects and resolutions?

International conflicts are clashes which spread beyond national borders. At any one time there are several international conflicts going on in different parts of the world. It could even be said that conflict is the normal state of affairs!

A sample of international conflicts involving the UK's armed forces

Conflict	Where	When
Second Boer War	Africa	1899–1902
First World War	Europe, Asia	1914–18
Second World War	Europe, Africa, Asia	1939–45
Korean War	Asia	1950–53
Suez Crisis	Africa	1956
Falklands War	South Atlantic Ocean	1982
Gulf War	Asia	1990–91
Yugoslav Wars	Europe	1990–2001
Afghanistan War	Asia	2001–*
Iraq War	Asia	2003–**

A

*Still ongoing at the end of December 2008
**In December 2008 it was announced that all troops would be withdrawn by the end of July 2009

Objectives

You will be able to:

understand the long-term and short-term causes of international conflicts

understand the effects of international conflicts and how attempts are made to resolve them.

Activity

1. a Look at Source A and decide in which decades the UK has not been involved in an international conflict.

   b Use an atlas to find out where Korea, Suez, the Falkland Islands, Yugoslavia, Afghanistan and Iraq are. What does this tell you about the UK's involvement in international conflicts?

B UK soldiers on patrol in the Helmand Province, southern Afghanistan

C Iraqi women fighters

Causes of international conflicts

Countries often have agreements with each other that if any of them are attacked they will come to each other's assistance. This is what happened in both the First and Second World Wars when Britain had agreements that she would come to the assistance of Belgium in 1914 and Poland in 1939 if they happened to be attacked. Belgium was invaded by Germany in 1914, while in 1939 Poland was invaded by the same country. Therefore, on both occasions Britain ended up fighting against Germany.

International conflicts are frequently over the economic and political power of land. A country has more power when it extends its national borders. Land may have natural resources such as oil, or it may be of strategic importance. Hitler and his Nazi Party invaded other countries in Europe before they were driven back and defeated in 1945. Hitler wanted increased political power in the world. The land the Nazis took over also had resources such as coal and iron. These were vital for boosting economic power and making it one of the wealthiest countries in the world.

Some counties may want to impose their political ideology on other countries. After the Second World War, Russia wanted to impose Communism on other countries in Eastern Europe. By making many of its neighbours follow Communism it could feel safer from the outside world.

Religious beliefs can also lead to international conflicts. Al Qaeda is the Islamic organisation led by Osama Bin Laden (Source **D**) which ordered the attack on the US on 11 September 2001. It

D   *Osama bin Laden*

believes that **Shari'ah** law should be restored throughout the Muslim world. British soldiers are fighting against another religious group, the Taliban, in Afghanistan, who also want the return of **Islamic fundamentalism**. Al Qaeda and the Taliban are good examples of religious causes of conflict.

Activity

2   Imagine you are one of the soldiers in Source B. What problems do you think you might have when patrolling in Afghanistan? Think about:

■ culture and language
■ identification of the enemy
■ weapons and equipment
■ climate and landscape.

Key terms

Shari'ah: Islamic law based directly on the Qur'an and Sunnah.

Islamic fundamentalism: the belief that Shari'ah law should be used over and above any laws made by elected politicians.

Activity

3   Give three reasons why international conflicts occur.

Going further

1   Research the events leading up to the Falklands War in 1982. General Galtieri was the head of a small group of army generals which ran Argentina as a dictatorship. Find out his political and economic reasons for deciding to invade the Falklands Islands when he did.

Did you know ??????

Almost all wars are fought by men but countries with women leaders have also been involved in conflicts. Queen Elizabeth I ruled during the defeat of Spain in 1588. Margaret Thatcher was Prime Minister during the Falklands War.

International conflict – the Iraq War

For the past 30 years Iraq has been in conflict. In March 2003, Iraq was invaded by a **coalition** of forces led by the US and Britain. It remains in a state of conflict today.

Long-term causes

In the 1980s, Iraq's leader, Saddam Hussein, was determined that Iraq should not be taken over by people who believed that Iraq should be run by Sharia law. He launched a war against Iraq's neighbour, Iran, which was run by Sharia law under its religious leader, Ayatollah Khomeini. The Iran–Iraq war lasted for eight years and cost over 40,000 lives. This is a conflict which had a religious cause.

At first, the US had good relations with Saddam Hussein because, like him, it did not want the growth of countries run by Sharia law. In 1990, however, Saddam ordered the invasion of another of Iraq's neighbours, Kuwait. This is an oil-rich country that is also strategically important. The causes for this conflict were economic and political because Saddam knew Kuwait's oil would make him richer and, therefore, more powerful.

This time the US and the UK came to the aid of Kuwait. Operation Desert Storm forced the Iraqi forces out of Kuwait. For the next 12 years, international sanctions and military restrictions were imposed on Iraq by many countries. From 1998 to 2003, US and British aircraft bombed Iraq to force Saddam to comply with the terms of his defeat of 1991. The United Nations sent inspectors to Iraq to find out if Saddam was building **weapons of mass destruction (WMD)**, whether nuclear, chemical or biological. It was desperate to prevent yet another conflict involving Saddam and Iraq.

E *Saddam Hussein's portrait on an Iraqi banknote*

Key terms

Coalition: a combination of two or more countries which join together, for example, the US and UK in Iraq.

Weapons of mass destruction (WMD): weapons that are intended to cause huge loss of life and property (nuclear, chemical and biological weapons).

Activity

4 **a** Why was religion an important factor in the causes of the Iran–Iraq war of 1980–88?

b Explain why the US supported Iraq in its conflict with Iran but not in its conflict with Kuwait.

c Which methods were used to try to avoid another conflict with Iraq and other countries?

d Explain why these methods may have only increased the chances of yet another war involving Iraq?

Did you know ???????

The USA is responsible for almost 50 per cent of all the money in the world spent on weapons and warfare. The Iraq war could cost USA over $2 trillion, says the Nobel prize-winning economist Joseph Stiglitz.

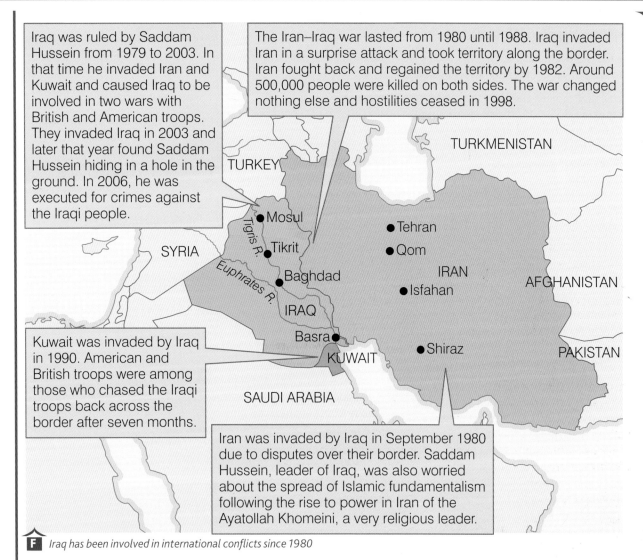

Iraq was ruled by Saddam Hussein from 1979 to 2003. In that time he invaded Iran and Kuwait and caused Iraq to be involved in two wars with British and American troops. They invaded Iraq in 2003 and later that year found Saddam Hussein hiding in a hole in the ground. In 2006, he was executed for crimes against the Iraqi people.

The Iran–Iraq war lasted from 1980 until 1988. Iraq invaded Iran in a surprise attack and took territory along the border. Iran fought back and regained the territory by 1982. Around 500,000 people were killed on both sides. The war changed nothing else and hostilities ceased in 1998.

Kuwait was invaded by Iraq in 1990. American and British troops were among those who chased the Iraqi troops back across the border after seven months.

Iran was invaded by Iraq in September 1980 due to disputes over their border. Saddam Hussein, leader of Iraq, was also worried about the spread of Islamic fundamentalism following the rise to power in Iran of the Ayatollah Khomeini, a very religious leader.

F *Iraq has been involved in international conflicts since 1980*

Short-term causes

Following the attack on the US by Al Qaeda on 11 September 2001, President Bush vowed to defeat the terrorists who believed in a holy war with God on their side. Bush thought that Al Qaeda had bases in Iraq and that Saddam had given his support to the attack on the US. Tony Blair, the UK's Prime Minister, agreed with President Bush to invade Iraq. Bush reportedly told Palestinian officials that God inspired him to end Saddam's dictatorship.

Did you know ???????

11 September 2001 was the second time that the US had been attacked without warning. The first was 7 December 1941 when Pearl Harbor in Hawaii was attacked by Japan. On both occasions, the result was involvement in long drawn out wars costing many lives and dollars.

The Iraq War (continued)

The invasion of Iraq in March 2003, led by US and UK forces, signalled the beginning of yet another war involving Iraq.

Bush and Blair both claimed that Iraq possessed weapons of mass destruction. Some US officials also accused Saddam Hussein of supporting Al Qaeda and therefore being partly responsible for **9/11**. No evidence of any such relationship between Saddam and Al Qaeda was found. In fact Saddam had no liking for any such religious fundamentalist groups. Saddam's record on the violation of the human rights of Iraqi citizens was also given as a reason for invasion. Others claimed that the invasion was due to Iraq's huge oil reserves, otherwise why didn't they invade other countries with poor records on human rights? Many millions around the world took to the streets to protest against the invasion.

The effects of the invasion

The invasion led to the quick defeat of the Iraqi armed forces. Saddam was captured and later executed by Iraqis who had suffered at his hands. President Bush posed on the aircraft carrier USS Abraham Lincoln in front of the banner 'Mission Accomplished'. He did not realise this was just the beginning of the conflict, not the end.

The US and UK troops tried to establish a new democratic Iraqi Government. However, there were new enemies they had had not counted on among various groups who resented the presence of foreign soldiers occupying their country. These groups, the Iraqi **insurgents**, were divided among the many Sunni and Shia Muslims. Many more people were to die in a conflict which quickly spiralled out of control as the various groups and foreign troops tried to impose themselves on a country increasingly torn apart by conflict. Hundreds of thousands died while millions lost their homes to the conflict.

Activities

5 Explain why the US and UK invasion of Iraq in March 2003 was partly due to religious causes.

6 What were the other reasons for this invasion? Think of political, moral, economic and social reasons.

H *US troops on patrol in Iraq*

G *Mission accomplished? May 2003*

Iraq soon became a place where human rights were easily abused by people in power. In 2004, the world saw shocking pictures of Iraqi people held at the Abu Ghraib prison. An estimated 90% of detainees in the prison were innocent. What's more, they were being tortured and humiliated by members of the American forces, the very same people who were supposed to be bringing freedom and democracy to Iraq.

The US began the practice transferring people it regarded as a threat to its base in Guantanamo Bay in Cuba. This practice, called **extraordinary rendition**, and the stories of torture and unjust detainment of prisoners in Guantanamo are more effects of the Iraq war on the lives of people.

I *A hooded and wired Iraqi prisoner at Abu Graib prison. He was told by US soldiers that he would be electrocuted if he fell off the box.*

Attempts at resolution

In 2003, without the support of the UN, the US and the UK launched their invasion of Iraq. The United Nations could do nothing to stop the US-led coalition from their invasion of Iraq. This demonstrated the limitations of the UN as a means of preventing and resolving international conflict.

In February 2007, the US sent an extra 30,000 troops to Iraq in an attempt to reduce civilian conflict-related deaths running as high as 4,000 per month. By the summer of 2008 this troop 'surge' had reduced civilian casualties to 500 a month, and some limited withdrawal of US troops began. However, in 2008, full peace and stability with Iraqis responsible for their own security still seems a long way off, although President Obama has promised to bring all American troops home by the summer of 2010.

- Estimates of the number of people killed in Iraq range from over 150,000 to more than one million.
- The war has created 4.7 million refugees which is 16 per cent of the population of Iraq.
- Conflict is still a way of life in Iraq.

Activities

7 Draw a timeline for Iraq from 1980 to the present showing the key events relating to conflict.

8 Explain why the message in Source **G** could be seen to be an error.

Going further

2 The end of one international conflict can sometimes lead directly to another. Research how the Versailles Treaty at the end of the First World War can be blamed for the Second World War only 20 years later.

Study tip

The case study of the Iraq war is just one example of the many international conflicts in the world today. You may choose to study and use your own example. Remember that most international conflicts, like the Iraq one, have long-term as well as short-term causes and that these may be political, economic, social or religious, or a combination. Remember too that resolutions are often hard to find and that the UN cannot always force its member states to do what it wants.

Check your understanding

1 Describe, with examples, the common causes of international conflicts.

2 Explain why the Iraq conflict has been so difficult to resolve.

3

■ Conflict and co-operation

Boy, 14, is latest victim of gang violence

A 14-year-old schoolboy was killed and his friend critically injured after being ambushed by rivals in London's spiraling 'postcode' gang war.

Paul Erhahon was attacked by at least 15 youths close to his home in Leytonstone, East London, on Good Friday. A post mortem confirmed that he was killed by a stab wound to the chest.

He was the seventh Londoner under 16 to be murdered in the past six months in attacks linked to gang violence.

It was claimed that they had been the victims of a turf war with rivals from the nearby Cathall Road area.

Adapted from David Brown, The Times, 9 April 2007

A   *Gang violence*

❝ *The responsibility lies with the parents. They should spend more time with their children telling them what is right and wrong. Gangs have replaced families as places of belonging to something.* ❞

Politician

❝ *If we had organised activities to do in the evenings we would not be bored and look for other kinds of excitement.* ❞

Teenager

❝ *Being in a gang makes me important and famous on my estate. I couldn't wait to be in a gang.* ❞

Gang member

❝ *Young people see violence on TV and in the cinema and they see the world of gangs as something normal* ❞

Social worker

❝ *I know teenagers who make a lot of money doing 'jobs' for gangs. With so much unemployment around here it's no wonder kids see joining a gang as better than having a part-time job.* ❞

Parent

   What do people say are the causes of gang violence?

Practice questions

3   **a)**   Name two basic rights.   *(2 marks)*

Study tip   Read the question at least twice and make sure you only answer what it asks you to do and no more.

     b)   Explain two reasons why people have not only rights but responsibilities.   *(4 marks)*

Study tip   If the question asks for two reasons or ways, write them separately so it is clear for the examiner.

     c)   Using Sources **A** and **B** and your own studies, give reasons why gang violence has become a part of local conflict in some communities.   *(12 marks)*

Study tip   If a question asks you to use two sources make sure you refer to both.

     d)   Explain the purpose of Amnesty International.   *(2 marks)*

     e)   Describe the various different effects of an individual or local conflict.   *(4 marks)*

     f)   Use your own studies to explain how individual or local conflicts can be resolved. You could refer to any of the following means:

         ■ Discussion

         ■ Negotiation

         ■ Arbitration   *(12 marks)*

Study tip   Your own studies can be anything you have learned from the television, Internet, radio or newspapers as well as in class.

In Question f, you could use more than one example for each bullet. It is much better to write a lot about a little rather than a little about a lot.

Remember to write a short conclusion for a 12-mark question.

Study tip   Make sure you have learned all of the key terms in the chapter.

Do not waste time writing out the question.

After you have written the answer, ask yourself if it would be easy for someone else to know what the question was.

4 Prejudice and persecution

4.1 What is meant by prejudice?

What are stereotypes?

Stereotypes are the fixed pictures we carry around in our heads of various groups of people. When we stereotype a group of people we are giving them a label or category. We often find it convenient to make complicated things more straightforward by grouping and labelling them. This is why we use stereotypes to help us understand a very complex world. Stereotyping is a part of our **socialisation** and in every culture there are different stereotypes.

You may decide there is some truth in many of the stereotypes you have discussed. The problem is that sometimes people think stereotypes are totally true because it simplifies the world for them.

'Boys like fighting'

'Women like cooking' 'Men watch football'

'Girls cry a lot'

A *Some commonly held stereotypes*

Key terms

Stereotype: a fixed, general view of a whole group of people which does not recognise individual differences. Stereotypes are usually negative.

Socialisation: the process by which a child learns the ways of its culture. It can be seen as a process of stages.

Activity

1 a Copy the grid and describe the common stereotypes for each group.
   b Compare your grid with other students. If there are lots of similarities it proves how widely held stereotypes of these groups of people are.
   c Do you think stereotypes are useful? Explain your answer in a short paragraph.

Social groups	Toddlers	Parents	Elderly
Nationalities	Spanish	Americans	Japanese
Occupational Groups	Builders	Cleaners	Lawyers

Group activity

1 Divide into groups. Look at the pictures in Source A.
   a Decide which common stereotypes they illustrate.
   b Do you think there is any truth in any of the four stereotypes?
   c Can you think of other stereotypes about men, women, boys and girls?

Stereotypes affect the way we think about the world. They can trick us into thinking the world is a much simpler place to understand than it really is. Stereotypes can be a little like small child's painting of a house – one-dimensional.

■ Why can stereotypes be harmful?

While many stereotypes can be quite innocent and inoffensive, many of them can be harmful. Stereotypes which apply to representations of gender, ethnicity, social class, age, sexuality and disability are often negative and therefore offensive.

Source **B** is an example of a stereotype which has led the adults to blame a whole group of people, in this case, teenagers, for something they have not necessarily done. While some teenagers may be noisy, rude and violent, they are certainly not all like that. What is more, it is not true that most crime is caused by teenagers. These adults are blaming teenagers for all violent crime – which is clearly not true.

Activity

2 Look at Source **B**. Explain in a short paragraph why these adults are mistaken to hold this stereotype of teenagers and why it maybe harmful and offensive to you.

Scenario

Imagine you heard two adults talking about teenagers in the following way.

'There is so much violent crime committed these days.'

'Yes, and it's all because of teenagers.'

'I agree with you there.'

'Teenagers these days are all noisy, rude and violent. I can't stand them.'

'I wouldn't employ one of them if I owned a business, that's for sure. They are nothing but a bunch of louts.'

B

Going further

1 a Research how much violent crime is, in fact, committed by teenagers. Decide for yourself how much truth is in the stereotype that teenagers are the main cause of crime in Britain. Use the British Crime Survey.

b Keep a log of the television that you watch in an evening. Record all the instances when you believe a character is being treated as a stereotype.

■ Why are people used as scapegoats?

Using a stereotype to blame a whole group of people for something they have not necessarily done is called **scapegoating**. The word comes from a story in the Bible which tells how a high priest would place his hand upon a goat's head and transfer the sins of the people to the goat which was then released into the desert. The goat was blamed for the mistakes committed by others. It is common to blame others for our own mistakes, and especially those who are unable to defend themselves.

Minorities, or **outsider groups**, are often the targets of scapegoating because they are the weakest groups in society with less power to influence popular opinion. The majority are more easily convinced about the negative characteristics of a minority with which they have no direct contact because they do not hear the opposing points of view. Unemployment, rising prices, diseases and crime are all examples of problems which have been blamed on minorities. The mass media often helps to form and influence stereotypes and scapegoats.

Key terms

Scapegoating: blaming a person or group for things they did not necessarily do.

Outsider groups: people whose culture is new or different to those who hold most power in society.

Activity

3 Look at Source C.

a Match the newspaper headings on the left with the sub-headings on the right.

b Which three groups of people are being scapegoated?

c Why do you think scapegoating is a common reaction to problems and why is it unhelpful in solving them?

Did you know ???????

The average foreign worker in Britain is earning about £2,000 a year more than the average British-born worker, according to Government figures. This means they are paying taxes which the government then uses to pay for lots of services such as hospitals and schools.

Did you know ???????

The Office for National Statistics reported that 385,000 people emigrated in the year to July 2006, the highest figure since current counting methods were introduced in 1991.

1 Government fails to hit education targets

2 Eastern Europeans flock to new jobs in Peterborough

3 Council taxes rise to spend more on litter collection

4 London on terrorist alert

a Another unwelcome visit by caravan dwellers

b Immigrants add to unemployment amongst Brits

c Britain's mosques fuel fundamentalism

e More and more children don't have both parents as role models

Going further

2 Research the trial of Sacco and Vanzetti – a famous case of scapegoating from American history.

C *Newspaper headings and subheadings*

A working mother's first job is to be a scapegoat

A recent Cambridge University report says that most people now believe that a mother who works harms family life. We hear that increasing teenage crime is primarily the fault of the parents, especially the mother who juggles home and work unsuccessfully. The message is that a mother's place is in the home.

'When it comes to the clash between work and family life, doubts about whether a woman should be doing both are starting to creep in. The idea of mothers with careers who also bake cookies and read bedtime stories is increasingly seen to be impossible.'

This adds to the many other messages about how inadequate we are every single day.

We work too hard, which makes us heartless. We work too little, which makes us an item of property. We're too fat. We're dangerously thin. We're exercise addicts. We can't find time for the gym. We're too old. We're too young. We have worn out skin. We have Botox. We can cook, which makes us old fashioned. We can't cook, which makes us a disgrace. We're too trendy. We're too dowdy. We have cellulite. Or have we had lipo? It's a wonder women don't commit mass suicide, frankly.

It is true 75 per cent of mothers work. They work because they have to. You can think that harms the family, or think it does the family good, but it's irrelevant. Most of us don't have any choice: if we stopped working, our place wouldn't be in the home but in the trailer, or in the cardboard box on the pavement, and our children wouldn't have any clothes to wear or food to eat.

Adapted from India Knight, The Times, 10 August 2008

D

E   *Juggling children and a career*

SAY NO TO RACISM

■ What are prejudices?

Prejudice means to form an opinion of someone before knowing anything about them i.e. to pre-judge them. It is often a negative opinion and it often stems from a stereotype. For example, if the stereotype of Americans is that they are loud and obese then it may lead to a negative opinion of Americans. Not wanting to get to know or accept anything positive about Americans is a prejudice because a whole nation is being pre-judged.

Where does prejudice come from?

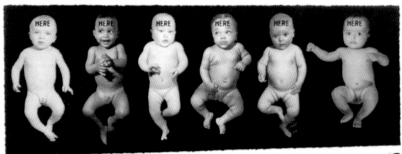

THERE ARE LOTS OF PLACES IN BRITAIN WHERE RACISM DOESN'T EXIST.

COMMISSION FOR RACIAL EQUALITY

F

Key terms

Prejudice: a negative opinion formed against a person or group based on a stereotype.

Racial prejudice: a belief that one race or ethnic group is superior to another.

Tribalism: the existence of people who share a strong group identity.

Nationalism: the belief that one's country is superior to other countries.

Imperialism: the act of creating an empire by invading other countries.

Propaganda: information which is used to influence others' opinions. It may 'bend' the facts or not tell the whole story.

Insider group: people who hold most power and influence in a society.

G

Activity

5 At some time in their lives, many people experience some form of prejudice.

a Using the images in Source **G**, list the types of prejudice the people represented might have experienced in their lives.

b Ask other students to see if they have ever been the victims of forms of prejudice: **racial**, ageist, sexist, sexual, disability or religious. Find out how the prejudice was expressed.

c Can you think of prejudices you personally have towards others?

Activity

6 a What does Source **F** tell us about where our attitudes to others come from?

b List the various places and people we get our attitudes from.

Throughout history, people have formed prejudices which have led them to carry out aggressive actions. **Tribalism** occurs when people come together in groups called tribes because they have a shared identity. This can be an ethnic or religious group, or a group with strongly held beliefs such as football fans. When one tribe comes into contact with another tribe, they can be suspicious or afraid of each other. Aggression often results from their opposing attitudes.

Some countries have believed they are superior to others and this **nationalism** has prompted them to invade other countries. Many European countries did this when they colonised most of Africa in the 19th century, a phenomenon known as **imperialism**. Countries building their empires, such as Britain and France, often used **propaganda** to persuade people of their reasons. They presented empire-building as a kindness to their colonies, helping them 'get started'. However, their motives were usually more selfish. British propaganda frequently showed Africa as the 'white man's burden', suggesting that the British had a duty to educate and civilise a primitive and backward people. The British sent people, the **insider group**, to run the colonies. In India this was the British Raj. The Indian people, who vastly outnumbered the British, were the outsider group, with next to no power or influence.

> Spanish students on an exchange trip to taste British culture in Sheffield were ambushed by a hooded gang who hurled bricks and bottles at them.
>
> *The Times, 19 July 2008*

> The leader of Zimbabwe, Robert Mugabe, has frequently expressed the view tht homosexuals are "worse than pigs and dogs" and have "no rights at all". He has dismissed criticism of his policies from the British government, calling it a "gaymafia" and in need of lessons on human reproduction.
>
> *The Independent, 9 June 2008*

> In November 2007, a Year 9 Sikh student was excluded from school for refusing to remove a Kara bangle. Sarika Singh said the bangle was very important to her, as a symbol of her religious faith.
>
> *BBC newsonline July 2008*

Check your understanding

1 What is a 'stereotype'?

2 What is a 'scapegoat'?

3 Describe two ways people form prejudices.

4 Explain how prejudice can lead to aggressive behaviour.

Activity 8

7 Read the news stories in Source **H**. Decide what type of prejudice is involved in each case.

Study tip

Not all stereotypes are negative but in this topic on Prejudice and Persecution you only need to use the ones which are.

Look out for stereotyping and scapegoating in your everyday life. You can use these examples when a question says 'using your own studies'.

Going further

4 Research the Milgram experiment at Stanford University (look up 'milgram experiment' on Wikipedia). Think back to Source **F** at the start of this chapter. What does the experiment tell us about how people can learn prejudices?

4.2 How do prejudices lead to discrimination?

From prejudice to discrimination

We have seen how stereotyping can lead to scapegoating and prejudice. When these attitudes are taken further, they can lead to **discrimination**. Discrimination is when prejudices are acted on and the attitudes become actions. Discrimination exists in many areas of life and affects many kinds of people. Look at Source **A** for examples of prejudice in action. What kinds of discrimination can you see?

Objectives

You will be able to:

understand how many prejudices can lead to types of discrimination

understand that prejudice and discrimination are all around us

understand how discrimination prevents people enjoying their basic human rights.

'You boys are in detention'

'May I help you sir?'

'I need to search you.'

No Gypsies or Travellers Allowed.

A *Where does discrimination exist?*

Key terms

Discrimination: unfair treatment of a person or group on the basis of prejudice about things such as age, gender, sexuality, disability, race, religion or class.

Discrimination in society: race, gender, class

There are various types of discrimination which can arise from stereotyping and prejudice.

B

Racial discrimination

Captain Doug Maughan says racial comments by his colleagues at British Airways are common and treated as normal. He was not successful in persuading BA's management to take racism among its senior staff seriously. He lodged his first complaint after hearing a senior training captain use the word 'coon'. Another pilot referred to men from Saudi Arabia as 'rag-heads'. On one flight a colleague, referring to Asians in Britain, said to Captain Maughan, who lives in Scotland, 'I don't suppose there are many of them up your way.' Captain Maughan replied: 'Well, there's my wife'. He comments, 'racism is as prevalent now in BA as it was in the RAF 25 years ago.'

Andy McSmith, The Independent, 26 March 2008

Gender discrimination

Under current rules, women are not allowed to serve in either the infantry or the Royal Armoured Corps. A spokesman for the Ministry of Defence said: "Women serve bravely on the frontline in many ground combat support roles. For combat effectiveness reason though, women do not serve in roles where they may be required to engage the enemy deliberately face to face in combat, often at the point of a bayonet."

Sean Rayment, The Telegraph, 2 October 2008

Class discrimination

State school pupils are still being 'ignored' by top institutions. Britain's leading universities are making slow progress in admitting more students from state schools and from poor backgrounds. Only 6 of the 20 top universities met the Government target for the proportion of state school pupils they admit. Only 7% of children are educated in private schools but they fill approximately 25% of university places.

At Oxford under 10% come from the poorest families.

Figures from Higher Education Statistics Agency

■ Discrimination in society: disability

F

Disabled people have often been viewed with a mixture of suspicion, **ridicule**, fear and pity. The mass media still frequently presents disabled people as those who deserve our pity or as those who deserve extra attention because they have achieved superhuman feats. Disabled people are also ridiculed in everyday language. Terms such as 'spaz', 'mong' or 'retard' are sometimes used as insults which reflect deeply held prejudices.

People with disabilities are often seen as having a problem which makes them less than complete human beings. Such attitudes have led society to treat them separately in almost every area of life. Source **G** identifies some of the ways attitudes have had an impact on people's lives.

> **Key terms**
>
> **Ridicule:** words or actions which make fun of people to hurt their feelings.
>
> **Barriers of access:** ways of preventing disabled people participate fully in society.

Activity

2 Look at Source **F**.

a What image of disability does each photo give?

b In what ways do these photos confirm or challenge stereotypes of people with disabilities?

> **66** *In the past, disabled children were not educated alongside non-disabled children. There were schools for the crippled and the deaf and the blind. This was educational segregation. Nowadays there are still special schools for severely disabled children but many are educated in mainstream schools.* **99**
>
> *Disabled students were prepared for jobs which paid less as they were not considered capable of doing the same jobs as able-bodied people.*
>
> *Steps, heavy doors and small toilets meant many places were inaccessible.*

G

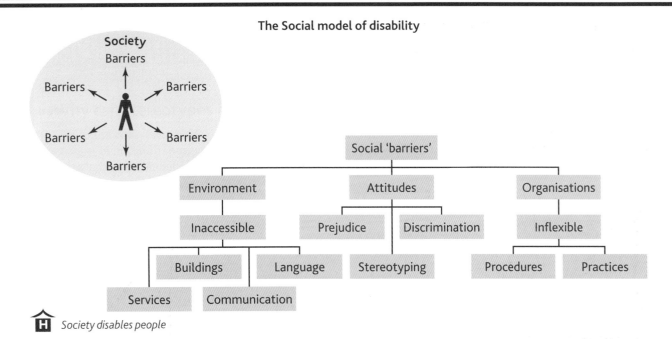

The Social model of disability

H   *Society disables people*

Source **H** illustrates the fact that it is society which disables people by presenting them with barriers which too often stop them from realising their potential. These barriers lead to unfair treatment which is called discrimination.

Society should be encouraged to give up the idea that disability is a medical problem requiring 'treatment', but to understand instead that disability is a problem of exclusion from ordinary life.

Tanni Grey-Thompson winner of the London Marathon six times, breaker of world 28 records and holder of 11 Paralympic gold medals

> By the age of seven, I was paralysed, but I think the head teacher chose not to tell anyone in the education authority that I was using a wheelchair, otherwise I would have been packed off to a special school. Special education didn't provide a real education: there was no way I would have done the same O-levels or A-levels or gone to university.
>
> At 15 I saw a careers adviser who said, 'The only job you're going to get is answering the phone'. I got 9 O-Levels and 4 A-levels. I spent a year looking at universities for their wheelchair access. In athletics, I'm not disabled. If there are two steps, then I am disabled.

I

Tanni Grey-Thompson's autobiography Seize the Day

New laws have led to improved facilities for the disabled in schools, shops and businesses and changing attitudes are slowly reducing the barriers for disabled people. Changing steps into ramps, providing information in Braille, providing textphones and minicoms are examples of breaking down the barriers which discriminate.

Activity

3   Use Sources G, H and I.

a   Draw up a list of the barriers which disabled people come up against.

b   How have people with disabilities been discriminated against in the world of work?

c   Explain what Tanni Grey-Thompson means when she says, 'If there are two steps, then I am disabled.'

Going further

2   Do an audit of the facilities in your school for people with disabilities. Find out what **barriers of access** there are for people in wheelchairs (physical disability) and for those who are deaf or partially sighted (sensory disabilities).

SAY NO TO RACISM

■ The impact of discrimination

Case study

Discrimination in employment

In a suburb north of Paris, 31-year-old Sadek quit his job delivering food. Sadek has finished his school education but he knows he will not be considered for certain jobs because of his name and his Muslim background. 'With a name like mine, I can't have a sales job.' If he wanted a job selling on the phone he would have to use a different name.

This is typical of many people living in Paris who have to try to disguise their culture and religion if they are to improve their career prospects. They may have a French passport but this does not mean they are widely accepted along with all other French citizens. A young man called Ali or Rachid is much less likely to get a job interview than someone called Alain or Richard.

Nearly a third of French Muslims with a university education are unemployed, compared to a national average of 5 per cent. Yazid Sabeg, a French Muslim graduate sums up the situation with the comment 'doors are closed'.

Help Wanted
No Irish need apply

 Discriminatory job advertisement

Activity

4 Read the Discrimination in employment case study.

a Why might Sadek need to change his name if he works in telemarketing?

b What do you think may be the impact of prejudice and discrimination on the rest of Sadek's life?

Activity

5 Source J was taken from a sign where people were invited to apply for jobs in Britain in the 1950s. How does the photo relate to the situation in France today?

Discrimination in the police force

Discrimination exists in lots of places in society and so it is no surprise that it should exist in both the public and private sectors. It is not always easy to identify because it is not necessarily intentional. It is not merely a matter of individuals having prejudices and expressing them. The discrimination is often a result of many years of not recognising old-fashioned practices when certain prejudices were more accepted by society in general.

K *Stephen Lawrence*

In 1999 a report by Sir William Macpherson followed an inquiry into the Metropolitan police's investigation of the murder of black teenager, Stephen Lawrence. The 18-year-old A-level student was fatally stabbed in an unprovoked attack as he waited for a bus in south London, in April 1993. Nobody was convicted of his murder.

Police officers in charge of the case were accused of being incompetent and racist. The Macpherson report said the Metropolitan police and, policing generally, was guilty of 'institutional racism'. Macpherson discovered that many officers would assume black people, especially young black males, were more likely to be involved in crime than other ethnic groups.

The report made 70 recommendations, many aimed at improving police attitudes to racism. It stressed the importance of a rapid increase in the numbers of black and Asian officers. The Government pledged to increase the number of officers from minority ethnic groups from around 2,500 to 8,000 by 2009. Retention and career development of officers, as well as recruitment, were also to be given greater attention.

The Secret Policeman, a BBC undercover documentary revealed that racism still exists within the police force. The programme told the story of eight police officers, five who had resigned and three who had been suspended, all for racist remarks and behaviour. One of the policemen could be seen dressed like the Ku Klux Klan and making offensive racist comments. The police forces were very critical of such behaviour and promised they would root out such racism amongst their officers.

L

Activity

6 Divide into groups, then use the text and Sources **K** and **L** to answer these questions.

a What might be the reasons why there has been such a small number of ethnic minority police officers?

b What areas of policing have been highlighted for improvement following the Macpherson report and the BBC documentary?

c Explain why the Macpherson Report recommended there should be more police officers from minority ethnic groups.

Going further

3 Research the existence of **institutional discrimination** in other institutions and services, such as education, prisons and housing.

Check your understanding

1 Name two groups of people who are victims of discrimination in society.

2 What is 'institutional discrimination'?

3 Explain how discrimination can affect a person's education.

4 Give two reasons why discrimination should be eliminated.

4.3 How can prejudice and discrimination lead to persecution?

Case study

Nazi persecution of different groups of people

People killed by the Nazi genocide (figures are approximate)

Jews	5.5 million
Slavs	550,000
Undesirables (including homeless, criminals, prostitutes, 'asocials', blacks, Freemasons)	1.8 million
POWs (many were branded as Communists)	5 million
Roma gypsies	350,000
Homosexuals	220,000
Disabled	250,000
Jehovah Witnesses	5,000

A

The Nazis also murdered Catholics, Protestants, protesters, musicians, students and trade unionists who were seen to be enemies of Nazism.

Objectives

You will be able to:

understand how prejudice and discrimination can lead to different kinds of persecution

understand the effects of persecution.

Key terms

Intolerance: the lack of willingness to respect differences among people.

Systematic persecution: the deliberate and organised harassment and murder of people.

Genocide: (geno = people, race; cide = murder) the destruction of a large number of people (racial, social, political, cultural or religious group).

Violence: an act of aggression which is intended to cause pain.

Holocaust: the persecution of millions of people, mainly Jews, by the Nazis.

The worst case in history of prejudice and discrimination leading to the persecution of millions of people was in Europe in the 1930s and 1940s. In the 1930s in Germany, a political party called the Nazis came to power. It was led by Adolf Hitler who was proud of his racism and **intolerance.** He wrote a book called *Mein Kampf* (My Struggle) in which he said society was a fight between different kinds of people, 'a struggle for survival'. He was determined to get rid of those people he believed would destroy Germany if they were not destroyed first. He stereotyped Jews and other groups such as the disabled, homosexuals and blacks as being inferior and trouble-makers. Jews were scapegoated as the cause of all Germany's problems including mass unemployment and defeat in World War One. Hitler's prejudice towards these so-called 'inferior people' led him to pass laws which discriminated against them. Within 12 years, between 12 and 14 million people were murdered through a process of **systematic persecution.**

B *Nazi rally*

The Nazis saw themselves as the only true Germans with a strong group identity. Indeed, Nazism was an extreme kind of tribalism. The Nazis were nationalists who believed in a strong, aggressive nation which should continue to grow stronger and stronger. They were also imperialists as they planned to take over as many other countries as possible and build a new Empire. Hitler was a great believer in fighting and conflict and he was proud of the Nazi 'achievement' of killing millions of 'inferior' people through **genocide**.

The Nazi mastermind responsible for whipping up people's emotions and encouraging discimination was Joseph Goebbels. Goebbels was the master of the 'big lie' tactic and propaganda. He said that if a lie, no matter how outrageous, is repeated often enough, it will eventually be accepted as truth. Many people were indeed fooled by the propaganda into believing that all Germany's problems had been caused by a few, very small, minority groups. These groups, it was said, needed to be removed by **violence**, as Hitler saw life as the 'survival of the fittest'.

According to the Nazis, the perfect racial characteristics were white skin, a tall figure, blonde hair and blue eyes. These characteristics were known as 'Aryan'. Yet neither Hitler nor Goebbels had Aryan characteristics. Hitler was dark-haired, not blonde and blue-eyed, and Goebbels was disabled. Physical education became the most important subject in schools because the Nazis wanted to give the impression of a nation full of fit, healthy young men and women ready for any future war.

links

Also see Topic 4.1 for tribalism.

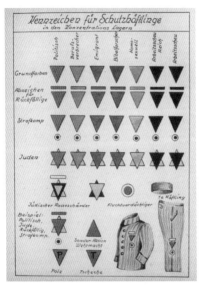

C *Nazi concentration camp badge system*

Activity

1 **a** Using Sources **A** and **C**, complete the table with the names of each type of group persecuted by the Nazis. You may decide that some groups could belong to more than one category.

Racial	Social	Political Religious	Sexual	Cultural

b How did Hitler use the phrase 'survival of the fittest' to serve his prejudices against so many different groups of people?

c Why do you think the groups of people the Nazis persecuted were made to wear the badges?

■ Genocide since the Nazis

People thought that after the Nazis had been defeated, genocide would never be allowed to happen again. Although there has not been genocide on the scale of the Nazi **holocaust**, there have been several examples since of the destruction of large groups of people in various countries.

Some more recent examples of genocide

Information

Cambodia 1975 – 79: 2 million

Bosnia 1994: 8,000 men and boys

Rwanda 1994: 800,000

Sudan, Darfur 2003: 350,000 killed

D

Activity

2 Research one of the examples of genocide given in Source **D**. Find out who carried out the genocide, if there any comparisons with the Nazi genocide and any statistics that are available. Present your findings to the rest of your group.

People who have suffered systematic persecution

The Roma people, known simply in Britain as **gypsies**, have been persecuted for hundreds of years. At least 500,000 were murdered by the Nazis. Wherever they have been, there has often been hatred and distrust.

Case study

The Roma gypsy people

Approximate populations of gypsies in some European countries today

Romania	2.5 m
Bulgaria	800,000
Hungary	600,000
Slovakia	520,000
Czech Republic	300,000
Poland	60,000
UK (includes travellers and circus workers)	120,000

E

F *Roma prisoners in Belzec concentration camp*

The past

UK

- The 1530 Egyptians Act required gypsies to leave England within 16 days. (The word gypsy is thought to come from the word Egyptian.)
- Henry VIII made it a capital offence to be a gypsy in 1531.

Nazi Germany

- The Nazis persecuted the gypsies throughout the 1930s:

1933	Gypsies identified as one of the various groups of 'inferiors' and 'undesirables'
1934	Individuals arrested as 'asocials' and 'habitual criminals' and sentenced without trials
1935	Nuremburg Laws forced sterilisation and made it illegal for gypsies to have sexual relations with non-gypsies
1936	Many gypsies arrested and removed to camps in the countryside before the Berlin Olympics
1937	Gypsies used for forced labour in the camps; very limited freedom of movement; curfew imposed
1938	Gypsy males over 16 sent to concentration camps
1939	Gypsies forced to wear black triangular patches, the symbol for 'asocials' or green for 'professional' criminals
1940	As Nazis invaded other countries, gypsies were rounded up and sent to ghettoes
1943	All gypsies, men, women and children sent to Auschwitz and other death camps to be eliminated

G

UK

- Signs outside pubs bar gypsies, disregarding the Race Relations Amendment Act 2000.
- 15-year-old gypsy was beaten to death in Chester – called a ' Gypsy bastard'.
- The effigy of a gypsy caravan and family was burned in a Guy Fawkes display November 2007.
- Life expectancy of gypsies is 10 – 12 years less than average.

Eastern Europe

- In the Czech Republic, gypsy children are 23 times more likely than whites to be in special schools for the 'mentally retarded'.
- Hungary has a 'whites only' policy in some schools, barring gypsy children from entering canteens and gyms.
- In Slovakia, 50,000 gypsies have no access to mains water, and racist attacks are common.

The Insider Story, TES Teacher, 19 March 2008

Italy

Petrol bombs had been thrown from three cars causing an extensive blaze. The Government plans to fingerprint all gypsies, including children in its plans to take tougher measures on crime and immigration. The idea has been criticised by the EU.

The Times, 24 July 2008

Activity

3 a Using Source G, explain why systematic persecution can be used to describe the Nazis' treatment of gypsies.

   b Using Source H, describe two ways in which gypsies are still persecuted.

   c Carry out a survey of attitudes towards gypsies in class. Do you identify any stereotypes?

Going further

1 Before the 1936 Berlin Olympics, gypsies were forcibly moved. Before the 2008 Beijing Olympics, many poor people's homes were demolished and the people forcibly removed. Research details of what happened in Beijing on BBC news online.

2 Research gypsies and what makes them different from people who prefer permanent homes. Possible starting points are:

- The National Romani Rights Association
- Friends, Families and Travellers
- Gypsy Council for Education, Culture, Welfare and Civil Rights
- International Romani Union.

The stolen generation – Aboriginal children in Australia

Between 1900 and 1972, over 30,000 aboriginal children were taken from their parents by Australian authorities. Children were listed as 'full bloods' or 'mixed descent'.

The authorities considered the parents incapable of raising their children in a civilised way. The children were to be de-socialised as Aborigines and re-socialised as 'whites' and were taken to special camps and educated in English.

> They put us in the police car and said they were taking us to Broome. They put the mums in there as well. But when we'd gone about ten miles they stopped, and threw the mothers out of the car. They pushed the mothers away and drove off, while our mothers were chasing; they came running and crying after us.

The 'Stolen Children' report (1997)

Activity

4 a Explain why you think the Australian authorities used the terms 'full blood' and 'mixed descent'.

   b Using Source I and the text, explain why some aboriginal children were taken away.

Check your understanding

1 Name two groups scapegoated by the Nazis and then persecuted.

2 Explain, with examples, what you understand by the term 'systematic persecution'.

3 Describe the effects of persecution on a group of people.

4 How can prejudice lead to genocide?

4.4 How can prejudice, discrimination and persecution be challenged and reduced?

Prejudice, discrimination and persecution have long been a part of human behaviour. After the holocaust, the United Nations was formed. One of its most important objectives was to ensure that genocide was never again allowed to happen. The genocide in Cambodia, Bosnia, Rwanda and Sudan has demonstrated that mass persecution has not, however, disappeared.

In many countries, however, there have been successful attempts to challenge and reduce the various types of prejudice and discrimination you learned about earlier in this chapter.

Objectives

You will be able to:

understand how prejudice, discrimination and persecution have been successfully challenged at various levels

understand how society is improved when prejudice is challenged.

■ Individual, local and community level

Lessons from Auschwitz Project (LFA)

The Holocaust Education Trust invites students from every secondary school in Britain to get involved in the Lessons from Auschwitz Project. Students meet survivors of the Holocaust who live in Britain before going to Poland to visit Auschwitz where two million people, mostly Jews, were murdered by the Nazis. The students come face to face with the horrors of the gas chambers and the piles of human hair, shoes and glasses which are a cruel reminder of the way the SS guards hoarded every last possession of their innocent victims. On their return, the students share their experiences with younger students from their own schools.

A *Piles of shoes taken by the Nazis from their victims at the Auschwitz death camp*

66 *Seeing things in the flesh is more hard-hitting than reading a textbook.* 99

Nick

66 *We have to be aware of this and learn from it. If we don't, history could repeat itself.* 99

Rachel

66 *The project had a profound effect on me so I am glad I was given the opportunity.* 99

Rachel

66 *I want other people to recognise the extremes of this place. I want to pass on the message.* 99

Victoria

66 *I really wanted to come here because I feel the lessons should be passed on to other people.* 99

Mallika

B *Quotes from visitors to Auschwitz*

The story of the unnecessary destruction of millions of people's lives by the Nazis is one that every person in Britain now follows as part of their secondary school education. The national Holocaust Memorial Day is held every year on 27 January to mark the liberation of Auschwitz-Birkenau, the site of one of the Nazi death camps. Many towns and schools hold events which include the work done by local students. They may invite one of the remaining survivors of the Holocaust, perform drama, present art, story and poetry reading, or simply hold a few seconds of silence to remember those who lost their lives. Young people have become leaders in local communities in educating people of the horrors of what took place. While their message is 'Never Forget', it is also to make sure it never happens again.

Going further

1 Find out some of the things students have done to challenge prejudice on their return from Auschwitz.

Go to **www.het.org.uk** and click on Students, Lessons from Auschwitz project.

Activity

1 a   Give at least two reasons why you think every school in Britain is invited to send students on the project.

   b   When students see the piles of possessions that are shown in the photos in Source **A**, what do you think they must feel?

   c   Use Source **B** to help you write a letter to your head teacher explaining why you would like to be chosen for the Lessons from Auschwitz Project.

Kicking racism out of football

The Kick it Out (KIO) **campaign**, which started in 1993, not only challenges prejudice and discrimination wherever football is played, but also works for positive change so that future generations do not inherit an unequal society.

KIO is constantly working in schools and communities, playgrounds and parks, promoting events and competitions and providing educational resources. Many professional clubs and players are also greatly involved in such things as reducing racist chanting and harassment and encouraging the participation of minority groups in football. As it has grown, the KIO campaign has challenged and successfully reduced all kinds of prejudice in addition to racial prejudice.

KIO also plays a leading role in the Football Against Racism in Europe (FARE) network which organises community events all over Europe. KIO and FARE work alongside each other in the continuing fight against racism in Britain and Europe.

Football Against Racism in Europe (FARE) had an anti-racist activity programme for EURO 2008, where messages against racism and discrimination and for more respect were prominent. Racism is not uncommon in some European matches in the same way it used to be in British football matches not so long ago.

The FARE initiative at the UEFA European Championships was headlined 'Unite Against Racism'.

Activities included:

- pitch side advertising boards with the 'No to Racism' message at every game
- branded captain's armbands
- a Unite Against Racism message on every ticket – over 1 million in total
- a Unite Against Racism logo on steward bibs as well as substitute player's bibs.

The campaign reached its climax at the semi-finals in Vienna and Basel, where the four team captains delivered an anti-racism message that was beamed into homes across the world. Outside the stadiums, the 'StreetKick' game toured the five host cities with a programme of fans and ethnic minority communities taking part.

Adapted from Kick It Out 2007

C *Paul Ince, the first black British manager in the Premier League*

Did you know ??????

Black footballers account for more than 25 per cent of professional players in the English football leagues yet there are barely a handful of black managers, coaches or chairmen of professional clubs.

Other anti-racism in football initiatives

The KIO Pioneers exhibition

The exhibition celebrates the achievements of sporting heroes from ethnic minorities. It also raises awareness of issues such as racism and under-representation in areas such as management and coaching. The need for more professional Asian players is explored.

D *Groups in the community like Elite Youth in London work together to prevent and eradicate racism*

Elite Youth

Another group which has the backing of KIO, Elite Youth, has been a local youth and community organisation based in Tower Hamlets, London since 1973. Its target is very simple: 'To bring out the best in young people.' Its key aims are to work with the disadvantaged and disengaged ethnic minority community of Tower Hamlets and encourage them towards mainstream education, employment and training. Elite Youth gained FA Charter Standard in recognition of its commitment towards quality standards in football development within a school and community-based setting.

www.kickitout.org

E *Various groups and organisations work to fight against prejudice and discrimination in sport*

Activity

2 **a** Find out the various community events promoted by Kick it Out at www.kickitout.org

b Imagine your group are going to organise a Kick it Out event for your school or community. List your objectives and design a poster for the event.

c Contact a local football club or other sports club and find out what they are doing to challenge prejudice and discrimination. Is there an organisation like Elite Youth in your community?

■ National level

Equal rights legislation in the UK

These laws are examples of **equal rights legislation**.

- Disabilities Discrimination Act 1999
- Equal Pay and Discrimination Act 1970
- Race Relations Act 1976 (amended in 2000)
- Criminal Justice and Immigration Act 2008.

These laws make it illegal to discriminate against people on the grounds of race, ethnicity, gender, sexuality, age, religion or disability. Some of the consequences of this legislation include:

- Those who feel they are being discriminated against can receive appropriate support from such organisations as the Commission for Racial Equality.
- In 2008, the Wimbledon tennis event agreed to award the ladies' champion Venus Williams the same prize money as Rafael Nadal, the men's champion.
- All public buildings have to provide easy access for people with disabilities.
- It is against the law to incite hatred on the grounds of sexual orientation.

F

> 66 *Royal Mail is an equal opportunity employer, suitably qualified applicants with disabilities will be shortlisted.* 99

G A job advertisement

Affirmative action in South Africa

After the end of **apartheid** in South Africa, there was an imbalance in the jobs which different groups held. The majority black population held very few jobs with power and influence while the minority white population held the most influential positions. This was the result of many years of deliberate institutional discrimination. One of the main ways to 'level the playing field' was to use **affirmative action**, also known as positive discrimination.

After the end of apartheid the South African government implemented a quota system where sports teams had to have a certain number of non-white players to reflect the population as a whole where 80 per cent are black while less than 10 per cent are white. For a fixed period, this meant that the cricket and rugby teams had to have a minimum number of black players. The quota system has had a lot of criticism from both players and supporters. Like all affirmative action, it is only intended to exist until the 'playing field' is level.

Group activity

1. Divide into groups and discuss the following questions.
   a. How different would life be if there were no laws on equality of opportunities?
   b. Using Source **G** as an example, find other job adverts in newspapers where the equal opportunities laws are reflected.
   c. The national laws aim to get rid of discrimination. Why then has discrimination not disappeared?

Going further

2. a. Prepare a speech for a group debate: 'This house believes that equality of prize money at Wimbledon 2008 is proof that equality has gone too far.'
   b. Keep a log of the prejudices expressed by fellow students as you discuss this topic.

Activity

3. Explain what the quota system was intended to do.

■ International level

Europe

The European Union (EU) has launched these recent initiatives:

- MTV Competition for Diversity and Equality during 2007, the European year of Equal Opportunities For All. Two Russian students living in Ireland won with their entry, a design showing apples of all different colours, tastes and origins, which are all equal because they are all apples. The EU launched the competition to raise awareness of equality and the fight against prejudice and discrimination with a 30-second advertisement on MTV, the world's largest youth channel.

- Truck Tour For Diversity Against Discrimination. For four years the European Diversity Truck toured 32 cities and 19 countries to inform people of their rights under EU anti-discrimination legislation. The truck, which had an interactive exhibition inside it, stopped at schools, markets and job fairs with the message of equal opportunities for all.

H   *The European Diversity Truck on tour*

■ Global level

The International Criminal Court (ICC)

The ICC (sometimes known as the World Court) is a court that tries people accused of the most serious crimes of international concern, namely genocide and persecution. The ICC has over 100 member countries. The urgency for the ICC followed the genocides committed in Rwanda and Bosnia. The Court has its seat in The Hague, The Netherlands.

The ICC is a court of last resort which is used only when a nation is not able or capable of prosecuting its own citizens in a fair and just manner. The ICC has tried several former leaders of countries who have persecuted their own people.

I   *Bosnian Serb leader Radovan Karadzic was brought to the ICC for genocide in the former Yugoslavia*

Activity

4   a   Look at Source **H**. Why do you think the MTV competition judges awarded first prize to the 'apples' poster?

   b   Why do you think a truck tour is a good way of preventing and challenging prejudice and discrimination?

   c   Describe two ways in which prejudice has been challenged in the UK and at least one other country.

Check your understanding

1   Describe how prejudice can be challenged at an individual or community level.

2   Give two examples of how discrimination has been challenged at a national level.

3   Explain what you understand by 'equal opportunities'.

4   Explain why it is necessary to challenge prejudice, discrimination and persecution at all levels.

Study tip

If you are asked to give examples of how prejudice is challenged or prevented at a community, national or international level, the Kick it Out campaign can provide evidence at each of the levels.

Going further

3   Find out who has been tried by the ICC. What crimes they were they accused of committing?

4

■ Prejudice and persecution

A *Back to the days of segregation*

I don't feel comfortable wearing certain clothes to work as my boss makes suggestions that I am just looking to attract men.

Following a car accident when my face was disfigured, I notice people telling their children to keep away from me.

Ever since the London tube bombings in 2005 I have had comments about me leaving my bag in places at school.

When I am selling the *Big Issue* in the High Street, I get insults like 'parasite' and 'scrounger' even though I am actually working for my living.

B *Quotes from people who have experienced discrimination*

Practice questions

4   **a)**   Using Source **A**, state two places where people have been separated according to race.   *(2 marks)*

> **Study tip** Read the question at least twice and make sure you only answer what it asks you to do and no more.

      b)   Using Source **B**, briefly explain two types of prejudice people experience.   *(4 marks)*

      c)   Explain how prejudice and discrimination can affect people's lives.
Use Sources **A** and **B** and your own studies to answer.   *(12 marks)*

> **Study tip** If a question asks you to use two sources make sure you refer to both.
>
> For question c, you can use ideas from the sources and your other answers but you must not simply copy them.

      d)   Give the meaning of the term 'scapegoat'. Use your own studies to answer.   *(2 marks)*

> **Study tip** Your own studies can be anything you have learned from the television, internet, radio or newspapers as well as in class.

      e)   Briefly explain how discrimination can lead to persecution.   *(4 marks)*

      f)   Explain how prejudice and discrimination can be prevented and challenged. Use your own studies to answer. You could write about any of the following:

- equal opportunities legislation
- campaigns
- international action
- reconciliation.   *(12 marks)*

> **Study tip** If the question asks for two reasons or ways, write them separately so it is clear for the examiner.
>
> In question f, you do not need to try to write about all of the bullets. It is much better to 'write a lot about a little rather than a little about a lot'.
>
> Make sure you have learned all of the key terms in the chapter.
>
> Remember to write a short conclusion for a 12-mark question.
>
> After you have written the answer, ask yourself if it would be easy for someone else to know what the question was.

5 Global Inequality

5.1 What are the different features of global inequality?

Absolute and relative poverty

Market stall, India

Market stall, UK

Homeless man, UK

Refugee, Sudan

What does it mean to be rich or poor? Maybe you feel poor compared to Roman Abromovich, the billionaire Russian who owns Chelsea Football Club, but rich compared to people living on the edge of survival in parts of Africa. What does it actually mean to be poor? Poverty can be defined in many ways. You need to know the meaning of **absolute poverty** and **relative poverty**.

Absolute poverty is defined by the United Nations as 'a condition of severe deprivation of basic human needs – food, safe drinking water, sanitation, health, shelter, education and information.' If you are missing any two of these basic needs you would be classed as living in absolute poverty. Absolute poverty is often a feature in **less economically developed coutnries (LEDCs)**.

The World Bank defines absolute poverty as living on an income of less than $1 a day. This would apply to 1.1 billion people in the world as shown in Source **B**.

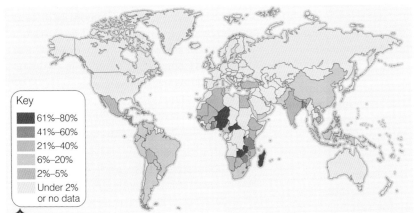

Key
- 61%–80%
- 41%–60%
- 21%–40%
- 6%–20%
- 2%–5%
- Under 2% or no data

B   *Map to show percentage of population living on under $1 per day from UN Human Development report 2007/8*

Activity

3   Draw lines to match up the UN deprivation factors on the left with the correct meaning on the right.

Food deprivation	No access to TV, newspapers, phones, radio
Water deprivation	No toilets
Deprivation of sanitation facilities	Four or more people in a room or a mud floor
Health deprivation	No schooling and illiterate
Shelter deprivation	Underweight
Education deprivation	Walk 15 minutes to get water from a pond or river
Information deprivation	No treatment for serious illness

In the UK you would not expect to find anyone living in absolute poverty as the UK is a **more economically developed country (MEDC)**. The government provides housing benefit so people have shelter and the NHS makes sure people have access to free health care. However, even in the UK, there are homeless people who are lacking food and shelter (see Source **A**).

Relative poverty depends on the society a person lives in. In the UK, data is collected every year on how many households are below average income (HBAI). In 2007 this included 2.9 million children and 2.5 million pensioners. Relative poverty may mean a child cannot afford to have a bicycle or go on holiday. In the UK about 14 per cent of the population are living in relative poverty.

Activity

2   Look at Source **B**.

a   Why are some countries shaded yellow?

b   Describe the pattern you see.

c   Explain the pattern you see.

Did you know ? ? ? ? ? ?

One person dies every three seconds as a direct result of extreme poverty.

Activity

4   Calculate how many people have died due to poverty during your lesson today.

Group activity   ▪▪▪▪

2   Discuss in what other ways the UK government helps to prevent absolute poverty in the UK.

Study tip

Make sure you know the difference between absolute and relative poverty.

Going further

1   a   Design a poster to show what poverty is. You could focus on one or several aspects of poverty.

b   Read the HBAI report at **www.dwp.gov.uk**

Development indicators

On the previous page you saw how within any country there can be very rich and very poor people. Development indicators are measures used to identify whether a country is an MEDC or an LEDC. The way to measure the wealth of a country is to use **Gross National Product (GNP)**. It is measured in US$ so all countries can be compared using the same currency. Obviously smaller countries may not earn as much in total, so to make comparison clearer the GNP is divided by the number of people to give GNP per capita (per person in the population).

The GNP influences how much money a country has to spend on making people's lives better in areas such as **calorie intake**, education and health. GNP is also influenced by the jobs people in a country do. **Occupation** is measured by the percentage of people working in agriculture. The higher the percentage, the less developed a country is. A country generally earns less money from agriculture than from industry.

Separate indicators are useful to show development in certain areas but the UN introduced the Human Development Index (HDI) which combines Gross Domestic Product (GDP: the same as GNP but does not include income from abroad), life expectancy, adult **literacy rate** and enrolment in education to give a score from 0 to 1. Above 0.8 indicates high development and below 0.5 indicates low development.

Key terms

Gross National Product (GNP): total Income in US$ from goods and services in a country for one year, including income from overseas.

Calorie intake: amount of calories obtained from food per person per day.

Occupation: jobs people do, measured by the percentage of population working in agriculture.

Literacy rate: the percentage of adults who can read and write simple sentences.

Activity

5 HDI from the UNDP 2007/8

Country	HDI
UK	0.946
Kenya	0.521
Nigeria	0.406
Egypt	0.708
Iceland	0.968
Sierra Leone	0.336
USA	0.951
South Africa	0.674
Ethiopia	0.406

C

Use the HDI data in Source D to put the countries in rank order. Then divide them into three groups of high, medium or low development.

Did you know ??????

All countries with an HDI below 0.5 are in Africa.

Activity

6 Using Sources C and D, list some problems of the HDI as a measure of development.

GDP — Adult literacy

HDI

Life expectancy — Enrolment in education

D HDO

Study tip

Make sure you know at least three development indicators. It is even better if you can quote some actual data for a country.

Health indicators

Health is a key indicator of development. MEDCs tend to have better health care facilities than LEDCs. There are four ways to measure the health of people in a country.

The first indicator is your chance of surviving your first year as measured by the **infant mortality rate**. High infant mortality can be linked to water or food deprivation but also poor health care of the mother during pregnancy or the child after birth. Once you have survived your first year, what are the chances of you being able to access a doctor? This is measured by **people per doctor**. Imagine a queue to see a doctor: the higher the number, the less likely you are to see a doctor.

The number of adults living with **HIV/AIDS** is another measure of health provision in a country. Countries with a high percentage of the population with HIV/AIDS often have poor health education linked to poor literacy rates. Treatment for people with HIV/AIDS is expensive and difficult to access. People with AIDS are often unable to work which further slows the development of a country. When they die their children are orphaned, putting a further strain on the country.

The final indicator is **life expectancy**. You can expect to live longer in a country with good health care.

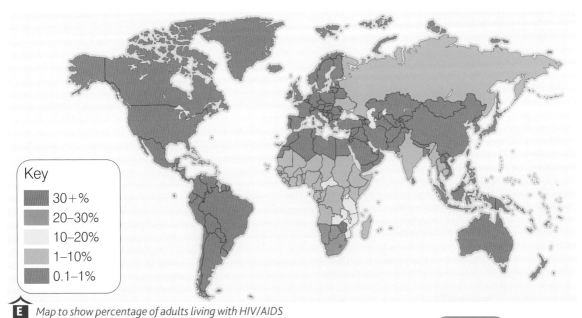

Key
- 30+%
- 20–30%
- 10–20%
- 1–10%
- 0.1–1%

E *Map to show percentage of adults living with HIV/AIDS*

Case study

'Average income = $32,602
GDP per capita is $33,238
1% employed in agriculture'

0.2% of adults with HIV/AIDS
People per doctor = 610

LIFE EXPECTANCY 81 YEARS

The average family has 1.84 children

'100% have access to clean drinking water
Calories per person = 3,412
14% children are obese.'

'99% of children go to primary school, 99% adults are literate'

F Nicola Smith

Comparing the UK and Ethiopia

UK

You live in the UK which is an MEDC. On the previous page you saw how the UK has a high HDI of 0.946 and is ranked 16th in the world. As of April 2009 the richest person in the UK, Lakshmi Mittal, is worth £10.8 billion and the country has some homeless people. 14 per cent of the population live in relative poverty and 1 per cent of the population is employed in agriculture. To compare countries, you need to use development indicators which are usually averages or percentages. They hide the difference between the richest and poorest in a country but allow you to compare countries. Compare the lives of these two 'average' people from each country.

'Infant mortality = 90
% adults with HIV/AIDS = 4.4
People per doctor = 37,397

The average family has 6 children

'Average income =$108
GDP per capita is $1,055
93% employed in agriculture'

'43% of children go to primary school, 35.9% adults are literate'

'22% have access to a clean water source
Calories per person = 1,857
38% of children are underweight.'

LIFE EXPECTANCY 48 YEARS

 Bereket Muluneh

Ethiopia

Ethiopia is classed as an LEDC. It has a low standard of living. It has a low HDI of 0.406 and is ranked 169th in the world out of 177 countries. The richest person from Ethiopia, Mohammed Al Amoudi, is worth $9 billion (£6 billion), but 44 per cent of the population live in relative poverty. 23 per cent live on under $1 a day and 78 per cent live on under $2 a day. 93 per cent of the population is employed in agriculture.

∞links

See Topic 5.3 to see how stereotyping in the media affects our views of MEDCs and LEDCs.

Going further

3 **a** To find out more about the culture, history and lifestyle in Ethiopia look at **www.ethioview.com**

b Choose another country and make your own 'average person' by finding development indicators from an atlas or website.

Did you know ??????

Ethiopia's official name is the Federal Democratic Republic of Ethiopia and its capital is Addis Ababa.

Check your understanding

1 What is 'absolute poverty'?

2 Give two ways that people in the UK can be relatively poor.

3 Briefly describe three development indicators.

4 Use development indicators to explain the main features of an LEDC.

5.2 What are the causes of global inequality?

■ Environmental causes

What has caused some countries to become LEDCs and others MEDCs? There are many different reasons.

Environmental crises may occur in any country. There are volcanic eruptions in Italy and earthquakes in Japan, for example. The UK experiences floods and **droughts**. The floods in 2007 killed 11 people, left thousands homeless and damaged crops. MEDCs are better able to cope with environmental crises, though, as they have the money to pay for stronger buildings, better warning systems, emergency rescue and insurance. Many LEDCs are in hotter climates and are not as able to cope with crises because of a lack of resources. Environmental crises such as **desertification** and **deforestation** are often made worse by human actions.

■ Historical causes

Many LEDCs were former colonies of Britain, France and Spain. These **colonies** produced raw materials such as sugar cane, gold, cotton and rubber which were sent to Europe and manufactured into goods that were sometimes resold to the colonies at a higher price. Land was often seized to allow production of a particular crop and these colonies then became reliant on imported food. Even when the countries became independent, their trade was still tied to the MEDCs. Independence also led to **civil wars** as tribal groups tried to re-establish boundaries. Money was spent on weapons instead of development. Buildings such as schools and hospitals were destroyed, making it harder for the LEDCs to develop.

" *The wages paid in the mines were very low and we got terrible diseases. On the plantations we sometimes had to work for nothing – it was almost like slavery.* "
Plantation worker, Mozambique

" *The roads only went to the places important to the Europeans, not to our local market.* "
Farmer, Malaya

" *Even though our children got an education, all the top jobs were saved for the whites.* "
Teacher, India

We have brought law and order, abolished slavery and introduced technology and democracy

A *Quotes from former colonial countries* **B** *Colonial administrator*

Objectives

You will be able to:

understand the environmental and historical causes of inequality

explain how primary product dependency, unfair trade and debt cause inequality

describe the poverty cycle

use a case study to describe a range of causes.

Key terms

Environmental crises: severe difficulties caused by natural disasters.

Drought: a long spell of dry weather.

Desertification: loss of productive land to desert due to climate change and overgrazing.

Deforestation: loss of forest due to climate change or cutting down trees without replacing them.

Colonialism: a policy where a country settles and exploits another country, for example, India was a former British colony.

Civil war: a war between sections of the same country or different groups within a country.

Activity

1 Match the following environmental crises with a country.

Flood	Turkey
Hurricane	Ethiopia
Drought	Jamaica
Volcanic eruption	Mali
Earthquake	Brazil
Deforestation	Bangladesh
Desertification	Montserrat

Case study

Ethiopia

Once a leading African nation, Ethiopia is rebuilding itself after years of civil war and famine. There are many reasons why Ethiopia is an LEDC.

Environmental causes

The country has a long dry season followed by a short rainy season. Long droughts have led to famines:

C *Famine in Ethiopia*

In 1973–4: 200,000 died.

In 1984–5: one million died prompting Band Aid and Live Aid to send humanitarian aid (Source **C**).

In 2008: drought affected 25 million people.

Desertification in the Ethiopian Highlands has displaced more than two million people since 2004.

Historical causes

1935–1941: The Italians invaded.

1962–1991: Civil war as groups in Eritrea fought for their independence.

1974: Last emperor overthrown. Military rule by the socialist Derg.

1991: The Ethiopian People's Revolutionary Democratic Front (EPRDF) took power (Source **D**).

D *Ethiopian rebels on tanks in Addis Ababa*

1994: Became a federation of nine states.

1998–2000: Ethiopia was at war with Eritrea.

2008: Peace-keeping troops are still monitoring the border.

Unfair trade

Ethiopian farmers sell coffee for $1 a pound.

It then sells in the USA for $10 a pound.

Primary product dependency

Coffee accounts for 60 per cent of Ethiopian exports. It relies on rain and is vulnerable to price changes in the world markets. Many farmers can earn more by selling khat (an illegal drug).

Debt

In 2006 Ethiopia had approx $6 billion debt. This was 80 per cent of its GDP. More money was spent on paying off debt than on education and health.

In 2005 the IMF agreed to write off $161 million debt.

Activity

2 Give three reasons why LEDCs cannot cope as well with environmental crises.

Did you know ??????

Each year 35 million people leave their homes due to natural disasters and wars.

Activities

3 Using an atlas or history books make a list of some former British colonies.

4 Use Sources **A** and **B** to explain how colonialism caused global inequality.

Activity

5 Draw the causes of inequality in Ethiopia as a spider diagram.

∞ **links**

Also see Topic 8.1 for information on drawing spider diagrams.

Going further

1 a Write a report on the effect of an environmental crisis in an LEDC such as the Boxing Day Tsunami in 2004.

   b Find out more about the colonies in the British Empire at

www.britishempire.co.uk and www.learningcurve.gov.uk/empire

Did you know ??????

Coffee was first discovered in Ethiopia by a goat-herd over 1,000 years ago.

Primary product dependency

One reason why many LEDCs are poor is because they get most of their income from exporting one particular product. These are usually **primary products**. Primary products are often exported to be used as a raw material in industries in MEDCs. Primary industries include agriculture, fishing, forestry and mining. The cost of exploiting some primary products such as timber and minerals is very high. Machinery and road-building are expensive, for example, the tyres on the trucks in Zambian copper mines (see Source **E**) cost over $25,000 each! LEDCs often look to multinational companies in MEDCs to provide financial investment and technical expertise.

E Copper mine in Zambia

Primary products include agricultural crops such as tea, cocoa, coffee and cotton. Because these crops are grown for export to bring in money rather than being consumed by the locals, they are called **cash crops**. Land that could have been used to grow food for locals is lost. Growing cash crops means the price the farmers receive can vary as it is dependent on the price set by world markets. Between 1999 and 2002 the price of coffee dropped by 50 per cent. Because farmers are only growing one crop, if there is a poor harvest they may lose everything.

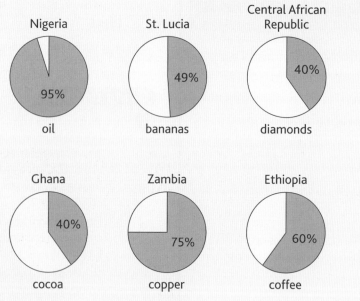

F Pie charts showing primary product dependency

⬤⬤ links

Also see Topic 7.3 for information on multinational companies.

Did you know ??????

Ethiopia is one of the top 10 coffee producers in the world.

Activity

6 Look at Source **F**.

a Name three countries that depend on a primary product for more than 50% of their exports.

b Name three non-renewable primary products.

Study tip

Remember one of the percentages from Source **F** to use in the exam.

Going further

2 a Find out how copper is 'undermining development' in Zambia at www.actsa.org

b Write a letter to the government of an MEDC explaining why their policies do not allow fair trade.

c Choose a product such as coffee, sugar, cotton or cocoa and find out about how it is traded.

Activity

7 Using the text and Sources **E** and **F**, what do you think will happen to countries like Zambia when their non-renewable products run out?

Unfair trade

Many of the primary products or cash crops exported from LEDCs to MEDCs are traded using **unfair terms of trade,** so that one of the trading partners, usually the LEDC, is not treated fairly. This leads to LEDCs remaining poor and the MEDCs becoming richer. These terms can range from unfair payment to workers to unfair **government policy** on imported or exported products.

> 66 *I have been forced to give up farming after 27 years. My sugar is rotting in the field as I cannot afford to harvest it.* 99
>
> *David*

> 66 *Last year we went on strike because we were working 10 hours a day without a break and if we didn't finish the work we didn't get paid. Now it's a bit better. I work 9 hours a day and earn 99p, but it's still not enough to buy clothes, medicines and school fees for my children.* 99
>
> *Joao*

 G *Quotes from sugar farmers in Mozambique*

H *Sugar cane workers in Africa*

Government policy can also mean that trade is unfair. The World Trade Organisation (WTO) was set up in 1995 to promote free and fair trade between countries. However some countries are more interested in putting their own interests first. Sugar is produced in both MEDCs and LEDCs. **Tariffs** make sugar from LEDCs more expensive to buy in the UK, but the extra money goes to the UK government, not to the sugar cane farmers. The government also pays UK sugar beet farmers **subsidies** to produce more sugar which gets 'dumped' on the world market and brings sugar prices down. However, the subsidies mean that UK farmers get paid three times the price of sugar on the world market. LEDCs are not able to or are not allowed to pay their farmers subsidies.

New trade agreements to reduce sugar subsidies have been accused of not going far enough so some sugar farmers in LEDCs will still lose out.

Key terms

Unfair terms of trade: policies that favour one trading partner, usually MEDCs.

Government policy: trade and agricultural policies such as tariffs and subsidies that protect their own industries against foreign imports.

Tariff: a tax on foreign goods when they are imported into a country.

Subsidy: money paid to a business or farmers to make their goods cheaper than foreign imports.

Activity

8 How many different uses of sugar can you think of?

Activity

9 Using Sources **G** and **H** describe the working conditions of sugar farmers in Mozambique.

Activity

10 Using Sources **G**, **H** and **I** explain how sugar is not traded fairly.

African farmer 'I only get £150 for this and we lost 22,000 jobs'

UK farmer 'I got paid £34,000 to produce this

I *The sugar mountain*

▪ Debt

The USA has the world's largest debt at $8.5 trillion, but debt is only a problem if it cannot be repaid. Today's **debt burden** for many LEDCs began in 1973 when the Organisation of the Petroleum Exporting Countries (OPEC) raised the price of oil, putting lots of money into banks, mainly in MEDCs. These banks were keen to invest their money and offered loans with low rates of interest to LEDCs. Between 1970 and 1994 the Democratic Republic of the Congo (formally Zaire) borrowed $8.5 billion, but most went into President Mobutu's personal bank account or was spent on weapons.

As some LEDCs had borrowed large amounts of money for useless projects or lost it through **corruption**, they were not able to pay back the loans. Meanwhile the banks were still charging interest, so the amount they owed was increasing. In 1982 the **World Bank** and the **International Monetary Fund (IMF)** took over the loans from the other banks. Countries were able to restructure their debts. To pay them off they had to reduce spending on health and education and export more primary products which meant they remained poor.

Many LEDCs spend four times more on debt payments than on health and education.

Bataan nuclear plant, Philippines

Case study

In 1976 the Philippine president, Ferdinand Marcos, borrowed $2.3 billion to build a nuclear power station. This was to save the country from importing oil. It took eight years to build. So far it has not produced any electricity because it was built near a major earthquake fault and the Pinatubo volcano. Thirty years later it was still costing Filipino tax payers $155,000 a day to pay back the debt. The debt was eventually paid back in 2007 and the government is deciding what should happen to the plant next.

J *Discussing the future of the Bataan nuclear plant*

Key terms

Debt burden: the amount of money owed by a country.

Corruption: abuse of public power for private gain, including bribery, influencing laws and favouring family.

World Bank: set up in 1945 to lend money to countries to pay for development projects.

International Monetary Fund (IMF): is a global financial organisation set up in 1945 to stabilise currencies and lend money in crises.

Activity

11 Explain how debt affects the lives of children in LEDCs.

Did you know ??????

LEDCs owe MEDCs $2 trillion in foreign debt.

Activity

12 a Using Source J and the information in the case study, explain who was to blame for the Filipino debt burden: Ferdinand Marcos, the banks in MEDCs or the construction companies?

b Have a class debate on what should happen to the Bataan nuclear plant.

Going further

3 Test yourself:

a Complete the corruption quiz at www.youthink.worldbank.org/issues/corruption

b Complete the debt quiz at www.newint.org/easier-english/money/debt.html

The poverty cycle

LEDCs remain poor because they become trapped in a neverending cycle where poverty only leads to more poverty. This cycle can apply to individuals as well as countries. Source **K** shows how an individual can be stuck in more than one type of **poverty cycle**. If a country is in a poverty cycle, it is often called a **development trap**. The country is unable to develop or improve.

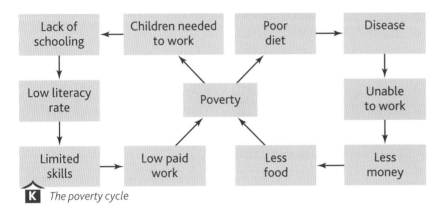

K   *The poverty cycle*

Some people blame the poor themselves for poverty. Comments such as 'they are lazy', 'they have too many children' and 'they do not educate themselves or accept change' are not helpful to people living in LEDCs. It is all the other factors mentioned in this topic that have caused their poverty in the first place. Once people are poor, they find it difficult to escape from poverty and must struggle just to stay where they are. The only way to escape is if there is some outside help to break the cycle.

Going further

4   **a**   Look at a range of reasons for global inequality at:
news.bbc.co.uk/
Use the search term: 'drought in Africa'.
Why is Africa poor?

b   Find out how population increase can lead to the poverty cycle at:
www.guardian.co.uk/world/2006/aug/25/uganda.mainsection
Draw a poverty cycle to include high infant mortality and high birth rates.

Check your understanding

1   What is meant by 'colonialism'?

2   Give two ways that trade is unfair.

3   Explain how debt can lead to global inequality.

4   For a country you have studied, explain why it is an LEDC.

Key terms

Poverty cycle: a set of factors such as low income and poor diet that cause poverty to continue.

Development trap: when countries are unable to develop or improve due to the poverty cycle.

Did you know ???????

80 per cent of Ethiopians live in poverty.

Activity

13   Draw a development trap (poverty cycle) for a country, using the following words and phrases:

■ Low literacy rate

■ High percentage working in Agriculture

■ Less money spent on education

■ Dependent on primary products and cash crops

■ Low GNP

■ Unskilled workers.

Tip: start with 'Low GNP'.

∞ links

Topic 5.4 will look at some of the solutions to the poverty cycle.

Activity

14   In what ways could the poverty cycle be broken?

Study tip

You can use diagrams like the poverty cycle in the exam.

5.3 How does global inequality affect LEDCs and MEDCs?

Objectives

You will be able to:

explain the effect of stereotypes on LEDCs and MEDCs

explain the impact of tourism on LEDCs and MEDCs

understand the role of multinational companies in globalisation

know the different views people have on globalisation.

Cultural stereotyping in the media

Unless you have visited an LEDC your views and ideas about those countries come from the **media** and socialisation by your parents. The newspaper headlines, TV reports and the Internet can give **cultural** stereotypes of the people living in LEDCs. They can be biased and often make assumptions about different cultures. An example of a stereotype might be 'all people in Ethiopia live in huts'.

A City in an LEDC

Key terms

Media: methods of communication including newspapers, radio, TV and Internet.

Culture: a shared set of beliefs, values, attitudes, norms, customs, traditions and practices.

Group activity

1. Write down a list of stereotypes people have about an LEDC such as Ethiopia and an MEDC such as the USA.

As you have already seen, there are people in the UK who are homeless and there are some very wealthy people in Ethiopia. These images are not always shown in the media.

UN Aid sent to Bangladesh after floods

House price crisis looms

East Africa food crisis looms

Retailers announce massive profits

£10 million lotter winner has not claimed prize

Somali refugees enter Ethiopia

 B Newspaper headlines

The media also helps spread these stereotypes around the world. A quarter of the world's population can speak English so UK and American news often dominate, while up to 4000 local languages may die out. Cultural goods from MEDCs such as books, CDs and fashion can easily be bought and sold around the world. Culture from LEDCs such as dancing and making music can not be 'sold' in the same way. Wealthy tourists may pay to watch them but they are in danger of being swamped by the culture from MEDCs.

Group activity

3. Look at Source **B**.
Decide if the headlines refer to an MEDC or an LEDC.
Explain how they reinforce cultural stereotypes.

⬭⬭ links

Also see Topic 4.1 for more information on stereotypes.

⬭⬭ links

See Topic 5.1 to compare the lives of people in the UK and Ethiopia.

Group activity

2. Look at Source **A**.

List the features in Source **A** that could also be found in a city in an MEDC.

Study tip

Remember cultural stereotyping works both ways.

Activity

1. Look at Topic 1.3. Does everyone in the UK have the same culture?

Explain your answer.

■ Expansion of tourism

People in MEDCs have more money to spend than before, so cheap flights have become popular. People also have more time so are able to travel further. The media and the governments of LEDCs help attract new tourists to their countries. Many tourists from the UK have become more adventurous and now travel to LEDCs for their holidays.

Tourism can affect MEDCs and LEDCs in a positive and negative way. Tourists in the UK benefit from cheaper holidays. However, fewer people may stay in the UK, which is a problem for the UK tourist industry. Tourists have a lot of money to spend while on holiday, but often stay in hotels owned by companies based in an MEDC. Profits from airlines and hotels often go back to the MEDC. The tourists may be enjoying a swim in their hotel pool while locals still have to collect water from a nearby well.

Did you know ??????
More than 80% of home pages on the internet are in English.

Activity

2 Using Source **C** and your own studies, explain why tourists want to visit LEDCs.

Did you know ??????
20% of the world's tourism takes place in LEDCs.

C *Tourist at Machu Picchu*

Activity

4 Look at Source **C**.

In what ways is tourism damaging sites like Machu Picchu?

Activity

The effect of tourism on LEDCs

3 Copy the table below.

Put the effects listed below in the correct box. Some boxes may have more than one effect.

	Positive effects	Negative effects
Economy		
Culture		
Environment		

Increased employment

Alcohol and sunbathing by tourists may offend locals in some resorts

Improved infrastructure, e.g. more roads built

Loss of agricultural land due to new buildings

Damage to ecosystems, e.g. coral reefs

Culture enjoyed by paying tourists so it does not die out

Low paid jobs

Wildlife reserves help preserve endangered species

Increase in prices for locals

Profits can be invested to protect the environment

Soil erosion due to new buildings

Group activity ▪▪▪▪

4 Have a class debate on the effects of tourism in LEDCs. Groups could represent tourists from an MEDC, environmentalists, farmers in an LEDC or holiday companies.

Popular tourist destinations in LEDCs include African safaris, beaches in Thailand and ancient sites such as the pyramids in Egypt and Machu Picchu in Peru. The impact of tourism is different in each location. In coastal areas, it could be destruction of the coral reefs. At historical sites, it could be building roads to access the site and damage to stonework. Machu Picchu is an Inca settlement built in 1450, high in the Andes Mountains. Nearly half a million visitors a year visit Machu Picchu.

■ Multinational companies

Multinational companies (MNCs) are businesses that operate in at least two countries. Many operate globally. They may have headquarters in an MEDC and branches or factories in LEDCs. They have an important role in globalisation. Their products are often recognised by **global branding**. Ronald McDonald promotes the value of friendly

D *Child labour in clothing factory*

service in McDonalds, but different adverts are used in each country to reflect different cultures. Some people in MEDCs accuse MNCs of exploiting workers in LEDCs, but often the workers are just happy to have a job. Many governments in LEDCs encourage MNCs to set up in their countries to provide employment. MNCs are happy to locate there as they can escape trade tariffs, expand their market and keep their production costs low.

> Amitosh was sold by his family to work in a clothing factory in India. 'I work 16 hours a day sewing individual beads onto clothes. I feel tired and sick. Sometimes if I lose concentration I get beaten by the manager. It is really hot where I work with the other boys. I have dust in my hair.'

E *Story of a child labourer*

MNC	Revenue US$billion	Country	GDP US$billion
Tesco	46	UK	2,772
Toyota	202	Kenya	29
McDonalds	22	Nigeria	166
BP	291	Egypt	127
Wal-Mart	387	Iceland	20
Microsoft	60	Sierra Leone	1
Exxon Mobil	404	USA	13,843
The Walt Disney Company	35	South Africa	282
Google	16	Ethiopia	19

Revenue: total income of a company in 1 year
GDP: Total income from goods and services in a country in 1 year

F *Table of nine MNCs and nine countries*

Activity

7 Using Source **F**, rank the countries and MNCs in order. Use a different colour for MNCs and countries. Describe the pattern you see.

Which do you think has more economic power: countries or MNCs? Explain, giving reasons for your answer.

Key terms

Multinational company (MNC): a business that manages production or delivers services in at least two countries.

Global branding: a set of values used to promote a product around the world.

Child labour: a child under 17 who is working more hours than legally allowed.

Did you know ??????

There are over 60,000 MNCs in the world.

∞ links

Also see Topic 7.3 for more information on globalisation and MNCs.

Activity

5 List two features of a multinational company.

Activity

6 Using Sources **D** and **E**, describe a child's day working in a clothing factory.

Going further

3 Find out more about Gap policy on **child labour** at www.gapinc.com

Produce a short report on the WTO and find out why people protest against it. Use the students' page at www.wto.org

Global interdependence

Global interdependence affects both MEDCs and LEDCs as all countries rely on each other for trade, jobs and resources such as food, oil and increasingly water. The MEDCs provide aid, manufactured goods and technical expertise to LEDCs. LEDCs provide cheap labour, food and other natural resources.

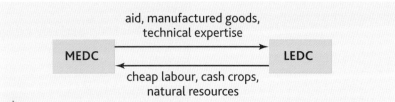

G   *Global interdependence*

The growing links and dependence on other countries can cause problems and benefits. The weather in other countries can affect the price of food we buy. Cheap labour in places like India may mean job losses in the UK, but means you can buy cheap clothes. Many countries depend on other countries for important resources. In the summer of 2008 Cyprus had to spend £35 million for Greece to deliver fresh drinking water by tanker. The UK spent $3.1 billion on Russian oil in 2007 as North Sea oil supplies run out.

Globalisation has increased the links between countries. The Pew global attitudes survey of 38,000 people in 44 countries found people in LEDCs were more positive about globalisation than people in MEDCs.

People protest about globalisation and the spread of MNCs whenever the **World Trade Organization (WTO)** has a conference. At the 2008 WTO conference, countries could not agree on fair trade because they were more interested in looking after their own needs.

Others say countries must act together over environmental and human rights. Supporters of globalisation point to rapid growth in India and China that has helped reduce poverty.

Check your understanding

1   Give two examples of a stereotype of people living in LEDCs.

2   Give two examples of a multinational company.

3   Describe two ways tourism can benefit LEDCs.

4   Read Source **H**. Explain in your own words whether you agree with this statement giving reasons for your answer.

Key terms

Global interdependence: the way that the countries of the world rely on each other for trade, resources and jobs.

Globalisation: where activities in one part of the world have consequences for people in other parts of the world.

World Trade Organization (WTO): set up in 1995 to promote free and fair trade.

Did you know ??????

Global trade is 20 times bigger than in 1950.

Activity

8   Draw a diagram to show the ways you are linked to other countries, such as charities you support, food you eat, clothes you wear.

Activity

9   Why do you think people in LEDCs are more positive about globalisation than people in MEDCs?

Activity

10   Using Sources D, E, F and G, explain why some people protest against globalisation.

Study tip

Make sure you can different views on globalisation.

> 66 *Globalisation itself is neither good nor bad.* 99
>
> *Joseph Stiglitz,*
> *Nobel Prize for Economics*

H

5.4 How effective are the methods used to reduce global inequality?

Aid

Aid is practical help. Donor countries give aid, which can be in the form of resources, gifts or loans to recipient countries which receive the aid.

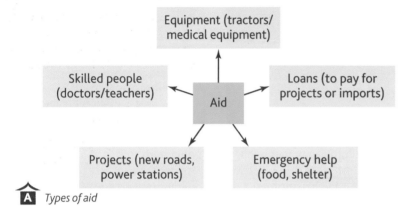

A Types of aid

The UK has a **government organisation** called the Department For International Development (DFID) which spends half its budget on **bilateral aid**. The main recipient countries are India and Tanzania. This is often 'tied' aid with conditions attached, meaning goods and services have to be bought from the UK. The DFID also gives **multilateral aid** to agencies such as the UN or the World Bank to distribute. After the 2008 cyclone in Burma, the Burmese government was reluctant to allow aid into the country but other countries sent aid anyway. This is an example of **unilateral aid**.

The Productive Safety Net Programme in Ethiopia is supported by £93 million from the DFID. People are paid to work on building projects and the money earned can be used to buy cattle or coffee trees to provide a permanent income. So far over 6,000 kilometres of road, 756 classrooms and 407 wells have been built and 15,000 people have benefited from increased income.

Activity

1 Look at the two countries below and explain which type of aid from Source **A** would be most useful.

Country 1: has had an earthquake. Many people have been left homeless.

Country 2: wants to develop more industry so it does not have to rely on primary products.

Activity

2 Decide if the following statements are TRUE or FALSE.

a Aid is always given freely by governments with no conditions attached.

b The UK gives bilateral aid to India.

c Five European countries, including the UK, have given 0.7 per cent of their GNP in aid.

d The Burmese government asked the UN for aid after the cyclone.

Objectives

You will be able to:

understand the different types of aid

evaluate the effectiveness of debt relief, fair trade and expansion of tourism in reducing global inequality

describe the Millennium Development Goals.

Key terms

Government organisation: for example DFID (Department For International Development) that manages aid to the World Bank and the UN.

Bilateral aid: resources given directly from one country to another, often with conditions attached.

Multilateral aid: money given by donor countries to the World Bank or UN who then distribute aid.

Unilateral aid: aid given by one country or organisation, whether the recipient country agrees or not.

Non-governmental organisation (NGO): an organisation that is not run by, or associated with, any particular government. It may operate at local, national or international level, for example, Amnesty International, Oxfam.

Humanitarian aid: resources sent to save lives or reduce suffering after a crisis.

The UN decided countries should give 0.7 per cent of their GNP in aid. So far only Sweden, Norway, Denmark and the Netherlands have met that target. The UK gave 0.51 per cent GNP in 2007.

Non-governmental organisations

Non-governmental organisations (NGOs) such as Oxfam are often associated with humanitarian aid following a crisis and with local development projects.

Activity

3   Using the text and Sources B and C, write five or six sentences describing how Oxfam provides aid to Ethiopia.

Oxfam in Ethiopia

Oxfam works in 70 countries worldwide. They try to ensure their aid goes directly to people who need it by working with local communities to help them develop. They have been working in Ethiopia since the 1970s in the following areas:

Agriculture: Helping people grow more food by providing seeds and tools.

Education: Working to achieve the Millennium Development Goal of all children in primary education by 2015. Providing training courses on beekeeping, woodwork and sewing.

Humanitarian aid: Trucking water to 15,000 people and feed for 30,000 animals during the drought of 2008. Training health professionals to help with the outbreak of 'Acute Watery Diarrhoea' (AWD) in 2008 which killed over 200 people.

Gender issues: Helping tackle gender-based violence that affects 70 per cent of women in Ethiopia.

Community- based organisations: Helping nomadic farmers to demand their rights from the government.

Case study

B Oxfam delivers water to refugees in Ethiopia

Ethiopian, Mohammed Ali went on a 15-day Oxfam training course on beekeeping. 'I used to produce 5 kg of honey a year. The course taught me how to look after the hives properly. Now I produce 25 kg of honey. From the income I can send all my four children to school.'

Adapted from Oxfam website

C Beekeeper's story

Some people criticise aid, saying it creates a dependency culture. LEDCs get swamped with too many aid programmes and LEDCs would rather have fair trade than aid.

Activity

4   Using the information you have read, which type of aid (government or NGO) do you think is the most effective and why?

Study tip

Do not confuse aid with HIV/AIDS.

Did you know ??????

The UK government gives £7,487 million in aid a year to LEDCs. Oxfam spends £213 million.

Going further

1   a   Find out how the DFID works at:

www.dfid.gov.uk

    b   Find out more about Oxfam at:

www.oxfam.org.uk/coolplanet/kidsweb

Cancellation of debt

Debt has caused many LEDCs to become trapped in a poverty cycle. Most of the money paid back to MEDCs is interest from the original loan.

D *Demonstrators at a Make Poverty History march during the G8 summit*

Jubilee 2000 was a campaign that started in 1996 and argued for $269 billion debt from 51 poor countries to be cancelled by 2000. It was supported by churches, NGOs and individuals such as Bob Geldolf. At the **G8** summit in 1998, 70,000 people took part in a protest march and 26 million people had signed the world's biggest petition.

In 1996 the World Bank and the IMF launched the **Heavily Indebted Poor Countries (HIPC)** initiative at a cost of $68 billion. They identified 41 HIPCs which had unsustainable debts. By 2008, 23 HIPCs had reached targets that allowed their debt to be partially or fully cancelled. Ethiopia has received $1.9 billion as part of this scheme, but the biggest success has been in Tanzania and Mozambique.

Tanzania has received $170 million from the HIPC initiative which means 1.6 million pupils are now going to primary school. Mozambique has received debt relief allowing it to spend money on vaccinating children, building new schools and supplying electricity to rural areas.

Because the aim of Jubilee 2000 was not met, and people argue that the HIPC initiative is still not enough, it is now called the Jubilee Debt Campaign. This supports the Make Poverty History campaign which has three aims: to cancel debt, make trade fair and get $50 billion more aid. The Jubilee Debt Campaign encourages people to sign petitions, wear white wristbands and take part in protests at G8 summits to remind the G8 leaders to keep their promise to end world poverty. Ten years after their first G8 protest the Jubilee Debt Campaign has a new demand to cancel $400 billion debt from 100 countries.

Going further

2 **a** Find out how you can support the Jubilee Debt Campaign and do some quizzes in the education section at: www.jubilee debtcampaign.org.uk

 b Write a letter to the leaders of the G8 explaining the demands of the Jubilee Debt Campaign.

links

Look at Topic 5.2 to find out more about the poverty cycle.

Key terms

G8: a group of the world's eight most powerful countries which meets annually to discuss world issues.

Heavily Indebted Poor Countries (HIPC): countries eligible for a debt relief scheme run by the World Bank and the IMF.

Cancellation of debt: relief from the burden of paying the original loan and the interest.

Did you know ??????

The UN estimates that seven million children's lives could be saved each year if debts were cancelled.

Group activity

1 Split into three groups. Have a debate on the effectiveness of **cancellation of debt** with groups representing NGOs, LEDCs and the HIPC initiative.

Activity

5 Using Source D and the text, explain why the Jubilee Debt Campaign supports Make Poverty History.

Study tip

Find out the latest information from the G8 summit before your exam.

Fair trade

E *Fair trade products*

Unfair payment to workers and unfair government policy causes global inequality. One way to reduce this is to practise **fair trade**. For a product to be sold as fair trade and carry the fairtrade logo, it must be approved by the **Fairtrade Foundation**. Fair trade gives farmers in LEDCs a guaranteed minimum price and provides a premium (extra money for social, economic and environmental development). This means farmers are able to send their children to school. The premium money can support new community projects such as building classrooms or wells.

Fairtrade product sales have increased dramatically over the past 10 years to half a billion pounds a year. 57 per cent of people are now aware of the Fairtrade logo. Many towns and schools have become 'fair trade'.

Governments can also reduce tariffs and subsidies to allow **free trade**, although some people argue this still benefits MEDCs more than LEDCs. The Trade Justice Movement was founded in 2000 by 80 charities, including Oxfam. It supports the Make Poverty History campaign by putting pressure on the WTO to change unjust trading rules.

In 2009 Tate and Lyle made the biggest ever switch to fair trade by selling 100 per cent of their sugar as fair trade. This benefits 6,000 growers in the Belize Sugar Cane Farmers Association by over £2 million a year. They will be paid an extra premium of $60 per tonne to help rebuild community centres and schools damaged by hurricanes.

Going further

3 a Play games and find out about Fair trade bananas at
www.oxfam.org.uk/coolplanet/kidsweb/banana/index.htm

   b Find out more about Fairtrade towns and schools at:
www.fairtrade.org.uk

   c Conduct a survey to see how many people know about or buy fair trade products.

Key terms

Fair trade: sustainable trade and improved working conditions for producers in LEDCs.

Fairtrade Foundation: organisation that gives companies the right to use the fairtrade logo, and checks up on them.

Free trade: trade without government tariffs and subsidies. Prices and products determined by supply and demand.

∞ links

See Topic 5.2 for more about the causes of global inequality.

Group activity

2 Working in groups and using Source **E** and your own knowledge, how many fair trade products can you list?

Did you know

There are over 3,000 fairtrade products available in the UK.

Activity

6 Design a poster to encourage people to buy fairtrade products.

Study tip

Use your own supermarket buying experience of fairtrade products to answer exam questions.

Expansion of tourism

Tourism can have a negative impact on LEDCs, but it can also be seen as a way to improve the lives of people living in LEDCs. **Ecotourism** appeals to people who are environmentally and socially aware, and are prepared to pay extra to reduce the impact of their holiday.

Community-based tourism (CBT) is concerned with the impact of tourism on the environment and the local community. Tourists can stay with local families and learn about their culture. CBT works best when it is supported by an NGO, and the local community owns and manages the project. The NGO can provide training on how to look after tourists in their own home and conduct tours.

Case study

Many mangrove forests in Kenya have been destroyed due to tourism. In Gazi, the women have built a 300 m boardwalk through the mangrove. They charge tourists a fee per trek. Women have been trained to conduct the tours. They provide local refreshments and show visitors the wildlife. The mangrove is preserved and 100 per cent of the profits go back into the village. The money has been used to:

- provide scholarships for poor children in the village
- improve health care
- improve the village primary school
- supply clean water.

F *Mangrove boardwalk – a community-based tourism project in Kenya*

There can be confusion over what the term 'ecotourism' means. Concern has been raised over the way some multinational travel companies have used it to advertise holidays while displacing local people and causing conflict over land use rights.

Activity

7 Using Source **F** and the text, explain how community-based tourism can help an LEDC like Kenya.

Activity

8 Produce a brochure for tourists interested in an ecotourism or community-based tourism holiday.

Did you know ???????

Money staying in local economy:
- Package holiday 20 per cent
- Ecotourism holiday 95 per cent

Study tip

Refer to a named resort in the exam.

Going further

4 a Find out more about the International Ecotourism Society (TIES) at: www.ecotourism.org
   b Find out more about community-based tourism at: www.mangroveactionproject.org/issues/tourism

Millennium Development Goals

The **Millennium Development Goals (MDGs)** were put forward by the UN. They were agreed by 189 countries who signed a declaration during the UN Millennium Summit in the year 2000. Some of the goals had targets set, to be met by 2015. The first goal to eradicate extreme poverty and hunger has a target to half world poverty by 2015.

Millennium Development Goals

- Eradicate extreme poverty and hunger.
- Achieve universal primary education.
- Promote gender equality.
- Reduce child mortality.
- Improve maternal health.
- Combat HIV/AIDS, malaria and other diseases.
- Ensure environmental sustainability.
- Develop a global partnership for development.

The first seven goals are to be achieved through Goal 8. The global partnership involves LEDCs promising to govern better by reducing corruption and to invest in their people through healthcare and education. MEDCs have pledged to support them by giving more aid, debt relief and fairer trade.

Campaigns like Make Poverty History and End Poverty 2015 focus on these goals and put pressure on world leaders to keep their promises. They say that although aid has increased it is not enough. Cancellation of debt has only benefited a few countries and LEDCs need to take more responsibility for reducing corruption and conflict.

H *Achieving the Millennium Development Goals*

Key terms

Millennium Development Goals (MDGs): eight goals agreed by world leaders to reduce world poverty by 2015.

Group activity

3 a Arrange the goals in order of importance, giving reasons for your answer.

  b Explain why the target for Goal 1 is to halve poverty and not fully eradicate it?

Study tip

Learn all eight Millennium Development Goals for use in a 12-mark question.

Did you know

The total cost of meeting the MDGs is $100 billion a year.

Going further

5 a Read personal accounts relating to the MDGs at:
www.bbc.co.uk/worldservice/ specials/ 1112_mdg/index.shtml

  b Find out more about the MDGs, and track their progress at:
www.undp.org/mdg

Check your understanding

1 Name two types of aid.

2 Give the meaning of the term 'ecotourism'.

3 Describe three things you could do to help reduce global inequality.

4 Using Sources **G** and **H**, evaluate which method will have the most impact on meeting the MDGs.

5

■ Global inequality

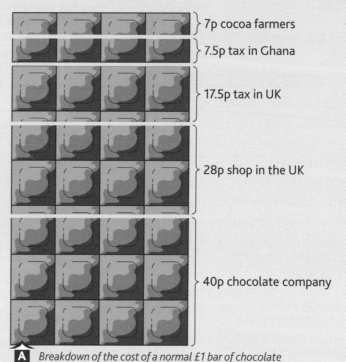

7p cocoa farmers

7.5p tax in Ghana

17.5p tax in UK

28p shop in the UK

40p chocolate company

A Breakdown of the cost of a normal £1 bar of chocolate

> ❝ I used to sell my cocoa beans to the Ghanaian government who often cheated me or paid me late. Most of my cocoa beans are sent to the UK to be made into chocolate bars. The Rica Gold Chocolate bars are sold in Oxfam shops. Since joining the fair trade company I can afford to send my children to school and we also have a new well in our village. I used to walk nine miles to collect dirty water from a river and people were always getting sick. Now we have the new well people want to stay in our village and that includes teachers. ❞
>
> Lucy, cocoa farmer, Ghana

B Fair trade cocoa farmer

Practice questions

5 **(a)** Using Source **A**, which two groups get the most money from selling a bar of chocolate? *(2 marks)*

(b) Using Source **B**, briefly explain two ways fair trade helps communities in LEDCs. *(4 marks)*

(c) How effective is fair trade at reducing global inequality? Use Sources **A** and **B** and your own studies to answer. *(12 marks)*

> **Study tip** Make sure you use both sources for Question c.
>
> You should aim to write about one side of A4. How does fair trade reduce global inequality? Are there other methods that are more effective?
>
> Try to link the sources together. How much would Lucy earn if her cocoa was not fairly traded?
>
> Use your own studies if you are asked.

(d) Give the meaning of the term 'Gross National Product'. *(2 marks)*

(e) Briefly explain two environmental causes of global inequality. *(4 marks)*

(f) Explain how globalisation affects both MEDCs and LEDCs. Use your own studies to answer. You could write about any of the following:

- Stereotypes
- Multinational companies
- Global interdependence
- Expansion of tourism *(12 marks)*

> **Study tip** Question f will assess the quality of your written communication. You should aim to write one side of A4.
>
> You could structure you answer into two parts, LEDCs and MEDCs, or take each bullet in turn and look at the effect each has on MEDCs and LEDCs.

> **Study tip** Make sure you use good English and clear presentation in all your answers.

Family and socialisation

6.1 What is meant by family?

Family and households

Two hundred years ago there were only two main types of **families** in the UK: The **nuclear family** and the **extended family**. Extended families were needed to help with jobs such as harvesting when many people were still involved with farming. Even when people moved into cities to work, there was no Welfare State. If people were ill or elderly, they needed the extended family to look after them. People were expected to marry. Single people and single-parent families were not encouraged. Gay relationships were illegal until 1967.

A Families and households in the UK today

There are many different definitions of what a family is. Giddens said 'the family is a group directly linked by marriage, blood or adoption where the adults take responsibility for the children.' This definition would cover all the families in Source **A**. But what happens when children leave home to go and live on their own and the parents are left by themselves? This is when the term **household** is used.

It describes who is actually living in a particular house. In this example there would be a household made up of a couple with no children (the parents) and a **single-person household** (the child who has left home). If you asked them if they were still family they would probably say 'Yes!'

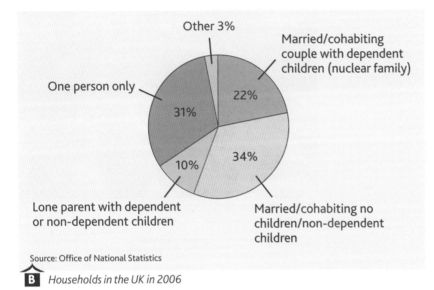

Source: Office of National Statistics

B   *Households in the UK in 2006*

Today there are many different types of families and households in the UK. There are several reasons for this:

1 **Changing attitudes** Changes in attitude to **single-parent families**, single-person households, divorce and gay relationships have led to different types of families such as **reconstituted families** and **civil partnerships**.

2 **Economics** Working women no longer have a financial reason to marry, as they can support themselves. Single-parent families have access to the Welfare State and other financial support. Divorce has become cheaper leading to more single-parent and reconstituted families. The high cost of childcare means many grandparents look after their grandchildren. The high cost of residential care means elderly relatives live with family members, showing that extended families are still important. Similarly young people often live in **student households** to reduce their cost of living.

3 **Immigration** Since the 1950s different ethnic and religious groups have settled in the UK. Many traditional Asians live in male-dominated extended families. Arranged marriages are still common. West Indian families are less likely to have married parents and are often female-dominated.

Going further

1 a Carry out further research into a type of household or family.
   - www.grandparentsplus.org.uk for extended families
   - www.adoptionuk.org.uk for adoption
   - www.youthinformation.com for arranged marriages (follow the Family & Relationships/Family and Personal link)
   b Do a survey to see the types of households and family in your class or school.

Key terms

Single-parent family: one parent (mother or father) living with their children often after divorce, separation or death of a parent. Also called a lone-parent family.

Reconstituted family: a family where at least one child is not common to both adults, for example, when parents divorce and one remarries to form a new family that may include step-brothers or sisters or half-brothers or sisters.

Civil partnership: since 2005 same-sex couples can become civil partners, giving them legal, financial and childcare rights.

Student household: a group of non-related students sharing accommodation, eating arrangements and bills.

Activity

2 Look at the pie chart in Source **B**.

a Which is the most common type of household in the UK today?

b What percentage are nuclear families?

c Give three different reasons for people to be in a single-person household.

d Give two examples of 'other' households.

Activity

3 Design your own 'soap opera' street containing as many different families and households as you can.

Study tip

Know the difference between a single-parent family and a single-person household.

Families in other cultures

Zulu family life

In the UK it is only legal to be married to one person at a time. This type of **marriage** is called **monogamy**. It is also legal to remarry after a **divorce**. This is called **serial monogamy**. However this is not the case in some cultures.

Three million Zulu live in the countryside in South Africa. Each village contains a large extended family with a chief as a leader. There are clear gender roles for the children in the village. The young boys help with looking after the cattle. The girls help their mothers with the cooking, looking after younger siblings, carrying wood and fetching water.

At age 14 girls can be married. A wedding must take place when the moon is bright to bring good luck. Offerings are also made to the spirits of ancestors for protection, health and happiness. No marriage is permanent until a child is born. In traditional Zulu culture a man can have several wives as long as he can afford to pay for them. This is called **polygamy**. The wives live in separate huts in order of importance.

Today nearly half of Zulus have moved to live in cities but polygamy continues. Jacob Zuma who is a potential candidate for president of South Africa in 2009, has at least five wives and three fiancées. He has 18 children in total.

C *A Zulu family*

Activity

4   Look at the Zulu case study and complete the following table:

	My family	Zulu family
Family size		
Marriage		
Childcare		
Religious beliefs		

Key terms

Marriage: the legal partnership between a man and woman.

Monogamy: marriage to one partner at a time.

Divorce: the legal ending of a marriage.

Serial monogamy: a series of relationships including a pattern of marriage, divorce and then remarriage.

Polygamy: marriage to more than one partner at the same time.

Study tip

Use actual names like Zulu or Jacob Zuma if you are asked to write using you own studies.

Did you know ??????

A Zulu woman can send a man subtle messages through her beaded jewellery.

Kibbutz

A kibbutz is a shared or 'collective' community in Israel. They were set up over 100 years ago as shared farms. The idea is that all property and work is shared. Men and women are seen as equal. Between 1,000 and 24,000 people live in each kibbutz.

Until the 1970s children were separated from their parents. They were raised in special units by trained nurses and teachers. It was thought that this was better than being raised by busy working parents. Parents would get to see their children for a few hours in the evening.

There were advantages to this system:

- No child felt lonely or neglected.
- All children had the same sort of clothes and amount of pocket money so there was no bullying.

But there were also disadvantages:

- Children became shy outside the group and were unable to develop relationships.

Read Source **E** for more disadvantages.

Today there are 266 kibbutzim in Israel and family life has changed over the last 25 years. Children still spend most of the day at school or in childcare, but now they live with their parents as a nuclear family in small bungalows or flats. Women are more involved in their children's activities. Working women are given an extra hour off work to do housework.

D *Children in a Kibbutz*

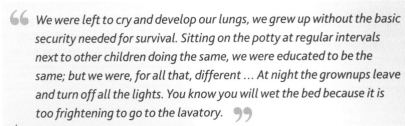

We were left to cry and develop our lungs, we grew up without the basic security needed for survival. Sitting on the potty at regular intervals next to other children doing the same, we were educated to be the same; but we were, for all that, different … At night the grownups leave and turn off all the lights. You know you will wet the bed because it is too frightening to go to the lavatory.

E *Quote from a child in a Kibbutz*

In a boarding school there's no privacy, no money, and no help, except from the larger family of the school itself. There's no dreamy solitude, no slack time, no lazing.

F *Quote from a child in a UK boarding school*

Activity

5 Use Sources **D**, **E** and **F** to describe how life at a UK boarding school is both similar and different to life in a kibbutz.

Check your understanding

1 Name two types of household in the UK today.

2 Describe the difference between a family and a household.

3 Explain two reasons why there are different types of family in the UK today.

4 Describe two differences between your own family and that of another culture.

Going further

2 a Research families in other cultures at:

www.zulu-culture-history.com

and

www.kibbutz.org.il/eng/

b Investigate life at a UK boarding school.

6.2 What are the functions of the family?

Functions of the family

You may be thinking 'what is the point of families?' In the kibbutz case study you read how children were not brought up by their parents. The function of looking after children was carried out by nurses. This topic will look at the five main functions of the family.

A *The five functions of the family*

The **economic function** is all about money. Families need money to pay rent, buy food and everything else you find in a home. Usually this means at least one person going out to work to earn money for the family. Sometimes the government can provide this function through benefits.

Families look after each other. This is the **caring function**. Parents look after children, and disabled or elderly relatives. In a nuclear family the adults also look after each other by providing emotional support.

The **sexual** and **reproductive functions** do not apply to all family types. Some adults within a family may not be able to fulfil the sexual function, for example if they are a single parent. Others may not be able to have their own children and adopt or remain childless.

Socialisation function

One of the main functions of the family is **socialisation**. This is where children learn how to behave in society from their parents. Small children like to copy what they see, so they easily pick up good and bad habits from their parents. If children did not learn how to talk from their parents, they would not be able to talk to anyone else in society. Children who have not been socialised by their parents may find it difficult to fit into society.

Children learn their behaviour by listening, watching, playing and talking. They listen to what their parents call them. For example they may call girls 'sweet' and boys 'tough'. They watch who does what in the house – is it the mum or dad doing the housework? They play with toys. Some children are encouraged to play with all types of toys. Others give dolls to girls and trucks to boys. They also learn how to talk and hopefully say the right things that society expects like 'please' and 'thank you' instead of being rude!

Children usually learn about religion first from their families. This is why children follow their parent's religion or lack of religion until they are old enough to make up their own minds. As you will see later, religion can have a big effect on you family life.

When children get older, the influence of their parents gets less. They are influenced by other socialisation factors such as friends, schools and the media, who often teach them different behaviours from their parents.

Did you know

The average family spends £155 per week on each person.

Group activity ▪▪▪▪

2   Divide into groups and discuss the behaviours your parents have taught you. Are they useful to you now? Have you changed your behaviour?

Activity

2   Draw a table like the one below to show how words and toys can socialise boys and girls. Add as many words and toys to the boxes as you can.

	Words	Toys
Boys	tough	trucks
Girls	sweet	dolls

Study tip

Make sure you understand the term 'socialisation' if you use it in the exam.

Going further

1   a   Draw a timeline from age 0 to 10 years old to show when you learned certain behaviours. Use child development websites as you may have forgotten when you learned to talk or eat.

   b   Investigate gender bias in toys and why it still exists in the UK today. Who is responsible: toy manufacturers, the media or parents?

Gender roles

Gender roles are the expectations about behaviour and the **division of labour** based on whether people are male or female. In the family this means tasks in the home such as looking after the children or doing the cleaning. Who decides who does these tasks? Most of the time it is due to socialisation by parents. The way we are brought up by our parents teaches us how we should behave and which tasks we should do in the house. Socialisation depends on the society we live in. Look at the case study below of gender roles in a different culture.

Case study

Chambri people of Papua New Guinea

Papua New Guinea is an island in the Pacific Ocean. The indigenous people are a society of hunter-gatherers. Approximately 1700 Chambri live in three villages on the shores of Lake Chambri. Their gender roles are almost the reverse of what we expect in UK culture. The women

B *Chambri man in feathered headdress*

have a dominant role in work and money, while the men spend their time shopping! Chambri lifestyle is now influenced by modern changes and some Chambri have moved to cities.

The table shows some gender roles of the Chambri people in Papua New Guinea.

Chambri Women	Chambri Men
Manage the money and business in the home.	Dependant on the women financially and emotionally.
Go fishing and weave mosquito nets to sell.	Receive money from the women to go shopping. They play the flute, dance and paint.
Shave their heads and wear no jewellery.	Curl their hair and wear fancy belts and head-dresses.

Activity

3 Look at Source B, the case study and the table. Describe what you can see and explain what this tells you about gender roles.

An experiment was conducted to show how children are socialised to learn their gender roles. Young children were asked if they preferred blue rocket pop or pink princess pop even though the drink inside was identical. The girls chose the pink and the boys chose the blue. This is because they have been brought up to expect to show a preference for those colours. The same applies to toys and jobs in the home.

C *Gender pop!*

Gender roles can change over time and in different cultures. In the 17th century cavaliers wore long hair and lace. Again in the 1970s long hair was popular for some men. These are roles we often associate as feminine. In UK society today men and women are expected to behave in different ways.

Activity

5 Who does these tasks in your house?

cleaning	washing	DIY
gardening	childcare	paying the bills

Compare your results with a partner and write down any patterns you notice.

Activity

4 Look at this list of behaviour. Which do you associate as male or female?

dominant	affectionate
aggressive	competitive
submissive	emotional

The 1970 Equal Pay Act and the 1975 Sex Discrimination Act meant women had more opportunities in the workplace. With more women working, men began to do more jobs in the house.

Today some women earn more than men and the man chooses to stay at home and look after the children. This is called a **househusband**. Change has happened so quickly over the past 30 years that men and women are still working out their new roles in the family.

Did you know ??????

The term 'househusband' was first used in the 1970s as a joke.

Activity

6 Match up these changes in society with changes in family gender roles.

Changes in society

- Equal opportunity laws
- House price and cost of living increases
- Raising children is expensive
- Changing attitudes to women at work
- Men and women working longer hours and shift-working

Changes in family and gender roles

- Women go to work to help pay the bills
- More women have the opportunity to go to work
- More men and women have to share the housework and childcare
- Families have fewer children
- Changing attitudes to roles in the home such as househusbands

Going further

2 a What do you think gender roles will be in 50 years' time? Explain giving reasons for your answer.

b Find out more about Margaret Mead and her study of gender roles in three different tribes in Papua New Guinea.

Care of the elderly

People in the UK are living longer due to improved lifestyles. The **life expectancy** for men is now nearly 77 years and for women just over 81 years. This means there are more elderly people in society. There will also be less young people like yourself, so when you get a job you will probably have to pay more taxes to look after the elderly.

Because people are living longer they often spend many years needing treatment or specialist care for long-term health problems. They may have conditions such as loss of hearing which prevents them listening to conversations or loss of vision which prevents them reading or watching TV. Many elderly people can feel isolated if they are not able to get out of their home. By the year 2025 there are expected to be over 1 million people suffering with dementia. Alzheimer's disease is a type of dementia. People lose their memory and find it difficult to look after themselves.

D *Elderly man helped by his son*

In the past the care of the elderly was the responsibility of the family. Grandparents often moved in with relatives and created an extended family. This still happens in some communities but there is another problem. Because families have fewer children, there are fewer relatives to look after the parents in their old age. Many of the women who would have done the caring function in the past are now too busy working. Elderly people may also live a long way from their family who find it difficult to visit them.

Activity

7 a Give two examples of improved working conditions.

b Give two examples of a healthier lifestyle.

Key terms

Life expectancy: the average length of time a person is expected to live.

National Health Service (NHS): provides nursing care for elderly people in addition to health services for the rest of the population.

Social Services: provides help for people in their own homes and help fund some residential care.

Residential care: for people who can not stay in their own homes. Meals and personal care are provided. Staff are usually available 24 hours a day.

Study tip

You can use your own elderly relatives as a case study.

Activity

8 Using Source D and the text, list the advantages and disadvantages if an elderly relative moved into your house.

Did you know ??????

There are 9.5 million people in the UK aged over 65.

The cost of looking after the elderly has risen rapidly and many families do not have the finances to support elderly relatives. Some people think it is the government's responsibility to pay for their care, especially if they have paid taxes all their working life. The government spends £17 billion a year on caring for people with dementia. Families themselves pay about £6 billion.

Under the **National Health Service (NHS)** and Community Care Act 1990, **Social Services** can give equipment to help people in their own homes, provide 'meals on wheels' or pay for **residential care**.

The NHS will cover nursing costs but social services or elderly people themselves have to pay for the accommodation, food and personal care. Personal care includes help getting out of bed and help with eating. Some people are campaigning to get free personal care for everyone.

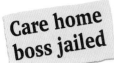

Care home boss jailed

Nursing staff neglected OAP

Elder abuse 'becoming common'

One in seven elderly are malnourished

Neglect leads to death of grandmother

E   *Newspaper headlines on care for the elderly*

RESIDENTIAL HOME

Included in bedroom...

- Telephone
- TV point
- Bring own furniture and pets

- garden
- organised activities

only £500 per week

F   *Advert for a residential care home*

Check your understanding

1   List two functions of the family.

2   What is meant by 'socialisation'?

3   Explain why gender roles have changed over time.

4   Describe two ways the elderly can be cared for.

Activity

9   Look at Sources E and F. Explain why it difficult for a family to decide where the elderly should be cared for.

Going further

3   a   Investigate facilities for elderly people in your area and produce a brochure. You could include health care facilities and social clubs provided by the government or voluntary sector.

b   Find out more about care of the elderly at: www.alzheimers.org.uk or www.helptheaged.org.uk

Influences on family life

Jack age 16

Religion
My parents are not religious. If I do get married I might have a civil ceremony or go abroad.

Family size
I live with my mum, dad and sister.

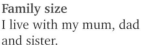

Media
I like watching football on Sky Sports. I like playing on my X-box and spend more time in chat rooms than with my parents!

Environment
I live in a detached house in a village in Northumberland.

It is very quiet and there is not much to do.

Government and law
My mum gets child benefit and working family tax credit.

I will apply for a provisional driving licence when I am 17 so I can see more of my friends.

Health
I go to a private dentist and get private health care through my dad's work. I play in a football team every Sunday and practise three times a week.

Class
My dad is an architect and my mum works as a GP practice manager. We are middle class.

I would like to go to university and become a sports physiotherapist.

Lifestyle
We have two cars in the family so it means there is always someone to give me a lift to football.

In the holidays I go to a villa in Italy with its own pool.

Objectives

You will be able to:

understand that families are influenced by a range of factors

understand the influence of religion and media on family life

understand how and why the government influences family life.

Key terms

Family size: the average number of children a woman has.

Class: the way society is divided into groups based on job, power or wealth. The three main classes are upper class, middle class and working class.

Activity

1. Draw a diagram for yourself and the influences on your family life. Use the headings: family size, environment, government, lifestyle, class, health, media and religion.

Aisha age 15

Religion
I am a Muslim. I pray at home, but I take my younger sister to mosque every evening between 5 and 7 p.m.

My parents had an arranged marriage. I want to get a job before I think about marriage.

Family size
I live with my mum, dad, grandma, two brothers and three sisters.

Media
I like watching Bollywood dramas on TV and use the internet for my homework and emailing friends.

Environment
I live in a terraced house in Bradford with a small garden. It can be quite noisy on the street.

Government and law
My mum gets child benefit and working family tax credit.

Next year I will apply for EMA (Educational Maintenance Allowance) so I can stay at school and do A-levels.

Health
I go to an NHS dentist.

I am in the school rounders team.

Class
My dad is a taxi driver and my mum works as a dinner lady at a primary school. We are working class. I would like to go to university and become an optician.

Lifestyle
We have one car – my dad's taxi – so I get the bus or walk to school.

In the holidays I go and stay with my cousins in London.

Activity

2 a What are the differences and similarities between Jack and Aisha?

   b Which factors do you think have the most important influence on their family life?

Influence of religion on family life

The UK today has many different religions. Religion can influence your attitude to **cohabitation**, marriage, divorce and family size.

Cohabitation

The Christian Church has always taught that sex before marriage and extra-marital affairs are wrong. Cohabitation is not encouraged.

The Silver Ring Thing

This Christian organisation was brought to the UK in 2004 from America with an aim to reduce teenage pregnancy by promoting abstinence. Abstinence means no sex before marriage. Teenagers attend a meeting at a school or church where the pledge to abstain from sex is explained. If a student makes a pledge, they are given a silver ring to wear and sent emails which will constantly remind them of their commitment.

no sex before marriage

C *The Silver Ring Thing*

Marriage

Marriage and family life is important in all religions. Vows or promises are made between the couple and to their God. Traditionally Muslims and Hindus had **arranged marriages**. Today internet sites can play a part in arranging marriages rather than parents. Arranged marriages tend to have lower divorce rates than 'love' marriages.

D *An arranged marriage*

Divorce

Divorce is not encouraged in religion but is usually allowed in certain situations. The Church of England, Islam, Judaism and Hinduism allow divorce. Catholics allow an annulment. This is proving the marriage was never valid in the first place.

Family size

Larger families are common in religions which have teachings that do not allow **contraception**. Some religious people see contraception as a personal issue and have smaller families.

Going further

1 a Investigate a particular religion and its views on family life.

   b Make further notes on how religion supports family life at:

   ■ www.careforthefamily.org.uk for a Christian-based organisation that works in many areas to support the family

   ■ www.mha.org.uk (Methodist Homes for the Aged) for elderly care

   ■ www.catholicchildrenssociety.org.uk for adoption.

Key terms

Cohabitation: couples live together but are not legally married.

Arranged marriages: a marriage where the partners have been chosen by the parents of the bride and groom.

Contraception: use of birth control to prevent pregnancy.

Group activity

1 Make a list of religions in the UK today.

Activity

3 Using Source **D** and the text, design an advert for an arranged marriage internet site.

Did you know

In England and Wales, there are now more civil marriage ceremonies than religious ones.

Group activity

2 Discuss which of these you would think are suitable grounds for divorce:

a Partner drinks.

b Partner has mental illness.

c Marriage was based on fraud.

d Couple can not have children.

e Partner is sent to prison.

f Partner has an affair.

Study tip

Do not confuse religion and ethnicity.

Influence of the media on the family

Attitudes to the family are influenced by the media. This influence affects the family types you are prepared to accept in society and your attitudes to marriage and divorce.

Many adverts use a **'cereal-packet family'** to advertise their products. They influence our attitude towards gender roles as they often show a woman when advertising household or childcare products and men when advertising cars. The 'cereal-packet family' traditionally used to advertise Oxo is now being replaced with a 21st-century family that is multicultural, multiracial has three children, two parents and two grandparents.

TV soap operas focus their stories on family life. Sometimes they feature big family weddings, but often arguments and relationship breakdown attract more viewers.

E *Madonna and David Banda*

Magazines and celebrity culture also influence attitudes. Pop stars and TV presenters act as **role models**. Expensive celebrity weddings show marriage is still popular and many young people still want to get married. In 2008, pop star Madonna officially **adopted** David Banda from Malawi. This may encourage more people to adopt children from abroad rather than the UK.

Presenter Ulrika Johnson who has four children with four different fathers has created a lot of debate about family types and the role of fathers. The Internet has changed people's views on families and relationships. Many people find new partners through online dating websites.

The effect of media on family life can be both positive and negative. Email and webcams can help families stay in touch. Obesity, slow language development and sleep problems have all been linked to young children watching too much television. 15-year-olds spend on average 55 per cent of their waking lives in front of TV or computers, meaning many do not share family meals.

F *The impact of the media on children*

Key terms

Cereal-packet family: an ideal nuclear family used in advertising with a housewife and male breadwinner.

Role model: someone whom you use as a reference point for your behaviour. You want to be like them.

Adoption: taking legal responsibility for a child other than your own.

Activity

4 Choose a household product and design an advert using a 21st-century family.

Activity

5 Collect magazines or newspapers and cut out stories about families. Which types of families are portrayed by the media?

Group activity

3 Make a list of family movies. How are males and females portrayed?

Did you know

80 per cent of teenagers have a TV in their bedroom.

Activity

6 Does the media reflect family life or does the family reflect the media? Evaluate this question using all the sources and your own studies.

Going further

2 Investigate how long teenagers spend on computers or watching TV and how it affects their family life.

Influence of the government and law on family life

From the moment you were born, the government has influenced your family life. NHS policies determine where you can be born: hospital or home? From age three, the government has learning objectives for children in nurseries. The government is also increasing the age you have to stay at school to 18. For elderly people there is the issue of who pays for their care: the government or the family? Laws determine what types of family are allowed. For example it is illegal to be married to more than one person at a time.

The government supports families financially. A form of **Child Benefit** was introduced in 1945. Parents or carers receive a weekly payment for every child they are looking after. More recently the **Child Support Act** ensures absent parents support their children.

The **Divorce Reform Act 1969** has made divorce cheaper and easier to obtain. This has led to different types of families such as single parents and reconstituted families. In 2002 laws to allow same-sex couples to adopt children were introduced and civil partnerships in 2005.

Information

16	Dads now get two weeks paternity leave
21	Child benefit up 26 per cent
22	2,200 Sure Start children's centres opened
24	Winter fuel payments for pensioners
30	600,000 children lifted out of poverty
31	Child Tax Credit introduced
32	Civil partnerships introduced
49	Free nursery places for 3- and 4-year-olds.

www.labour.org.uk website

G *Some of Labour's Top 50 achievements since 1997*

❝ *Our family-friendly agenda is our plan to try and help families get more time as well as money.* ❞

Speech by David Cameron MP

H *Conservative family policy 2008*

Despite the Equal Pay Act of 1970, women are still paid on average 17 per cent less than men. This can have an influence on family life as it can determine which members of the family go out to work and which stay at home to look after the children. This can be responsible for reinforcing gender roles. There are also plans to force single parents to return to work when their youngest child reaches age of 12.

I *Women are still campaigning for equal pay*

⚭ links

Also see Topic 6.2 for care of the elderly.

Activity

7 Look at Source G. Which policy, if any, do you think has been the most important for family life?

Group activity

4 Decide if you were in government what laws would you change or new laws would you bring in to support families? Use Sources G, H and I to answer.

Truancy

A couple have been jailed for failing to send their four children to school.

The children had not attended school for nearly seven months. The local education authority had sent letters, made telephone calls and carried out home visits. The parents had housing and health issues which made family life difficult. They claimed one child was bullied at school. The education authority only take parents to court as a last resort. They would prefer children to attend school regularly. The father has gone to jail for 12 weeks and the mother for 8 weeks. The children will be looked after by other relatives while the parents are in jail.

J *Parent in court over truancy charges: 'It's not my responsibility, not guilty'*

Activity

8 a Write a letter from the education authority explaining why the children must attend school.

b Write a reply from the parents explaining their point of view.

Did you know ??????

7,500 parents go to court each year over their children's truancy.

Some people argue that the government interferes too much in family life. By sending children to nursery at three years old, it removes **parental responsibility**. They argue children are better off with their parents and should not go to school until they are six or seven. The **Children Act 2004** is carried out by the education system and social services. Many parents are unaware of it. Others argue the government should do more to support all types of families by providing more financial support and free personal care for the elderly. Some politicians like to blame single-parent families for anti-social problems in society. They would like to see a return to Victorian values where parents are married and divorce is limited. Others want to see more equality laws for all types of families and solve the problem of poverty rather than blaming certain families for problems in society.

Going further

3 a Find out more about political parties' family policies at:

  ■ www.conservatives.com

  ■ www.labour.org.uk

b Look at Source I. Explain how the lack of equal pay and gender roles are linked.

Activity

9 'The government should leave families alone.'

How far do you agree with this statement? Explain, giving reasons for you answer.

Study tip

Don't be biased! Try and give balanced views from different political parties.

Check your understanding

1 What is a 'cereal-packet family'?

2 Briefly describe three influences on family life.

3 Describe two ways religion can influence family life.

4 Explain how government influences family life.

Marriage

In 1900 it was expected that most people would marry. Divorce was difficult and expensive. The laws favoured men, so many women stayed in unhappy or violent relationships. During the Second World War women did jobs done by men and started to gain their independence and rights in society and within marriage. The 1969 Divorce Reform Act made divorce easier and cheaper to obtain.

**Marriages and divorces[1]
United Kingdom**

1 Divorce data from 1955 to 1970 are for Great Britain only. Divorce became legal in Northern Ireland from 1969. Includes annulments.
2 For both partners.
3 For one or both partners.

Source: Office for National Statistics; General Register Office for Scotland; Northern Ireland Statistics and Research Agency

A *Graph showing number of marriages and divorces in the UK*

There are many reasons for these changes:

- Changing attitudes as people become less religious and more tolerant of divorce and cohabitation.
- Changing opportunities for women such as women going to work and having equal rights.
- Legal changes such as the Divorce Reform Act and civil partnerships.
- Economic changes such as increased cost of weddings, decreased cost of divorces and financial support for single parents.

Activity

1   Use Source **A** to answer the following questions:

a   How many marriages were there in 1955?

b   How many marriages were there in 2005?

c   Describe what has happened to the number of marriages.

d   How many divorces were there in 1955?

e   How many divorces were there in 2005?

f   Describe what has happened to the number of divorces.

Key terms

Marriage rate: the number of marriages per 1,000 people.

Divorce rate: the number of divorces per 1,000 people.

Did you know ??????

The average cost of a wedding is between £16,000 and £25,000.

Although the statistics show the **marriage rate** is in decline, many people still want to get married. The average age at which people marry has increased to 36 years old for men and nearly 34 years old for women. Weddings do not have to be religious and can now take place in many different venues. One of the most popular venues is the BA London Eye, which costs over £2,000 to hire for a wedding. Celebrities continue to have expensive, high-profile weddings. They act as role models to younger people thinking about marriage, who then think they need to have expensive weddings too. The wedding of Coleen and Wayne Rooney cost £5 million. Unfortunately the **divorce rate** has increased and 45 per cent of marriages now end in divorce.

Divorce

The increase in divorce has led to many different types of family in the UK today. If a couple get divorced and have no children, they will form single-person households. If one of them has children, a single-parent family will be created. If a divorced person marries a new partner they will form a reconstituted family.

B *Celebrity couple Coleen and Wayne Rooney*

Some people still view divorce as wrong, often due to religious beliefs. They say it causes problems for the children and adults involved. Other people argue that making divorce easier means women (and men) can escape from violent or abusive relationships.

Group activity

1   Make a list of celebrities you know. Decide if they are single, married, divorced or cohabiting. Is there a pattern?

Activity

2   Decide if these quotes show positive or negative aspects of divorce.

'I find it hard to concentrate on revising for my GCSEs with my mum and dad divorcing' – Sam aged 16

'I find it difficult to work and look after the children now my husband has left' – Jackie aged 38

'My parents do not agree with divorce and they are not supporting me' – Zara aged 24

'I had no children so it gave me a chance to start again' – Mike aged 33

'I'm glad to be away from my husband who used to drink and beat me up' – Kath aged 46

'It's much better now I don't have to listen to my parents arguing all the time' – Rizwan aged 10

Going further

1   Go to www.divorce-online.co.uk to find the latest news and stories on divorce. Make notes and use them as case studies.

Different types of family

Life expectancy has increased from under 50 years in 1901 to nearly 80 years today mainly due to improved health care. This has changed family life. Many people who got married young are finding it difficult to spend 60 years living with the same person. More people in their 50s and 60s are getting divorced. More elderly people need care by the family or in care homes.

Family size has also changed. In the past, women had more children as they were needed for work, there was no contraception and many children died. Today children are expensive to raise and with many couples both working in **dual-income households**, families are getting smaller. However with an increase in migration and some cultures having larger families, it is a changing situation.

Date	Number of children per family
1851	6.25
1900	3.3
1930	2.06
1960	2.7
1964	2.95
1976	1.70
1980	1.89
1990	1.80
2001	1.63
2006	1.84

C ONS

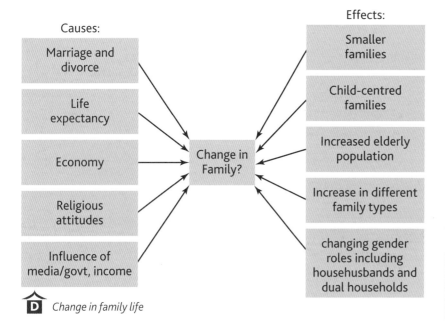

D *Change in family life*

∞ links

You have already looked at the difference between a family and a household in Topic 6.1 and some of the reasons why there are so many different types in the UK today in Topic 6.3.

∞ links

See Topic 6.2 for care of the elderly.

Group activity

2   List all the households and family types that you can remember.

Key terms

Life expectancy: the average length of time a person is expected to live.

Dual-income households: a household or family where both partners go out to work.

Surrogate mother: a woman who becomes pregnant with a child, usually for a couple who are unable to have their own children.

Teenage mums: girls who have children when they are under the age of 20.

Activity

3   Draw a graph using the data in Source C. Explain the trend in family size since 1851.

Activity 6

4   Look at Source D. Which of these causes do you think has had the most effect on family life? Give reasons for your answer.

Study tip

Make sure you understand all the different effects on family life. Be able to evaluate them. That means look at advantages and disadvantages of each effect.

Teenage mums

Hannah White, age 16, sat her GCSEs 11 hours after giving birth to Ebony. Her 19-year-old boyfriend was very supportive, but she was treated badly when she went to the chemist in her school uniform. The centre for teenage mothers helped her apply for housing benefit. The government 'Care to Learn' scheme provides childcare for Ebony while Hannah attends sixth form. Hannah does her homework while Ebony is asleep. Eventually she wants to get a job so she won't have to rely on benefits.

E *Teenage mum*

Gay dads

Tony and Barrie Drewitt-Barlow were the first dads in the UK to be both named on their children's birth certificates. They paid £200,000 to have donor eggs from the biological mother Tracy McCune implanted into a **surrogate mother** Rosalind Bellamy. Twins Aspen and Saffron were born in the USA. On their return to the UK, the Drewitt-Barlows received a lot of media attention and had to turn their house into a fortress. However, they have since repeated the process and now have another boy – Orlando.

F *Tony and Barrie Drewitt-Barlow*

Confessions of a househusband

As a househusband having a conversation with a bunch of 'blokes' can be fairly challenging. They say: 'So, what have you been up to lately?' This is what I want to say: 'My life has changed completely and I'm frantic, what with making the kids' breakfast, getting them off to school on time, keeping my three-year-old occupied, fed and clean during the day, getting clothes washed and hung out to dry, making sure the kitchen is tidy, picking up the kids from school, taking them to a park afterwards, trying to listen to each one of them when they are all speaking at once, and then keeping them occupied again until my wife comes home in the evening.'

The Daily Telegraph, 21 November 2007

G *Househusband*

Childhood

H *Childhood*

Childhood is not always decided by your biological age. It varies depending on where you live. In some societies for example, when a girl reaches puberty she may be classed as an adult and able to marry. Boys in war zones are often forced to become soldiers at a young age.

In the past, children were part of the adult world. They wore adult clothes and were expected to help with work. During **industrialisation**, children as young as five years old used to work down mines or in factories. Children were seen as cheap workers and often died, so parents did not get too attached to their children. This tells us that childhood is not decided by your biological age but by the society you live in. This is called a **social construct**.

Group activity ▪▪▪▪

3 Look at Source H and then copy and complete this sentence.

A child is age _____ to age _____ .

Explain how you arrived at your answer.

Key terms

Industrialisation: the change from a farming society to a society based around production of goods in factories.

Social construct: an idea, such as the age of childhood, which is decided by society.

Child-centred: treating the needs of children as important.

Pester power: the power children have over parents to make them buy or do something.

Tweenager: a fashion-conscious 8- to 12-year-old.

UN Rights of the Child: 54 rights that all children in the world should be entitled to, according to the United Nations.

Study tip

Remember not everyone has a childhood like yours.

By the 20th century, there were laws in place to stop children working and they had to attend school. Once children did not have to work, and because of better health care, fewer children died. This meant families had fewer children. Children became important in family life and we now live in a **child-centred** society. The 1988 Children's Rights Act gave children more rights today. Charities such as the NSPCC support children to get these rights. Children also have increased spending power through '**pester power**'. This is where children pester or hassle their parents to spend money. This starts when toddlers ask for sweets at the checkout and before long they are **tweenagers** asking for the latest electronic devices.

Information

The UN defines a child as anyone under 18. There are 54 rights of the child. Here are four:

- The right to be educated
- The right to freedom of religion
- The right to medical care
- The right to be protected from conflict and cruelty.

UN

 UN Rights of the Child

Activity

7 Match these responsibilities with the **UN Rights of the Child** in Source I.

- To respect other people's religion.
- To not bully or harm others.
- To learn as much as they can.
- To take care of themselves.

Some people say that childhood is disappearing again. Children are growing up too fast. Tweenagers are dressing like adults and have to cope with constant exam pressure. However, recent studies show that although childhood is more complicated today, most children are happy, they just need more support.

Check your understanding

1 What is 'cohabitation'?

2 List three different family types in the UK today.

3 Describe how changes in marriage and divorce have affected family life.

4 Explain why we live in a child-centred society today.

Group activity

4 Discuss the following legal age limits in the UK today. Do you agree? Would you change any?

- Drink alcohol at home – age 5
- Draw money from a bank – age 7
- Be convicted of a crime – age 10
- Buy a pet without an adult – age 12
- Drive a car, go to prison – age 17

Activity

6 Describe a time when you have used pester power. What was the outcome?

Did you know ???????

Children in the UK can work for up to two hours on a school day.

Activity

8 a Using Sources H and I, draw a table to show advantages and disadvantages of childhood in the UK today.

b Do you think childhood is better today than in the past or compared to other countries?

Going further

3 a Conduct a survey into spending habits of children today and their parents.

b Investigate charities that support children's rights at

www.savethechildren.org.uk and www.nspcc.org.uk

Family and socialisation

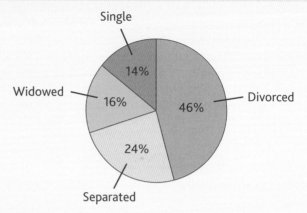

Single

14%

Widowed 16%

Divorced

46%

24%

Separated

A Percentage of lone dads

> 66 *Other mums do not invite me to their coffee mornings and I feel isolated and lonely. There is no childcare in the evening so I can't go out and socialise then either.* 99
>
> Dave, aged 27

> 66 *My wife died two years ago and my daughter really misses her mum. I find it hard to support her emotionally when she gets upset.* 99
>
> Mike, aged 45

> 66 *I find it hard to work all day then come home and sort out the discipline with the children on my own. I have no time for my own hobbies.* 99
>
> Majid, aged 26

> 66 *You have to do your best as a father and a mother as there is no one else to help you. It is a big responsibility and very exhausting as the children rely on you 24/7.* 99
>
> Noel, aged 35

B The views of some lone dads

Practice questions

6   **a)**   Using Source **A**, give two ways that men can become lone dads. *(2 marks)*

      b)   Using Source **B**, briefly explain two problems that lone dads face. *(4 marks)*

      c)   How important is it for both parents to have contact with their children?
Use Sources **A** and **B** and your own studies to answer. *(12 marks)*

> **Study tip**
>
> Make sure you use both sources for this. You should aim to write about one side of A4. Does everyone have a choice about having both parents? Can one parent do the job of two parents effectively?
>
> Try to make links between the sources. What type of lone dad might be giving his views?
>
> Use your own studies if you are asked.

      d)   Give the meaning of the term 'cohabitation'. Use your own studies to answer. *(2 marks)*

      e)   Briefly explain two reasons why life expectancy in the UK has increased since 1900. *(4 marks)*

      f)   Explain how family life in the UK compares with family life in a contrasting culture. Use your own studies to answer. You could write about any of the following:

- Family size
- Religious beliefs
- Life expectancy
- Childcare
- Care of the elderly
- Marriage. *(12 marks)*

> **Study tip**
>
> This question will assess your quality of written communication. You should aim to write one side of A4.
>
> Make sure you specify which contrasting culture you are using in your answer.
>
> Remember there are differences in family life in the UK too. For example, people have different religions.
>
> Good answers will make lots of comparisons. Remember to include similarities and differences when comparing families.

> **Study tip**
>
> Make sure you use good English and clear presentation in all your answers.

7 People and work

7.1 Why is work important to individuals?

Your humanities course covers many issues that arise from human interaction. Today economic activity, or **work**, in a range of forms will take up much of your life. It is a major area of human interaction, usually involving people outside the immediate family. It has not always been like this. Work in primitive societies was for survival, largely involving hunting animals for food and skins and gathering food such as berries and roots. Work was shared by family members and a division of labour emerged. The men and boys hunted for animals and the women and girls were more involved in ensuring food was collected and prepared.

A Bushman hunting

■ Why do people work?

In the more complex societies that exist today, this question produces a wide range of responses.

■ Why work is important

- The culture you live in expects you to work because it means you are contributing to society and helping it function. If you work, you are said to be employed. If you are training, you are a student or an apprentice. If you do not work, you are unemployed.
- Whenever you are asked who you are, between the ages of 18 and 65, you are likely to reply with your name and the job that you do.
- The kind of work you do often depends on your education.
- The work you do provides you with an income. The income generally determines where you live and the lifestyle that you can afford.

I like working with children.

I've always been interested in cars.

I like helping people solve their problems.

My mother was a doctor so I followed the family tradition.

It's good money and I like outdoor work.

It gives me freedom.

My job is interesting and pays well.

B *Why do people work today?*

- Work influences your health. Some types of work carry health risks.
- Working can be satisfying and very fulfilling, giving you a good feeling.
- Work normally involves you in working with others in a group. Work is a very human activity.

What is work?

The word 'work' has been used in this topic already, and you certainly know what it means. However, an exact definition of 'work' is very complex. When most people think of work, they tend to think about the work they know members of their family do. They usually leave home in the morning and then, using some means of transport, go to their place of work. This may be a hospital, a school, a factory, an office or a shop, for example. You may even think of going to work when you go to school. Teachers go to school to work.

Activity

3 Try to answer the following questions.
a Does anyone remain at home and work?
b Name some jobs that are done outside buildings.
c Do people work all day when they are outside the home?
d Are there groups of people who do not work? Who are they?
e How do people spend their time when they are not working?
f How many hours a week do you think most people spend working?

Activity

2 Do you see going to school as the equivalent of work? Make a list of the differences between what you do at school and what the teachers do.

Study tip

Make certain you can define 'work' and **'leisure'**.

Going further

1 Using the internet, see if you can find out about work, leisure and unemployment in another European country. France is an interesting contrast to the UK. You can use

en.wikipedia.org/wiki/Economy_of_France

but be careful with this site in general. At the top of each page of the site there is a warning that incorrect information might have been added to the site.

Does work dominate our lives?

Work is important to society but does it take up too much of our time?

Country	Legal maximum hours per week in one employment	Actual average hours worked per week	Legal minimum holidays in days
UK	48	42.1	20
France	35	41.0	36
Spain	41	40.8	35
Austria	50	44.1	38
Sweden	48	42.1	34

C *The working week and statutory holidays (by law) (2007)*

In the past

The average working week before the Ten Hour Act of 1847 is estimated at 72 hours work a week. This Act restricted the working week to 60 hours for children and, in 1878, to 60 hours for women.

Before 1750, most people worked in their homes. They could start and stop when they wanted. Most worked in farming and there were long days at harvest time in the summer and shorter days in winter when weather limited activity. Craftsmen worked in small workshops at their homes producing clothing and general goods such as knives. Working from home was called 'cottage industry'.

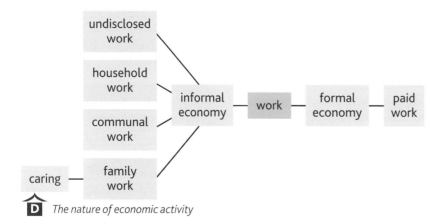

D *The nature of economic activity*

Today economic activity is much more complex.

The **formal economy** employs people in full-time and part-time work. The **informal economy** consists of work done as unofficial employment. These are unpaid tasks such as childcare and housework that could be someone's paid employment (as a nanny and housekeeper). It also includes money that is earned outside of the law, so avoiding payment of tax (often referred to as the 'black economy').

Group activity

1 Using Sources **D** and **E**, answer the following questions.

a In which country is the actual average hours worked per week the greatest?

b Write a sentence that describes the actual average hours worked per week in the five European countries.

c Why do you think the UK has the least statutory holidays? Find out if this is to change?

d What else do you notice from the table?

Activity

4 Decide which of the following activities can be defined as work or leisure:

- walking to work
- sleeping
- eating meals
- cutting the lawn
- washing
- looking after the children
- playing football
- visiting a relative
- reading a newspaper
- doing the housework
- going shopping for clothes

E *Leisure time activities*

Some people believe the effects of work spill over into our leisure. If work is physical, then leisure will need to be restful. If pay is low, then our leisure activities will be limited by the lack of spare money. Leisure requirements may influence work. A number of people have more than one job with the second job paying for their leisure pursuits. Others argue that age is the dominating influence on leisure.

Activity

5 Can you think of an exhausting job that will mean leisure time has to be for recuperation?

a Which jobs might spill over into leisure where people will talk about their work to each other?

b Do you think that work influences leisure in your home or is it more influenced by people's age?

Activity

6 Create a list with the headings shown below.

Work time	Travelling to/from work
Sleep	Going out–leisure
Family responsibilities	Staying–in leisure
Personal hygiene	Other

Calculate how you usually spend the 168 hours in a week and fill in the list.

Activity

7 Using a heading 'work' and one 'leisure' make two lists from the words below which characterise either work or leisure.

payment/no payment

specific duties/choice

free time/committed time

enjoyment/provides moneywork role/leisure role

Extension
- The job is interesting
- Work friends are frequently leisure friends
- Good wages provide for good leisure activities

Neutrality
- Money from work enables leisure activities which will brighten up a working life that is routine

Opposition
- The job is physically exhausting
- Workers turn to a quite different leisure to recuperate

F *Linking the nature of work with leisure*

Childhood
- Play

Youth
- Meeting people
- Sport and music
- Travel

Young couples
- Money needed for housing and young children
- Leisure is family based

Middle-age
- More disposable income
- Holidays and home-based leisure

Retirement
- Physical abilities decline
- Leisure more sedentary

G *Linking age and leisure*

Going further

2 Try to develop a timeline from Victorian times to now, linking leisure and work in terms of hours per week worked, amount of holiday time per year and popular leisure pursuits of the time.

Study tip

Remember that someone's work is often someone else's leisure, for example football, gardening, home decorating, modifying cars.

What influences job satisfaction?

Satisfaction at work is about enjoyment and fulfilment. It is not easy to measure this because each individual has different expectations of what they want from work:

- Working conditions and safety
- Ability to use own initiative and creativity
- Opportunities for promotion
- Level of wages
- Attitude of employer
- Technological support
- Holiday entitlement
- Perks and benefits
- Serving the public and helping others
- Danger, excitement and challenge
- Benefits

Activity

8 a Using the list of factors above can you identify particular satisfaction factors that might fit these occupations?

artist	soldier	bricklayer
doctor	solicitor	policeman
teacher	journalist	care worker
refuse collector	bar-worker	office cleaner
nurse		

   b Now rank the jobs in order from high to low job satisfaction.

A survey of 1000 workers in 2006 in the UK by the Work Foundation found the following:

- 75% of workers found their work satisfying.
- 9% found their work meaningless.
- 78% said their work was stimulating and challenging.
- 51% of the 1000 workers said 'work was a means to and end.'
- Women were more likely to be satisfied than men.
- The over 55s were more satisfied than younger workers 16–34.
- Managers and professional workers were more satisfied than other workers.
- People earning over £50,000 a year were most satisfied.

www.hrmguide.co.uk/general/job-satisfaction.htm

H *Different jobs have different satisfaction factors*

Work perks and benefits

- Company car
- Expense account
- Free health insurance
- Pension
- Discount purchases
- Free uniform
- Free parking

Activity

9 What does this information tell you about the level of work satisfaction in the UK at the start of the 21st century?

> ❝ *Okay the job is lousy but it's steady work and the pay is good, if you do your job there is no hassle. I know that there's money every month to pay the mortgage and we can afford to go abroad every other year.* ❞

 I   *Coming to terms with a dull job*

> ❝ *I'm a railway man through and through, I started work at 15 and I've never imagined doing anything else. Of course, the job has changed and it's not what it was. When I started there were still a few steam engines left and there were many more of us at the shed. We were all mates and no-one would let anyone else down. There's something about being around engines even the 'electrics'. I suppose for me they need love and attention.* ❞

 J   *The end of an era – a railway worker speaks*

Activity

10   Decide whether the experience of each worker in Sources I to L is **intrinsic** or **extrinsic satisfaction**. Explain your reasons.

> ❝ *I enjoyed my short time on the Apprentice programme and it was a shame I was fired. I know I'll make it. My target is £100,000 a year by the time I'm 30. I'll do whatever it takes as long as it's legal. I must spend 10 hours a day in the office, working lunch and then communication catch-up on the phone for an hour every night. I'm also taking another accountancy qualification. My salary is £40,000.* ❞

 K   *I know what I want from work*

> ❝ *I've always wanted to be a social worker. I've had my troubles when I was young and I believe this helps me make a difference. It's not an easy job but it is really rewarding when you help someone make good.* ❞

 L   *Helping others counts*

Study tip

Do not confuse intrinsic (in work) with extrinsic (outside of work).

Activity

11   Ask your parents or grandparents what their experience of work has been. Have they gained satisfaction from it? If they have had several jobs, ask whether they experienced differences in job satisfaction. What might have been done that would have improved the level of job satisfaction?

Going further

3   a   If you have the opportunity to undertake work experience, ask those you work with about job satisfaction.

   b   Using the internet, find out, about the work of Abraham Maslow who said that we have a hierarchy of needs which influence our level of work satisfaction. This following site is one of the easiest: www.learnmanagement2.com/maslow.htm

   c   Find the happiest workers at: http://news.bbc.co.uk/1/hi/business/4296975.stm

Is unemployment inevitable for some people?

Unemployment statistics

If being employed is so important to people, then imagine not being in work when you want to be. In the UK population, in the spring of 2009, 29.3 million people were in paid employment and 2.02 million people were seeking work and currently experiencing **unemployment**.

There are a number of people 'unemployed' because they are between jobs, a number of people unable to work because of sickness or disability and then there are those prevented from taking up work because they are too young or too old. The law, for example, prevents you taking up full-time employment until you are 17 and have completed your full-time education.

The Government collects **official statistics** on those people who unemployed and who are registered as seeking work. The official figures in the graph below have their limitations because a number of people are excluded.

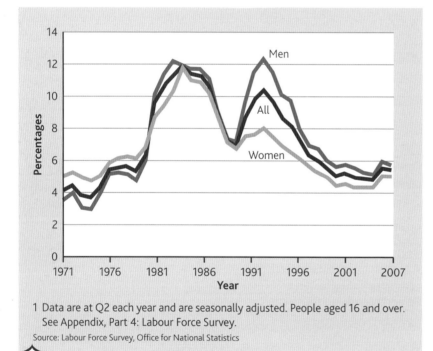

1 Data are at Q2 each year and are seasonally adjusted. People aged 16 and over.
  See Appendix, Part 4: Labour Force Survey.

Source: Labour Force Survey, Office for National Statistics

M *Unemployment rates – United Kingdom*

The causes of unemployment

Types of jobs come and go and always have done, dependent on technology and the increasing development of a culture. In 1800 it is estimated that 80 per cent of people were employed in agriculture. As agriculture became mechanised, there was countryside unemployment. People made their way to the growing towns for work in the newly developing industry, made possible by the harnessing of water and steam power.

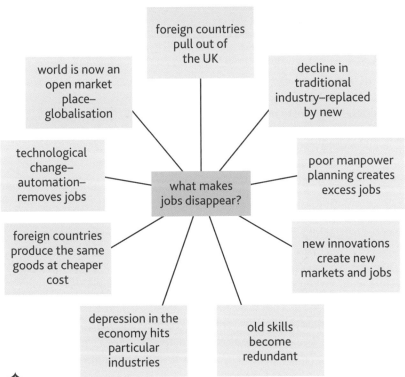

Activity

14 Using Source N to help you, make a list of jobs that you think are in decline today.

a Thousands of UK call centre jobs have been lost due to which cause shown in Source N?

b A shortage of nurses and doctors is the result of which cause shown in Source N?

Going further

4 Up-to-date figures on unemployment can be found at:

■ www.hrmguide.co.uk/jobmarket/unemployment.htm

■ www.poverty.org.uk

People without work

Facing up to unemployment

John worked in one of the few remaining shipyards in the north-east of England. The shipbuilding industry has been in decline for many years because of foreign competition. In other parts of the world the wage costs are lower so ships are cheaper to build. The shipyard where John worked as a gas welder had been hoping for a government contract but it went to an overseas shipyard. With no ships to build, the shipyard owners had no alternative other than to close the yard and its offices, making workers redundant over a six-month period.

> *I don't know how it came to this. I've worked hard all my life. I was good at my job. There were others who lost their jobs before me and who couldn't care less. They were near retirement and the redundancy payout was good for them. The young ones were young enough to retrain. Some even saw it as an opportunity to get out of a rut and change jobs. Others had jobs to go to because they were multi-skilled. Unfortunately gas-welding ships is highly specialised and no one around here needs gas welders, especially if they are 53 years old!*
>
> *Our lass worked in the offices so she'll be out of work in a month when the yard closes completely. She got her job about ten years ago after the kids left home. She'll go mad being at home all day but at least she has a chance of another job. It's getting to me already. It's being at home all day. I've no mates to talk to and all this time and no spare money to enjoy it. We only bought a new car two years ago and there's still two years of payments left. The unemployment benefit won't cover our bills when Sheila finishes. But we are being careful. I've cancelled the satellite channel for the sport. I was hoping to keep my redundancy for my retirement.*
>
> *It's been 12 weeks now and there are absolutely no vacancies for my trade. I've applied for 10 jobs and had two rejection letters and the other eight companies never replied. You begin to feel useless. I can't stand it at times. I've been getting headaches and I've never had them before.*
>
> *I'm not alone I suppose, in being unemployed, but that does not help. I'm no longer the breadwinner. My grown-up children call round, always talking about their jobs and I have nothing to say now. You walk down the street to the supermarket during the day when others are at work and you see the looks. 'He must be unemployed.'*
>
> *The whole area is affected. A couple of local shops have closed already because there just isn't the trade. So more jobs are lost! I can only see things getting worse. If the supermarket goes we'll have no local food shop and that will mean going up to town. We haven't the money to try and move at my age. Anyway there are lots of houses up for sale already so that must say something about the area.*

P Gas welder

Shipyard

Activity

15 Read the case study and then answer the following questions.

a Why is John unemployed?

b Is unemployment always a problem for people?

c Make a list of the effects of unemployment on John.

d How might unemployment impact on the local community?

Going further

5 a Investigate this site which looks at the decline of a number of industries including ship-building:

www.makingthemodernworld.org.uk/learning_modules/history

b There is also an interesting site including interviews of ex-shipyard workers by students from a local school:

www.bbc.co.uk/nationonfilm/education/school-clips/interviewees/

c Film clips of the shipyards:

www.bbc.co.uk/nationonfilm/topics/ship-building/

Did you know ???????

■ In 1914, British shipyards produced more new ships than the rest of the world put together. There were 3,000,000 men working in the shipyards.

■ In 2006, there were 24,000 men working in specialist ship repair and ship conversion. The key ship builders today are South Korea and Japan.

Did you know ???????

The reasons why the shipbuilding decline took place were:

■ failure to modernise and adopt new technology

■ failure to produce the right ships for the market

■ reliance on government subsidies

■ unable to compete with low-wage workforces in other countries.

Check your understanding

1 What is the function of work in simple societies?

2 Give five reasons why people work.

3 Explain the difference between work and leisure.

4 Explain the difference between intrinsic and extrinsic work satisfaction using examples.

5 List four effects of unemployment.

What impact does technological change have?

Does technological change bring benefits?

The stone you see in Source A is an early tool which was used to help people tear through animal skins. Many years later, a spinning wheel was invented to spin yarn to create wool that could then be formed into clothing. Prior to this, the process had been done by hand. After the spinning wheel, other inventions appeared which meant the country was on its way to an industrial revolution.

A *Handaxe*

Craft industry has not died out but is no longer a dominant technology. The worker with craft skills can produce a unique individual item for a customer that processes using machines cannot. There are still factories with workers at machines producing goods but much of this intensive labour is now transferred to developing countries where wages are lower.

Workers in the motor industry for some 50 years worked on **assembly lines**. The pace of the line drove the work and there were few opportunities to avoid the boredom and monotony.

Objectives

You will be able to:

describe the main production technologies over the last 200 years

understand the nature of alienating work

explain some consequences of automated technology and the impact of information technology on working practices.

∞ links

Also see page 176 for a case study about the automobile industry and alienating work.

Pre-1800 Craft production e.g. thatching a roof	■ Complex skills requiring long training ■ Production is slow ■ Products are expensive	■ Hand-made ■ Working for a customer ■ Provides a high level of job satisfaction
1800s Machine production (mechanisation) e.g. textile industry	■ 'Machine minding' – may be boring ■ Requires little skills in comparison with craft production ■ Provides less job satisfaction	■ Production quick & efficient ■ Products cheap ■ Products to defined standard ■ Working for a market
From 1910 Assembly line production e.g. car industry	■ Production assembly in lines ■ Worker has no control of the pace of production ■ Often isolated from other workers	■ Production very quick ■ Production maximised ■ Production as cheap as possible
From 1950s Automated production e.g. chemical industry	■ Automated machines produce products with minimum supervision ■ Continuous process managed by workers in control rooms	■ Removal of human error ■ Quality controlled ■ Cheap price – less labour costs

B *Key technologies*

When the experience of work becomes extremely bad, the term **alienation** is used. This means being 'separated from something'.

- On the assembly line, the work has no meaning anymore, only the wages count. The work is repetitive and it is difficult to take pride in the finished product because you are separated from it. 'There goes a Model T Ford and I put a bolt in the rear bumper!'
- Work is in isolation. The line ties the worker to a position and so physically and socially the worker is separated from other workers on the line and elsewhere in the factory
- Work is managed by other people and the worker is powerless to control the pace of the line.
- Work separates the worker from their true self. This is referred to as 'self-estrangement'. The worker is no longer a human but more like a part of a machine.
- There are still some industries that operate assembly line production.

A new technology began to take over in the 1950s. **Automation** involves a self-regulating process. The simple example in your own home is the immersion heater. You switch the heater on and thereafter it will heat the water, switch itself off and turn itself on if the temperature of the water falls too low. The process self-regulates until you intervene and switch it off. This is a simple device compared to the complexity provided by micro-chip technology. This allows very complex self-regulation of machines and robots. Some industries such as the chemical industry rely on separation of people from the product and use automated **continuous process technology**.

C *Chemical plant: continuous-process technology*

Going further

1 You can visit a continuous process plant by taking a virtual tour of a Coca Cola plant at this site:

www.coca-colabottling.co.id/eng/ourbusiness/index.php?act=virtualplant

Key terms

Assembly line: a series of machines in a factory where each worker assembles one small part of the finished product.

Alienation: a state of separation of the worker from themselves and other workers.

Automation: a process which is self-regulated with the help of electronic technology.

Continuous process technology: a process (often in the chiemical industry) which is started electronically by a person and then continues until it is shut down electronically.

Activity

1 Can you think of other automated devices you have in the home? Can you think of anything else that might become automated in the future?

Activity

2 Ask some people what is the most boring job they have ever done. How did it make them feel?

Study tip

- Remember the key technologies: craft production, machine production, assembly-line production and automated production.
- Link the idea of alienation with the case study of the motor industry that follows.

Technological change

Technological change in the automobile industry

The manufacture of cars is an example of the pattern of technological change outlined on pages 174 and 175. The 20th century saw car production move from craft production to automated production.

The first cars were built by former carriage makers in small workshops. Car builders gained great satisfaction by making each car individually to order. This kind of small-scale craft production, relying on parts crafted by many others, did not survive long. It made cars very expensive.

In the early 1900s, a new approach in the USA to car manufacture was developed by Henry Ford. He introduced assembly-line production and his aim was to build large quantities of identical cars that were simple enough for consumers to operate. By 1916, he was employing 40,000 workers, producing a million cars each year.

In this new approach, the assembly of a car took place on a moving track or line. The car's chassis moved down the line and parts were brought to the chassis and fitted by relatively unskilled individuals. One person did one task. Payment to workers was based on how many repetitions of the task were undertaken.

D *Assembly line success story*

One Ford worker recounting his time at Ford in the 1920s said, 'We're numbers. Ford class you more as a machine than as a man.'

Assembly-line production quickly took hold in Britain as well, in the factories of William Morris. The men worked just for the money. The pace of the line drove the work and there were few opportunities to offset the boredom and social isolation of the repetitive work. The worker could not abandon their place on the line.

In the 1930s in the car industry, there were no trade unions to intervene to help workers improve their conditions and laws did not protect the worker's employment. Work was seasonal around the annual motor show. Many workers were 'laid off' and received no pay. Any worker that had been a troublesome or a poor worker might find that he was not taken back on.

This kind of production method and technology was undoubtedly a successful one for the manufacturer in terms of output. The consumer too was pleased with it because it meant that cars became cheaper.

The continuing nature of technological change, however, brought about a solution as some of the tasks began to be taken over by robots. No longer might a worker have

to attach eight nuts to the same part every minute of the day, a robot would do it. The downside to this in the car industry was a drastic reduction in the workforce. Automation had arrived.

The use of robots, programmed to copy the physical movements of humans, is referred to as computer-aided manufacture. Robots are now used to weld car bodies and paint the cars. This has health and safety benefits and also removes repetitive jobs. This is good for the consumer but not for the gas welder and the skilled paint-sprayer whose jobs have disappeared. However, new jobs have emerged such as quality control inspectors. The quality of each car leaving the factory is now guaranteed to be the same.

Computer technology is also used extensively in car design. Software packages allow the designer to manipulate a 3D image of the car and its component parts. They are able to determine, for example, whether a brake pipe will rub against the chassis. This saves time and costs.

Car plants are now clean, quiet and more pleasant places to work. The improved working experience means workers can go to their leisure time with good wages, able to enjoy it. The same number of cars can be produced in less time at a lower cost.

Activity

3 After the introduction of assembly-line production, attempts were made by employers to try and ease the boredom. The Volvo car plant in Sweden in the early 1950s, introduced team-working on the line, with groups of workers sharing the responsibility for a group of tasks. Some workers were also made 'worker directors' and were involved in management decision-making. Profit-sharing was also introduced so that if the company was successful the workers would receive a bonus.

List the measures introduced by Volvo. Why might they prove successful?

Activity

4 Make a list of the positive and negative outcomes for the car industry, the consumer and the car workers brought about by the technological changes in the later half of the 20th century.

Going further

2 To find out more about the car industry, visit a site about the troubles at British Leyland as the British car industry went into terminal decline. Chapter 5 on the website is good reading for information on industrial disputes. You have to be interested in motor vehicles!
www.aronline.co.uk/index.htm?wsindexf.htm

The impact of information technology on working practices

The introduction of computers and microprocessor-controlled machinery has resulted in changing patterns of employment and work practices.

Activity

5 Investigate how **information technology** has impacted on your school

a Look at the use of information technology in your school. If you investigate the impact it has made with others in your class this could be your IT case study.

b Find out in what ways information technology is used. Add to the list below if your school uses it in any other ways.

video conferencing	email pupil to teacher	teachers with laptops
information screens	electronic whiteboards	electronic registration
electronic whiteboards	school website	software packages for learning
digital measurement– gym equipment	intra-school links	computer-aided design packages
electronic office	virtual learning environment (VLE)	
email teacher to teacher	dedicated computer rooms	

c Now make a detailed list of the benefits you think information technology has brought. (You need to remember that few schools had computers until the early 1980s.) Are there any disadvantages? Ask your teachers and students their views.

d Imagine there are no computers at school. How would this change your education?

E School computers

Activity

6 What are the benefits of the new information technology enabled by **silicon-chip** technology? Can you add to the list below, thinking of additional ways that it has changed the world and particularly work? Try to find an example for the suggestions below and also add your own suggestions.

- Society needs less skills as electronic devices can do things for us, for example calculator.
- It makes work more interesting and reduces the amount of boring work.
- It allows people to work from home and provides a home library.
- It increases the number of hours that people engage in work and has created IT jobs.
- It has influenced the role of women in the workplace.
- It has created more time for leisure and is itself a leisure pursuit for some people both young and old.
- It has led to cleaner working environments, saves work space and improves communication between people.
- The globalisation of industry has been made easier.

F Silicon chips

Key terms

Information technology: a term that encompasses all forms of technology used to create, store, exchange and use information in its various forms (data, voice conversations, still images, motion pictures, multimedia and other forms including those not yet conceived).

Silicon chip: an electronic device made from a piece of silicon that holds millions of microscopically small electronic components.

Information

Results of a recent survey into the use of computers across the European Union shows the use of computers has increased substantially year-on-year, especially in office work. The use of a computer results in less physical work. However, those who work with a computer permanently show more signs of back and repetitive strain injury.

G *The use of computers among workers in the European Union and its impact on the quality of work*

Information

Household income, education, employment status, age, gender, family size, and attitudes toward technology are all important in determining computer use among working-age adults. Many employers now expect prospective new employees to have basic computer skills.

Compared to even five years ago, many more people have a laptop and can connect with their office by email from home. This has been particularly useful for women. Some people, however, find that their employers expect them to do more work in their own time from home. Some people, for example, use laptops on trains on the way to work and access work email during their official holidays. Computers have helped people with difficulties and impairments access employment.

By 2008 65 per cent of households in the UK have an internet connection with many people making use of online shopping, instead of shops. More and more flights and holidays are booked online, as are event bookings. Books, DVDs and all manner of consumer goods are now purchased this way. However some 21 per cent of people fear internet fraud more than they do burglary.

Many employees in large firms have reported they had received little training in information technology at work and mainly used their computers for email and word processing. They also admitted to using their computers to contact friends by email and to order goods in work time.

Some people aged under 30, working for IT companies, reported earning over £50,000 a year.

H

Check your understanding

1 Explain the meaning of the term 'alienation'.

2 Draw a diagram to illustrate how technology has changed the nature of production over the last 200 years.

3 State the meaning and list four benefits of automation.

4 List five changes to work brought about by the introduction of information technology.

Activity

7 After reading Sources G and H, explain and evaluate how information technology has affected people's attitudes to work.

Did you know ??????

Microsoft is a multinational company that develops software for computers. Bill Gates founded the company in 1975 when he was only 20 years old. By 1985 Microsoft had linked with IBM, a computer manufacturer, to create 'Windows' which now runs on 95 per cent of the worlds computers. Gates is one of the world's richest men worth US$58 billion.

Study tip

If you visit a hospital or watch a hospital programme on TV think of all the technology that is being used. Look out for BBC series called 'Casualty 1907' for comparison. This could give you some interesting examples.

Going further

3 Bill Gates' Microsoft Corporation has financed several pieces of research about the impact of computers on society. You can find details on the Microsoft website. Some articles are quite detailed.

What changes have there been in patterns of employment?

Employment sectors

Primary sector

The primary sector of the economy of a country makes use of the raw materials of the land and sea. This includes mining, farming the land and rearing animals on it and catching fish in the sea.

Secondary sector

The secondary sector turns raw materials into products that we need. From iron we can make steel and then cars. From raw cotton and wool we can make clothes. From trees we can cut and process wood for use in the construction of houses. We also commonly call the secondary sector the manufacturing sector.

Tertiary sector

The tertiary sector covers all the services we receive. This includes education and health sectors, retail and banking sectors and travel and tourism sectors. It also includes the information technology services although some people believe this is such a growing sector that it should be called the 'quaternary' sector.

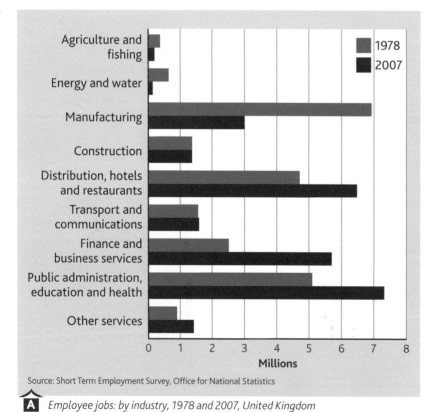

Source: Short Term Employment Survey, Office for National Statistics

A *Employee jobs: by industry, 1978 and 2007, United Kingdom*

Social Trends 2008 National Statistics website: www.statistics.gov.uk
Crown copyright material is reproduced with the permission of the
Controller Office of Public Sector Information (OPSI)

Objectives

You will be able to:

describe the primary, secondary and tertiary sector of an economy

explain globalisation and the role of multinational companies

evaluate some of the benefits and costs of economic migration

explain some of the changes in employment patterns.

Activities

1 Using Source A, identify the key changes between 1978 and 2007. Copy and complete the following sentences.

a The fall in manufacturing jobs is from _____ to_____

b The fall in agricultural jobs is from _____to _____

c The increase in finance and business jobs is from _____ to_____

d The increase in public administration, education and health jobs is from _____ to_____

e The increase in distribution, hotel and restaurant jobs is from _____ to_____

2 What explanations can you put forward for the changes you have identified?

Globalisation

Globalisation is not new. In earlier centuries there were empires built around trade with colonies. What makes globalisation so special now is the speed at which it has developed over the last 50 years. This is because transport and communication improvements have made trade much easier. There are thousands of containers of merchandise going to and from the UK at any one time.

Governments used to restrict trade in order to protect their own markets by preventing imports. Gradually the advantages of free trade are being seen to outweigh the disadvantages.

The information technology revolution has greatly improved communication around the globe and spread the market place for goods. Companies employ people abroad as part of their workforce. For example, some UK companies use call centres based in India to serve customers in the UK because it is cheaper to employ Indian workers than British ones.

Multinational companies (MNCs)

Some companies now have factories, shops or provide services across the world. These companies are called 'multinational' because they operate in several countries.

These are the characteristics of multinational companies:

- They originate in the economically developed world for example US.
- They have money to invest.
- They see advantages in using raw materials and cheap labour in other countries.
- They are large and can benefit from economies of scale.
- They often do not have to meet such stringent health and safety legislation or regulations on working conditions in foreign countries.
- They actively seek new markets for their products.

These are the benefits of multinational companies to the host country in which they operate:

- They bring employment where there is often none and develop skills in the people.
- Working conditions are often better than the average for the host country.
- They bring foreign currency to local communities and help provide resources for things like education and health.
- They bring new cultural ideas to help development.

> 66 *The reason I don't like multinational companies is that they come and go. If they can find another country where they can pay lower wages, they'll move on and leave lots of people without jobs. They also drive small businesses in our country out of business. The profits go back to the foreign country they come from.* 99

C

Key terms

Globalisation: where activities in one part of the world have consequences for people in other parts of the world.

Group activity

1. Can you think of five reasons why free trade is a good idea? Can you think of any disadvantages?

   Share your ideas with the other groups.

B *Shell and General Motors are examples of multinational companies*

∞links

See Chapter 5 for additional material on globalisation and multinational companies.

Study tip

You can use abbreviations in the exam such as MNCs and LEDCs.

Activity

3. Join with a partner. Present a counter-argument to the African man speaking in Source C.

Going further

1. The Coca-Cola web site is interesting if you want to find out more about how a multinational company operates.

Is economic migration a cause for concern?

People have always moved to find work. Sometimes this is within a country and sometimes it involves a move across national boundaries.

- Whcn machines came to agriculture in the 1800s unemployed workers were forced to seek work in towns.
- When there was a potato famine in Ireland in the 1830s and 1840s many Irish people migrated to England.
- When there were iron and steel closures in north-east England in the 1970s many workers transferred to Corby in the midlands.

Why do immigrants come to the UK?

There are two reasons why people migrate to a particular country.

- **Push factors**: These drive people to leave their country. For example persecution (**asylum seekers**), unemployment and a poor standard of living.
- **Pull factors**: These attract people to a country. For example better wages, security, new opportunities and a shortage of their skills.

Since 1994, there has been a net inflow of **immigrants** into the UK. This means more people came into the country (as immigrants) than left (as **emigrants**). The graph in Source **D** shows the pattern over recent years. It is equivalent to adding more than 500 people a day to the UK population.

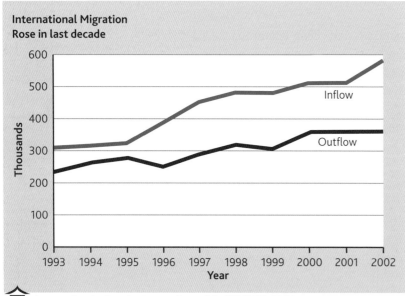

D International migration into and out of the UK 1995–2004

Office of National Statistics 2005

With the formation of the European Union, it is now possible for people to move from country to country for employment, becoming **economic migrants**. In the UK, these new arrivals have settled across the country but certain areas have received more economic migrants than others. The areas with the highest numbers have been London and the south-east. Both these areas have low unemployment and a strong economy (economic pull).

Activity

4 Try to find out about some other examples of **economic migration** to or within the UK.

∞links

Also see Topic 1.3 for more information on the history of British immigration.

Key terms

Asylum seeker: a person classed as a refugee fleeing persecution. He or she is not an economic migrant.

Immigration: the movement of people into an area across a national boundary.

Emigration: the movement of people out of an area across a national boundary.

Economic migrant: a person who moves to live in another place for work.

Cause for concern?

If more people of working age arrive in a country than leave, this contributes to population growth. A steadily rising population is usually considered to be good for a country's economy. This is because it means there are more people wanting to purchase goods and services. It particularly helps when a country has an increasingly ageing population as does the UK. Older people spend less and contribute less in taxes. Immigrants can bring new skills and help alleviate skills shortages. Recent examples are construction workers and doctors from Poland and nurses from the Philippines.

E   *In 1952, many West Indians came to the UK to work on London's buses and the underground*

Many immigrants are prepared to work in low paid jobs where there are vacancies because the unemployed have not wanted this work. Low wages here are still better than the wages they received in their country of origin. The UK does experience extra social costs in terms of the provision of health, education and housing.

F   *Many people have emigrated from the UK to work in Australia*

Going further

2 The BBC news site archive (news.bbc.co.uk) has a number of interesting stories. Use the search function on the BBC site to find the relevant article from the list below.

- Harming communities
- Migration is good for everybody
- Secret life of the office cleaner

Key Chronology

Some people claim that migrant workers take UK national people's jobs. The evidence suggests otherwise. The jobs they take, British people are not prepared to do.

A survey of companies in 2004 found the UK migrant worker policy was good for business.

Britain has many foreign cleaners who clean while we sleep. London alone now has an estimated 250,000 immigrant cleaners.

Many stress that they could not survive without their foreign workers.

G

Key Chronology

In a BBC documentary in 2005, some cleaners in London claimed the cleaning industry is 'run on fear' and that there are problems regarding the minimum wage and hours worked.

H

Key Chronology

In February 2004 at Morecambe Bay, 19 Chinese cockle pickers lost their lives. The cockle industry relies on casual workers, many of whom are migrant workers and some are illegal immigrants.

I

Did you know ??????

The World Bank says Britain has lost more skilled workers than any other country. Of 400,000 people leaving the country in 2006, 207,000 were skilled workers. It is equivalent to 1 in 6 graduates. In contrast France lost 3 in 100.

Did you know ??????

- In 2008 the UK introduced a new points scheme for immigrants. Migrants from the EU and people with skills received more points.
- A census is held every 10 years in the UK. At the 2001 census, there were 57,103,331 people in the UK. Some 4,301,280 were born abroad.

Activity

5 What do Sources G, H and I tell you about the work done by many migrant workers?

Is there a working revolution?

Key changes in the patterns of work

Some of the major changes in work have been identified such as the decline in manufacturing and unskilled work, an increase in non-manual work in the service sector and a continuing increase in the proportion of the labour force who are women.

A number of trends associated with these changes are emerging:

- **Flexible working**: From 2008, all parents with children under 16 have the right to make a request to work flexible hours. The employer has to give fair consideration to the request.

- **Job sharing**: Job sharing is a way for two people to both fill one job. Each person fills one part-time post. They split the holidays, pay and any benefits that go with the job. This potentially gives employers a wider range of skills and experience and there is less stress for the employees, particularly if they are parents or carers.

- **Tele-working and working from home**: Tele-working is when someone works from home or from a tele-centre closer to their home, making use of information technology. The home-worker can often work flexible hours as well to suit their circumstances.

- **Retraining increasing**: The idea of a 'job for life' is becoming more and more unlikely. Workers are encouraged to develop themselves and to continue to update their skills.

- **Deskilling**: Deskilling is when particular skills are no longer required, often as a consequence of new technology. A spellchecker on a computer means a secretary does not now need to be good at spelling. Deskilling is taking place in some service sector industries. McDonald's is an example; all the outlets have the same design. They all offer the same service and the same food. They all have workers doing the same tasks who treat customers in the same way because that is how they have been trained. This makes for workforce efficiency and easy staff transfer. Work is routine and has been simplified. Several supermarkets in the UK have also followed this approach. Checkout operators are given a script to follow with each customer. It is a standard service response and all individuality is removed.

- **Women have returned to the workforce**: Before the Industrial Revolution, women worked alongside men in all forms of agricultural work and even at the start of the Industrial Revolution they worked underground in the mining industry. As the Industrial Revolution progressed, women were more and more confined to the home. Over the last 50 years, the movement of women into paid employment has gathered pace.

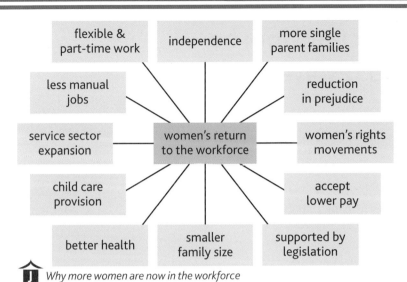

flexible & part-time work

independence

more single parent families

less manual jobs

reduction in prejudice

service sector expansion

women's return to the workforce

women's rights movements

child care provision

accept lower pay

better health

smaller family size

supported by legislation

J *Why more women are now in the workforce*

For women to return to the workforce there are three key factors. They need the **motivation** (the desire), the **capacity** (free of child care, constant pregnancy, good health) and then access to work **opportunities** that they can take up.

Activity

6 Put the branches in the spider diagram in Source J under the appropriate heading of motivation, capacity and opportunity.

Activity

7 What do you think the figures in Source K are saying?

Going further

3 **a** You can find out about job sharing and flexible working at www.equalityhumanrights.com/en/Pages/default.asx

b Also search for part-time friendly on news.bbc.co.uk

Check your understanding

1 Name two employment sectors.

2 Explain three benefits of globalisation.

3 List four reasons for the increase in the proportion of women in the workforce.

4 Name three 'pull factors' which have attracted economic migrants to the UK.

K

7.4 How can conflict at work be prevented and resolved?

Equality and equality legislation

The idea of equal opportunities at work is:

- a relatively new idea
- meant to create a fairer society
- not about treating all people the same, but ensuring that everyone has a chance to contribute
- based on the concept of fairness
- based on legislation that has been introduced to eliminate unfairness.

There has been a considerable amount of equality legislation, some of which is outlined in this section.

Objectives

You will be able to:

describe the purpose of key equalities legislation

describe male/female inequalities in work

describe the purposes of trade unions

explain the methods of preventing or resolving conflict at work.

Key legislation

1970 Equal Pay Act	2000 Race Relations (Amendment) Act
1974 Health and Safety at Work Act	2001 Special Needs and Disability Act
1975 Sex Discrimination Act	2003 Employment Equality (Religion or Belief) Regulations
1996 Employment Rights Act	
1997 Protection from Harassment Act	2003 Employment Equality (Sexual Orientation) Regulations
1998 Human Rights Act	
1998 Working Time Regulations Act	2006 The Disability Equality Duty for the Public Sector
1999 Sex Discrimination (Gender Reassignment) Regulations	2006 Employment Equality (Age) Regulations
	2007 Gender Equality Duty for the Public Sector
2000 Part-time Workers Regulations	2008 Equality Act

Why is there so much legislation?

The answer is that the early laws listed above were not successful enough. Legislation does not necessarily make anything happen. It does mean that a person who feels they have been discriminated against, harassed or unfairly treated has the right to go to law for redress (for example compensation, their job back or in some instances both).

More recent legislation has been aimed at creating a situation where organisations have a duty to put in place a strategy to prevent unlawful behaviour before it happens. This is what the equality duties established since 2000 are all about. The new duties attempt to create a situation where discrimination, harassment or unfairness does not take place, from the initial job advert through the subsequent employment stages. These include: the application form, the interview, job contract, pay and conditions, treatment at work in line with other legislation to leaving the employment and being given a fair reference.

Key terms

Discrimination: unfair treatment of a person or group on the basis of prejudice about things such as age, gender, sexuality, disability, race, religion or class.

Going further

1 To find out more, go to the website for the Equality and Human Rights Commission: www.equalityhumanrights.com/en/Pages/default.aspx

> *A mature experienced woman is required for general office duties.*

> *Required – youthful energetic man, recently graduated to join sales team.*

 Job adverts – Monthly Times

Activity

1 Working with a partner, decide why the job adverts in Source **A** are likely to fail recent equality legislation and some other legislation. Try rewording them so that they conform.

In 2006, the Equal Opportunities Commission (now the Human Rights and Equality Commission) produced a gender equality index to gauge how long it would take for women to be equally represented at work in terms of their occupation, job role and pay. This period of time was based on current trends.

Information

- Percentage of women with directorships compared to men
  Current: 10 per cent
  Equality: 65 years

- Percentage of women high court judges/senior judges compared to men
  Current: 9 per cent
  Equality: 60 years

- Percentage of women MPs compared to men
  Current: 20 per cent
  Equality: 195 years

- To achieve the same full time rate of pay as men
  current: 17 per cent below men
  Equality: 20 years

- Part-time women workers to achieve the same hourly rate as full-time men
  Equality: 25 years

- Retired women to achieve the same income as retired men
  Equality: 45 years

- For men and women to be equally represented in occupational groups
  Equality: Never, unless action is stepped up
  (currently 65 per cent of occupations are dominated by either men or women)

  Equal Opportunities Commission 2006

 Gender equality index

Activity

2 What does the cartoon in Source **C** tell you about some of the work that women do?

Study tip

Here are some key words you could use if you wanted to promote equal opportunities:
Say 'NO' to:

- harassment
- discrimination
- unequal treatment
- unequal pay.

Group activity

1 Hold a debate on the statement: 'Women do not have the equality at work that they deserve.'

Research the inequalities in Source **B** and other work inequalities and prepare an argument that supports or disagrees with the statement.

The Class Ceiling
30 July 04   Nicholson

Did you know ??????

- Recent disability legislation requires employers to make reasonable adjustments for disabled employees. This might mean special toilet facilities, special chairs or extra equipment if the employee believes it will help them.

- If an employee makes remarks towards another employee about their sexual orientation in the workplace then the employer must take action. If the employer does not, they are at risk of being seen to sanction harassment.

Are trade unions in decline?

A **trade union** is an organisation of workers created to protect and advance the interests of its members by:

- negotiating agreements on pay and work conditions
- providing legal advice to members
- providing financial advice and assistance
- providing training opportunities and education.

As well as trade unions, there are professional organisations that represent particular groups of workers such as doctors, lawyers, architects and teachers. The common factors that link such occupations are the extended periods of education needed to gain the appropriate qualification, the occupational code of conduct (with the idea of 'service'), backed by a professional disciplinary body.

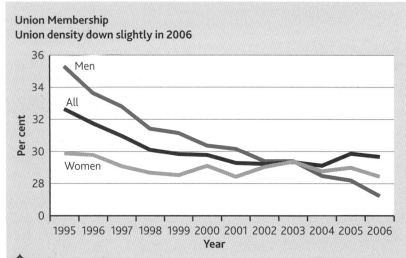

D Trade union membership

1 See Appendix, Part 4: Labour disputes.

Source: Office for National Statistics

E Labour disputes: working days lost

Key terms

Trade union: an organisation of workers created to protect and advance the interests of its members.

Activity

3 **a** Using Sources **D** and **E**, describe the pattern of decline in union membership and the number of working days lost in the last two decades.

b What do Sources **D, E** and **F** tell you about union membership today?

Did you know ???????

In 1984 there were 190,000 workers in the coal-mining industry in 170 pits. In 2007 there were 6000 workers in the coal mining industry in 12 pits.

Study tip

You need to be able to write about the work of one trade union in detail to explain what it does for its members. A useful site is: www.unionhistory.info and select the timeline tab.

Did you know ???????

- Some companies have worker representatives on the Board of Directors.
- Henry Ford fought to keep trade unions out of his car plants until 1941.
- Unison is the largest trade union with 1.3 million members. It acts on behalf of workers in the public services.

Sources **D** and **E** show the decline in union membership and the reduction in days lost due to industrial disputes.

 I used to be a union man. The union did a lot for us years ago. We wouldn't have the pay and conditions we have now but for the unions. But times have changed. Half the workforce here is part-time and they are not all in the union. The membership is much lower than it once was here, now that we are at different factories around the country. We do not have the muscle. In some ways it doesn't matter as much because the new laws over the years have given us protection.

F *One description of the state of trade unions*

G *Police and miners clash during the 1984 miners strike*

Case study

The miners' strike of 1984

Background

In 1972 and 1974 there were miners' strikes for better pay, involving all the miners in the UK. The strikes were successful and miners received large pay rises. In 1981, the Conservative Government wanted to close many pits as uneconomic but a wave of unofficial strikes by the miners led to the closure programme being dropped.

The cause

In March 1984, the Government announced the closure of five coal mines without any review and consultation with the National Union of Mineworkers (NUM). Official strikes were started in Yorkshire and Scotland. The union argued these were just the first of many closures. The union wanted an agreement there would be no more closures.

Miners went from the Yorkshire and Scottish pits to other areas to picket (try to persuade workers not to go into work) and spread the strike. This worked in some areas but not all. In Nottinghamshire, miners kept working because they thought their jobs were safe.

The struggle and outcome

The Government with Margaret Thatcher as Prime Minister were the employers. They now decided to stand firm and make closures. They had stockpiled coal in the event of such a dispute. The NUM were led by Arthur Scargill who was a determined union leader who was not interested in compromise. The police were used to help workers who wanted to go to work through the picket line. The struggle between the police and the miners was a main news story for months. During the strike more than 11,000 people were arrested and many were charged with a breach of the peace. The struggle ended in March 1985 when a conference of union representatives voted to return to work. After 12 months trying to manage on union strike pay, the men started returning because they could not afford to feed their families. The union was defeated. There was no agreement and the closure plan went ahead. By 1992 the pits that remained were in private ownership.

Activity

4 In pairs, look at Source **G** carefully. Who is fighting who? Why do you think this photograph was taken? How do you know it was not staged? Give the photograph a headline to go with it. Compare your headlines as a pair.

Group activity

2 Decide what factors led to such a long dispute and the National Union of Mineworkers defeat. Share your ideas with the rest of the class.

Going further

2 The BBC reviewed the miners' strike on 4th March 2004 on the twentieth anniversary of the dispute. Go to news.bbc.co.uk and search for: Miners Strike 1984

There is also a slideshow on the website.

Going further

3 Search the internet for the 'Tolpuddle Martyrs'

What causes industrial conflict and how can it be avoided?

The potential for conflict

Employers want quality work, high productivity and profits.	Employees want the best wage, work conditions and benefits possible and fulfilling work.	Consumers want a quality product or service and good value for money.

The differences between the priorities of these three groups are a potential for conflict in the workplace. For example to obtain high profits it is in the interest of the employer to keep wages low. If wages are low then workers' morale may be low. This is likely to lead to poor output and quality or even **industrial sabotage**. What the consumer wants is good quality and service at a value for money price. If the employer raises wages then the cost for the consumer may increase. The employer needs to obtain higher productivity to obtain the same profits. He may need to reduce the workforce. It is a very complex set of relationships.

Ways of preventing industrial conflict

Source H shows possible worker responses to industrial conflict. However, it is far better to avoid conflict if possible. Employees need to be able to talk to employers about their grievances and employers need to know how the workers are feeling. This can be done via trade union representatives where there is a union but another way is by having worker committees. Many schools have student councils which act in a similar way. When the two parties talk to each other a compromise can be reached through **negotiation**. A third party may arrange these talks as a form of **conciliation**, or it could judge both sides arguments and make a ruling, as an **arbitrator** of the dispute.

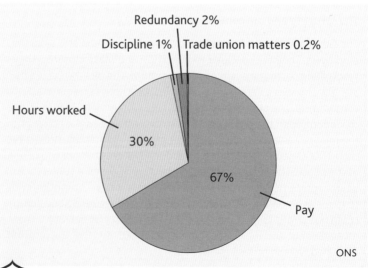

Working days lost by type of dispute: UK 2007

Employers need to keep their workforce up-to-date with new skills. For their self development and in order to take advantage of promotion opportunities, employees need to be up-skilled. It is of mutual benefit if there are good staff training and development programmes.

Employers can be generous to employees by offering incentive schemes, providing bonuses and improving the work environment. Research indicates that looking after the workforce has several advantages. Not only are there fewer conflicts but productivity can be improved and absenteeism and employee turnover can be reduced.

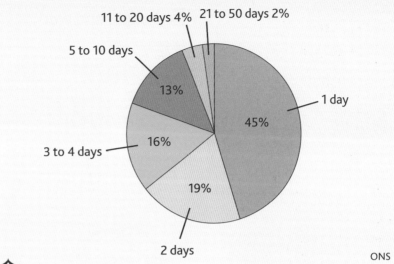

11 to 20 days 4%   21 to 50 days 2%
5 to 10 days
13%
1 day
45%
3 to 4 days
16%
19%
2 days

ONS

J *Duration of stoppages: UK 2007*

Reasons for reduced industrial conflict

- New legislation introduced in the 1980s and 1990s prevents some actions previously undertaken by unions to fight their cause (for example wildcat strikes and secondary picketing).

- Action has been taken to improve work environments to try to prevent industrial unrest.

- Legislation also helps prevent injustices at work. These include unfair pay, discrimination, harassment and unfair dismissal.

K   *Arbitration*

- Many jobs are not as secure. There are many more smaller businesses. Industrial action could mean lost business and in a competitive environment the company might go out of business. This does not help the employer or the worker.

Check your understanding

1   Name three pieces of equality legislation since 2000.

2   What is 'discrimination'?

3   Name four ways membership of trade unions can help people.

4   Name three strategies used to solve industrial conflicts.

Activity

5   Look at Sources I and J.

a   What is the biggest issue causing workplace disputes?

b   Explain how far the pie charts support the view that industrial conflict is not an issue in the UK workforce nowadays.

Going further

4   Acas (The Arbitration and Conciliation Service) is very successful at solving industrial disputes. The website has a useful section on solving disputes. See **www.acas.org.uk**

Going further

5   Use the BBC News website and type 'industrial conflict' into the site's search engine. This will bring up recent new stories about industrial conflict.

Study tip

Remember industrial conflict strategies: N C A
Negotiation, Conciliation, Arbitration.

7

People and work

A *A legal loophole?*

The Sex Discrimination Act and Equal Pay Legislation were introduced in the 1970s when the trend for more women working was already well under way. There were many reasons why women were entering the workforce. These included helping the family budget, supporting home-ownership, buying consumer goods or paying for family holidays.

With higher divorce rates and an increase in one-parent households in the last two decades, work has become a necessity for many women.

Some women have broken through the glass ceiling and reached the boardroom or obtained better paid jobs. However, many are still employed in occupations with lower than average wage rates, such as clerical, cooking, cleaning and caring work. Full-time women workers earn 17 per cent less per hour than men in full-time work. In 2007, the Head of the Equal Opportunities Commission said the pay gap was worsening. 'Employers need to address systematic pay inequalities.'

B *Has legislation brought real equality?*

Practice questions

7 **a)** Using Source **A**, explain the meaning of 'sex discrimination'. *(2 marks)*

   b) Using Source **B**, give two reasons for the continuing concentration of women in certain types of employment. *(4 marks)*

   c) Assess the view that the equality legislation has been a success in creating equal opportunities and equal pay for women. Explain your answer using Sources **A** and **B** and your own studies. *(12 marks)*

   d) Give the meaning of 'assembly-line' technology. Use your own studies to answer. *(2 marks)*

   e) Briefly explain the success of assembly-line technology. *(4 marks)*

   f) Explain some of the changes in employment patterns in the UK over the last 25 years. Use your own studies to answer. You could write about any of the following:
   - Manufacturing sector
   - Flexible working
   - Women in the workforce
   - Equality of workers
   - Experiences of employees
   - Information technology. *(12 marks)*

Study tip There are relatively easy marks for you to pick up in questions **a** and **d** as long as you know your definitions of the key terms.

Remember the 4Cs: cooking, cleaning, clerical, caring. These are the lower paid occupations for a majority of female employees.

Balance your time according to the marks available. In question **e** with four marks available and the instruction 'briefly', you should respond in four sentences.

8.1 Spider diagrams

Creating spider diagrams is a way to take notes, enhance your problem solving and revise. The technique holds information in a format that your mind will find easy to remember.

A personal spider diagram illustrates not only the scope of the subject but also the importance of individual points and the way facts and ideas relate to each other.

The Culture and beliefs module includes a section where you may have to examine a cultural, moral, political or religious issue. You are expected to look at a range of perspectives. Here, a spider diagram can be very useful as tool to organise your thoughts. Source **A** and Source **B** present the views some people hold towards abortion. You can see how Source **A** has been developed into Source **B**.

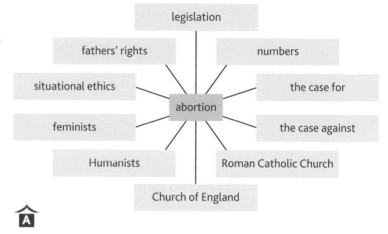

A

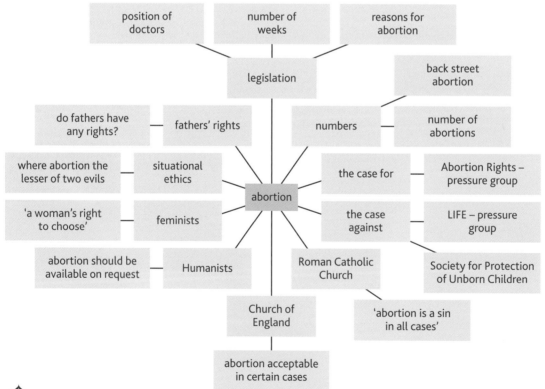

B

Activity

1   **a**   Design a spider diagram around the issue of punishment and the attitudes people have to those who break the law. You will obviously have had to study this issue for these words to immediately trigger a spider diagram. However, it would be possible to use the list of words below to research the topic using these words as your sub-headings.

   b   The following words could be your sub-headings: deterrence, rehabilitation, restitution, retribution, liberal thinkers, right-wing attitudes, Humanists, Amnesty International, NACRO.

   c   Then add in the next branches of the spider diagram as shown in Source B.

Source **C** is an example of a revision spider diagram showing the advantages of wind power on the left-hand side and the disadvantages on the right-hand side.

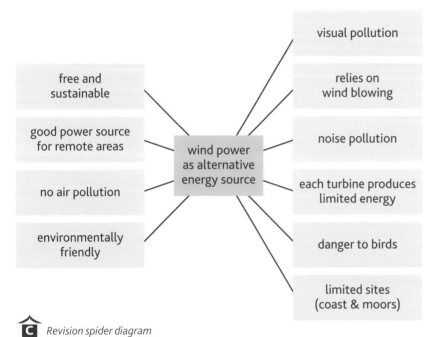

C   *Revision spider diagram*

Activity

2   Create your own revision spider diagram for different types of pollution.

   a   Fill in the centre with the title 'Different kinds of pollution'.

   b   Your first branches should include land, noise, light, air, visual and water.

   c   Then match each of the following statements to the appropriate branch:

- toxic waste land-fill
- excessive street lighting
- wind turbines in countryside
- heavy road traffic
- aircraft taking off and landing
- contaminated sewage.

   d   Add other ideas of your own as well.

What the question instructions mean

In your exam, you will find instructions like these in the questions:

- State...
- Name four...
- Describe the importance of...
- Explain how...
- Explain two reasons why...
- Explain the different views...
- From your own studies, explain...
- Explain and evaluate...

You cannot follow instructions unless you really know *what* it is that you have to do.

- When the instruction is **state** or **name**, the question is asking you to be brief and clearly give a fact or a name (or however many are asked for).

- When you are asked to **describe**, you must provide in words a 'picture' of what something is like or what has happened. You communicate this by using your own knowledge. You may have to **describe how** two things are different. In this case you need to provide a clear picture of a number of differences.

- If you have to describe **the importance** of something, you must concentrate on those aspects which you feel are important.

- A more complicated task is when you are required to **explain**. Explain is usually followed by **how**, **why** or **when**.
  - If you were asked: '**Explain how** cultures differ', this requires you to identify different ways in which people in different cultures organise their lives, their different norms and values, their different gender roles, their different socialisation practices and so on.
  - If you were asked: '**Explain why** cultures differ', you would have to give reasons why people organise their lives in different ways, e.g. different levels of development, different family size, differences in economic activity or environmental factors.

- Some questions ask you to use a case study or include examples **from your own studies**. In the Environmental Issues module, for example, you may have studied a large ecosystem, the Amazonian rainforest, in detail. This would help you answer a question such as: '**From your own studies**, explain how individuals and groups interact with a large-scale ecosystem.'

- The hardest instructions are when the question asks you to **Evaluate** (judge the evidence) or **Assess** (make a judgement). These instructions want you to give an opinion that is backed up by evidence or knowledge, e.g. 'I believe that the development of off-shore wind power is the best option for the UK because...'

- There are also words that you must not confuse or you will provide the wrong answer. In questions in the Conflict and Co-operation module, you must not confuse **cause** and **effect**.
  - Cause comes before effect.
  - A cause of something is why it happened (what went before).
  - An effect of something is what the event led to (what came after).
  - A **consequence** of something is when one thing leads directly or indirectly to another (when a cause leads directly to an effect).

The extended questions

There are some questions that require you to write an extended answer of one page (or more) of the answer book. These questions have a larger number of marks available.

Practice question

1   Explain how environmental pressure groups protect
       the environment and evaluate their effectiveness.
       Use your own studies to answer.

Activity

1 Here is a student response to
an extended question with
examiner's comments on it.
At each stage, write your own
comments on the response
and then give the whole
answer a mark out of 12.

Sample answer

There is a wide range of environmental pressure groups. They have different
aims. There are small and focused ones. For example, ones that wish to
protect the habitat for certain animals like 'Save our Otters' or which appear
suddenly for a cause such as saving local trees. Others are much larger with
many supporters and are national or international pressure groups for the
environment. They cover many issues. Examples are Friends of the Earth and
Greenpeace. Greenpeace tries to protect all aspects of the environment including
climate change, oceans and animals. It also has views on nuclear power.

This student made a quick start telling us
immediately about the different kinds of
pressure group and giving examples from
their own studies.

Pressure groups use a range of methods to get their ideas over to others. These
methods depend on the size of the pressure group and if it gets support from the
public. The more support the more money they are likely to receive in donations.
Greenpeace receives money from famous people and from wills and monthly
subscriptions. This money allows pressure groups like Greenpeace to work all
over the world. This has helped Greenpeace buy and run the ship Rainbow Warrior. They use it to try and stop the killing of whales. The ship now is a symbol
for them and helps advertise their views. Greenpeace has the money to provide
educational materials for schools and to run a website. On their website they
ask people to write to their MPs about many different issues. They have only
been successful in a small way with protecting whales but they have been very
successful in making people think green.

The student has told us about
Greenpeace from their own studies
and some of the ways that it works:
education, website, supporters writing
to MPs, support from famous people,
promotes itself with Rainbow Warrior.
They then go on to make a judgement
about Greenpeace's effectiveness.

In my area there is an environmental pressure group that wants to save some
trees where a builder wants to build apartments. The group have attracted
publicity from the Gazette and held meetings at the community centre. The
issue was also brought up at our School Council. A petition has been signed by
many of us at school. It will go to the local Council showing what our feelings
are. I think we will not be successful because the Council and the builder will
be able to afford legal people to help them succeed. There are also other people who
support the builder because there is a shortage of housing in the area.

The student writes about a real-life,
detailed example from their experience. A
judgement is made recognising obstacles
to a successful outcome.

Environmental pressure groups help to make the world a better place but they
need more money and support from famous people or MPs and help from the
government.

This is rather a brief conclusion, perhaps
the student ran out of time. Nevertheless
it does attempt to make a judgement
about effectiveness.

The examiner expected a high level answer to provide a thorough
explanation of attempts made by one or more environmental pressure
groups to protect the environment. The answer had to be developed
to show how environmental groups operate and might include an
explanation of the aims behind the methods used or an assessment of
their effectiveness. There had to be good use of own studies.

The student's answer relies on Greenpeace and a local pressure group.
By not concentrating on more permanent pressure groups, the student
has missed the opportunity to focus on the effectiveness of a greater
range of pressure group methods and their outcomes.

However, the answer is still impressive and the student has made
judgements about effectiveness.

What mark would you give out of 12?

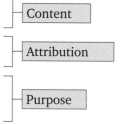

8.3 Interpreting written evidence

There are many kinds of written evidence, for example: documents, letters, official records, books, eyewitness observations and newspaper reports. When you look at a piece of written evidence, there are a number of questions you need to ask about it.

- Is the evidence relevant to what I am studying? What can it tell me?
- What can the evidence probably not tell me?

⎫ Content

- Who produced the document? Is the person likely to be biased?
- When was the evidence produced?

⎫ Attribution

- Do I need background information to tell me more about the evidence?
- Why was the evidence produced?

⎫ Purpose

Only then you can make a judgement as to whether the document can be relied on.

Study tip

An easy way to remember how to interpret written evidence is to use a memory device called a mnemonic. Think **CAP**.

1. Look at the **content** (**C**).
2. Ask who wrote it and under what conditions, i.e. who it is **attributed** to (**A**).
3. Ask what the writer's **purpose** was in writing it (**P**). Was the writer's purpose to inform, persuade, earn money or was it another reason?

Sources **A** and **B** are two pieces of written evidence from the Internet which relate to your study of the environment.

'Man is to blame' say scientists

In February 2007, a United Nations report blamed humans for global warming. The report said that the cause is 'very likely to be the use of fossil fuels'. The report was supported by 2000 of the world's leading scientists. The United Nations panel of scientists recommended urgent action by Governments on CO_2 emissions.

The Greenhouse effect is a myth

Scientists claim that the greenhouse effect is too simple an explanation for global warming and that there are other causes. The cause of global warming they claim is very complex. Professor Clark of the University of Ottawa in Canada, for instance, claims that warmer periods of the earth's history came around 800 years before rises in carbon dioxide levels resulting from the greenhouse effect. After the Second World War, there was a huge surge in carbon dioxide emissions, yet global temperatures fell for four decades after 1940. Other scientists say global warming could be caused by the activity of the sun or massive eruptions. Professor Stott of London University said that climate change was too complicated to be caused by just one factor.

You are studying climate change, so both extracts seem helpful but the headlines appear contradictory. Apply the CAP method and all may become clearer.

Source A

Content

- Greenhouse gases are to blame for global warming.
- This seems to be supported by many scientists.
- Many websites and textbooks take this view too.

Attribution

- United Nations – reputable body.
- Recent publication 2007.
- Supported by 2000 leading scientists but we do not know their names.
- The actual report was produced by a panel of scientists.

Purpose

- To inform governments of the need for urgent action to reduce CO_2 emissions.

Source B

Content

- Suggests the causes of global warming are complex.
- Warming began before increase in CO_2 emissions.
- Solar activity or massive eruptions are a possible contributor.

Attribution

- Some named scientists.
- Some attribution generally to 'scientists', not named or how many.

Purpose

- To indicate their findings to other scientists. In minority, so might come in for criticism.

◼ Conclusion

This analysis does not mean you have to decide if one extract is right and the other is wrong. However, if you used only one piece of evidence, you would have only part of the possible explanation for global warming. Behind the headlines of the extracts, there is not so much disagreement. In Source **A**, there is a strong message to governments with an emphasis on one cause and so a focus on what governments must do. Source **B** is more about adding extra possibilities to the debate and a preference for a more complex set of causes being responsible for global warming.

In the pre-release booklet, you will be provided with some written sources to study in advance of the exam. Use some of your time to look at them and check them as sources of evidence using the CAP mnemonic.

Did you know ???????

Following the release of the UN report there was controversy of a different kind. A number of the 2000 scientists who were actually named in the report as supporters protested because their names had been used without authority and they did not support the report.

Activity

1. Search the Internet for more reports or articles on global warming. Analyse them in the same way as the articles here, using the CAP mnemonic.

Interpreting cartoons

A cartoon is a visual attempt to capture the interest of the reader. It usually exaggerates something. The message in the cartoon has to be teased out like solving a puzzle. To solve the puzzle and correctly interpret the cartoon, you need to know the background that led to the cartoon being drawn in the first place. The cartoon in Source **A** appeared in the Daily Mail newspaper in June 2008. There had been violence in Zimbabwe, an African state, ruled by President Robert Mugabe.

Everything in a cartoon usually has a purpose. Sometimes there is some writing in the cartoon to help you. Look for signs and symbols as they may be significant. If there are characters in the cartoon, ask yourself what they are doing. In Source **A** there are arrows pointing to the key features of the drawing.

Dead bodies and blood – the violence that has occurred

Mugabe the president driving to victory

Mugabe's supporters – they hold sticks with which to beat the opposition

WE TOLD HIM STRAIGHT... ...IT'S UNACCEPTABLE BEHAVIOUR! WE SAID.

WE SAID, 'TUT-TUT' SEVERAL TIMES.

YOU'VE BEEN VERY NAUGHTY! WE SCOLDED

WHO FANCIES A NICE CUP OF TEA?

UN

AFRICAN NATIONS

EU

COMMONWEALTH COUNTRIES

Others looking on

African Nations – they disapprove but do not want to intervene and become involved. Many are not democratic themselves

Commonwealth countries such as Australia and Canada seem unconcerned – not their affair

ZIMBABWE

United Nations observers and the United Nations – the behaviour is unacceptable

Notice caricatures of the people, their skin colour and their dress

European Union – using words telling him they disapprove

A Daily Mail, 24 June 2008

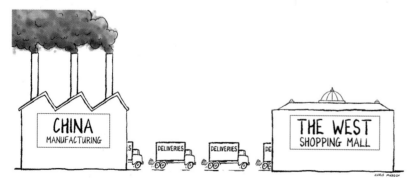

CHINA MANUFACTURING

DELIVERIES DELIVERIES

THE WEST SHOPPING MALL

WHY CHINA'S CARBON FOOTPRINT IS SO LARGE

B © Chris Madden

SEX IS WHAT YOU'RE BORN WITH, GENDER IS WHAT YOU'RE GIVEN

ACTION MAN

PASSIVITY GIRL

C © Richard Chapman

■ Interpreting photographs

As with a cartoon, you need to look closely at what is in a photograph.

D

E

Try to answer the following questions.

1 What do you see in Source **D**?

2 What do you see in Source **E**?

3 How do you think the photographs might relate to each other and to your course?

4 Why do you think the photographs may have been taken?

5 What do you *not* see in the photographs?

Now consider your answers in the light of the following information. The photos are part of a local pressure group campaign. They want to prevent wind turbines being located near their village. The photos were taken by residents. Wind turbines were added to the first photo after it had been taken, based on the scale in the plans and the planned location of them. The residents were open about adding the turbines to the photo and the scaling of them so they could not be accused of exaggeration. They also acknowledge that the use of zoom and the angle can alter the impression of size. For example, a low angle close-up can make wind turbines appear taller. The second photo is from the same campaign but it has been cropped so that you do not see the possible location of four wind turbines close to this house.

Going further

1 Find out more about the campaign from which these photos have been taken by going to the Cotton Farm Action Group at **www.stopthewindfarm.org.uk/**

Activity

3 Answer this 4-mark exam question that comes from a past paper.

Use Sources **F** and **G** to comment on the impact of tourism.

F

G

In your pre-release booklet, you will be asked to interpret simple tables or graphs or ones in their original format original but easily understood.

◼ Simple tables

Source A shows a simple table of the population of the UK. It has a title. There are two columns, one for the year and the other for the number of people. The table also has a scale, millions.

◼ Simple line graphs

The same data can be put in graphical form. Source B is a simple line graph drawn using the information from Source A. Graphs are used to demonstrate the relationship between sets of figures. They provide a visual indication of trends or movements.

UK Population 1961–2011 (estimate)

Year	Population (millions)
1961	52.807
1971	55.928
1981	56.357
1991	57.439
2001	59.113
2005	60.238
2011 (est)	62.309

A

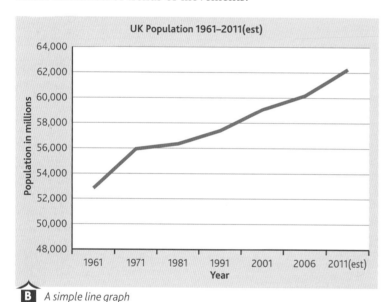

B *A simple line graph*

Activities

1 Using Source A, state the number of people in the population in 1981.

2 a Describe the trend of the UK population shown in Source B.

   b At what period was the population change at its lowest?

3 a Did more boys than girls obtain 5+ A to C grades?

   b Did more girls than boys obtain results that were not graded?

◼ Pie charts

Pie charts provide instant visual information about proportions. You will normally be just asked to interpret them, unless you draw one in your controlled assessment. They are easy to draw. There are 360 degrees in a circle and as a whole circle represents 100%, each 1% is represented by a central angle of 3.6 degrees (i.e. 360 divided by 100). The percentage of each component is worked out and converted to the appropriate number of degrees e.g. 5% requires an angle of 18 degrees (5 × 3.6 degrees).

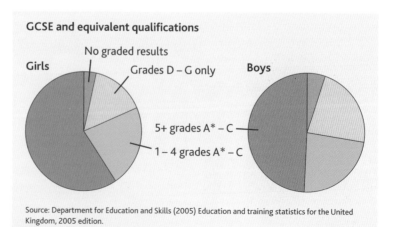

Source: Department for Education and Skills (2005) Education and training statistics for the United Kingdom, 2005 edition.

C *Pie charts show comparisons*

Bar charts

In the simple bar chart in Source **D**, the bars are erected from the same baseline and have equal width. Their heights are proportional to the values they stand for. In some bar charts, the bars are close together with no space between them. In some bar charts, the bars may be horizontal.

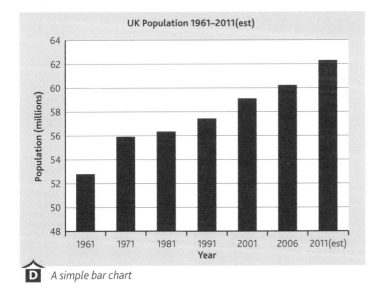

D *A simple bar chart*

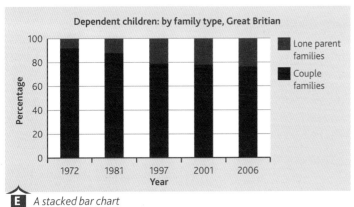

E *A stacked bar chart*

Activity

4 Look at Source **D**:

a What was the population in 2001?

b Why do you think the bars are not every ten years, e.g. 1970, 1980?

Activity

5 a State two trends illustrated by the bar chart in Source **E**.

b Can you think of any reasons for these trends?

Activity

6 Look at Source **F**:

a What trend can you recognise in marriages? How can you tell this?

b What trend can you recognise in divorces? How can you tell this?

Even more information can be provided if each bar is a 'component bar' divided into different elements. This type of bar chart is called a 'stacked' bar chart. Source **E** is a stacked bar chart illustrating the changing proportions of one parent-families and couple families.

Complex graphs

Graphs can be used to demonstrate the relationship between sets of figures and they can indicate trends or movements. In Source **F**, the graph illustrates very well changes in the family over the last 50 years of the 20th century.

1 Divorce data from 1955 to 1970 are for Great Britain only. Divorce became legal in Northern Ireland from 1969. Includes annulments.
2 For both partners.
3 For one or both partners.
Source: Office for National Statistics; General Register Office for Scotland; Northern Ireland Statistics and Research Agency

  A complex graph

Your controlled assessment task is an important part of your GCSE humanities course and is worth 25 per cent of the total marks. The topic will be chosen from a list provided by the examination board. In making a choice, your teacher will take into account the resources available at your school which will allow you to do your own research.

The process of doing the controlled assessment task consists of three stages as shown in the diagram.

■ Stage 2

During this stage, your teacher can give you feedback on the work you have done.

- You should create a file for your research for use in your final presentation. It is important that you include a bibliography which lists all the sources (including websites) that you have used.

- You need to acquire information and arguments using books, the Internet, videos, surveys, questionnaires and interviews. You need to make judgements about sources, deciding on the strengths and weaknesses of the information. When was it written? Who by? Is it a reliable source?

- You then need to begin to develop your own views. Phrases you might use are shown in the bulleted list below.

- Give some thought to whether you are using all your humanities subject skills. Would a map help to illustrate the topic even though you are mainly looking at a historical topic? Begin to formulate your conclusion in your own mind.

Useful phrases

- This evidence shows that…
- This argument is strong because…
- This evidence does not support the hypothesis…
- My own research suggests that…
- There is a connection between…
- There is a trend towards…

■ Stage 3

The person in charge of the Stage 3 session when you complete the assessment is not allowed to give you any help at all.

- When you begin Stage 3, your file will be checked to ensure it does not contain a prepared answer or skeleton answer which could just be copied out during the sessions. Your research material will be kept after completion of the task and can be inspected by the exam board. Your teacher is required to check whether any plagiarism (copying material from books/websites rather than using your own words) or unauthorised collaboration has taken place.

Stage 1: Preparartion

Teacher briefing to the class. Ideas and background to the topic you will investigate. Your teacher will set coursework deadlines.

This will involve a number of lessons.

↓

Stage 2: Doing it

The planning and investigation stage when you may work with others as well as developing your own individual approach to the topic.

8 – 12 hours class time, plus homework to investigate.

↓

Stage 3: Writing it up

Under exam-type conditions, and probably in a number of sessions, you use your notes to help you complete your final presentation. This can be up to 2000 words in length.

3 – 4 hours for writing final presentation.

A

B

- Once you have begun the final presentation (i.e. session 1), you cannot bring in additional material. At the end of the first session, your teacher will collect in all materials and return them to you at the beginning of the next session.

- You can handwrite or use a computer to produce your final piece. You will not be allowed to access email or the Internet while you do this.

- At the end you will have three pieces of exam evidence as shown in the margin box.

- You will be marked on your ability to investigate, apply and communicate your ideas and your ability to analyse and evaluate.

Exam evidence

- Your final presentation.
- Your research material you used.
- Your bibliography.

■ Example

Here is an example topic:

Economic migration has effects on people and societies. Choose one economic migration and assess its impact.

This topic could be done at a number of different levels:

- At a **personal level** it could involve a case study such as the experiences of a British family moving to Australia or an Asian family moving to Britain.

- At a **local community level** it could involve a case study of the experience of migrants and the host community. Peterborough, for example, has in recent years had an influx of East Europeans.

- At a **national level** it would be possible to investigate one economic migration.

- At an **international level** it would be possible to look at migration to the US.

Economic migration to the UK

- The Irish in the 1840s.
- West Indians in the 1950s and 60s.
- East Europeans over the last 10 years.

Economic migration to the US

- The early settlers in the 1840s and 1850s.
- Groups like the Italians who have migrated there since the 1880s.

Whatever you choose, you will then have to pose and answer a number of questions to explore the topic. Possible questions are shown in the margin.

Questions to pose

- What caused the migration? For example, in the case of West Indians in the 1950s, the British Government advertised for them to come to fill job vacancies.
- What was the experience of the migrants at first and after a number of years?
- Did the migrants integrate into the host society?
- What was the response of the host country?
- Who gained most from the migration?
- How reliable is the evidence you have obtained?

The important thing is always to listen to your teacher and follow their guidance.

Glossary

9/11: commonly used to refer to Al Qaeda's attack on the World Trade Center in New York, on 11 September 2001.

A

Absolute poverty: an individual lacking the basic needs to survive.

Acculturation: where members of one cultural group adopt the culture and beliefs of another group.

Acid rain: rain, snow, fog or dust with a pH below 5.

Adoption: taking legal responsibility for a child other than your own.

Affirmative action: actions and policies to improve situations for people disadvantaged by existing discrimination.

Agenda 21: a commitment to move towards sustainable development at government and local level.

Aggressor: someone who attacks another person.

Alien species: a plant or animal that moves from its original habitat into a new area.

Alienation: a state of separation of the worker from themselves and other workers.

Alternative energy: does not deplete natural resources and does not harm the environment, for example solar power.

Apartheid: 'separateness' – a system of segregation or discrimination on the basis of race.

Arbitration: when a body such as Acas gets a group of independent people to decide on the basis of evidence what the outcome to a dispute should be. The employers and employees have to agree in advance that they will accept the outcome.

Arranged marriages: a marriage where the partners have been chosen by the parents of the bride and groom.

Assembly line: a series of machines in a factory where each worker assembles one small part of the finished product.

Assimilation: when an ethnic group adopts the host culture as their own.

Asylum seeker: a person classed as a refugee fleeing persecution. He or she is not an economic migrant.

Attitudes: positive or negative feelings towards objects or people.

Automation: a process is self regulated with the help of electronic technology.

B

Bantu: the name given to Black South Africans.

Barriers of access: ways of preventing disabled people participate fully in society.

Beliefs: a set of ideas about the world that form the basis of a religion or other way of making sense of life.

Bilateral aid: resources given directly from one country to another, often with conditions attached.

Biodiversity: the variety of species found in a particular area.

Biofuels: energy generated from organic matter (biomass), including wood and crops.

Bullying: the act of intentionally causing harm to others, through verbal harassment or physical assault.

C

Calorie intake: amount of calories obtained from food per person per day.

Campaign: a series of coordinated actions which work towards particular objectives.

Cancellation of debt: relief from the burden of paying the original loan and the interest.

Carbon footprint: the impact of human activity measured in carbon dioxide units.

Carbon offsetting: removing the same amount of carbon from the atmosphere as produced by an activity such as air travel.

Caring function: looking after young, disabled or elderly members of the family.

Cash crops: crops grown for their monetary value, for example, coffee.

Cereal-packet family: an ideal nuclear family used in advertising with a housewife and male breadwinner.

Child benefit: a weekly payment to parents to support a child.

Child labour: a child under 17 who is working more hours than legally allowed.

Child Support Act 1991, 1995, 2000: controls the amount an absent parent must pay to the parent who cares for a child.

Childcare: the role of looking after the children. Can be carried out by parents, relatives or other providers such as nurseries.

Child-centred: treating the needs of children as important

Children Act 2004: 'Every Child Matters': five outcomes for children including to be healthy and to stay safe.

Civil partnership: since 2005 same-sex couples can become civil partners, giving them legal, financial and childcare rights.

Civil war: a war between sections of the same country or different groups within a country.

Class: the way society is divided into groups based on job, power or wealth. The three main classes are upper class, middle class and working class.

Coalition: a combination of two or more countries which join together, for example, US and UK in Iraq.

Cohabitation: couples live together but are not legally married.

Colonialism: a policy where a country settles and exploits another country, for example, India was a former British colony.

Colonisation: when one country goes to another country and takes over important aspects of its culture.

Community Based Tourism (CBT): local communities are supported to provide sustainable tourism that benefits the local community.

Conciliation: when independent people get the parties in conflict together and look for areas that they can agree on and work towards a solution.

Conflict: a verbal or physical clash.

Conservation: protection of the environment and natural resources of the earth including plant and animal life.

Continuous process technology: a process (often in the chiemical industry) which is started electronically by a person and then continues until it is shut down electronically.

Contraception: use of birth control to prevent pregnancy.

Coral bleaching: when sea temperatures rise, the coral die and lose their colour.

Corruption: abuse of public power for private gain, including bribery, influencing laws and favouring family.

Culture shock: when newly arrived immigrants find the host country's culture very different.

Culture: a shared set of beliefs, values, attitudes, norms, customs, traditions and practices.

Customs: the long-established habits of a society.

D

Debt burden: the amount of money owed by a country.

Deforestation: loss of forest due to climate change or the use of trees without replacing them.

Democracy: a political system in which power lies with the people who can vote for people to represent them, for example, MPs in UK.

Desertification: loss of productive land to desert due to climate change and overgrazing.

Deskilling: when particular traditional skills disappear, replaced by advanced technology.

Development trap: countries are unable to develop or improve due to the poverty cycle.

Dictatorship: a political system in which power lies with an individual who has total power and does not allow fair elections.

Diffusion: the idea of something spreading out gradually.

Direct action: the use of violent or non-violent methods to influence a political decision.

Discrimination: unfair treatment of a person or group on the basis of prejudice about things such as age, gender, sexuality, disability, race, religion or class.

Division of labour: how tasks in the home are organised and divided up between members of the family or household.

Divorce: the legal ending of a marriage.

Divorce rate: the number of divorces per 1,000 people.

Divorce Reform Act 1969: allowed a couple to divorce on the grounds of cruelty, adultery and mutual consent.

Drought: long spell of dry weather.

Dual income households: a household or family where both partners go out to work.

E

Economic function: families are units that earn and spend money.

Economic migrant: a person who moves to live in another place for work.

Ecosystem: all living and non-living things in a particular environment and the way they work together.

Ecotourism: responsible travel to natural areas that conserves the environment and the well-being of the local people.

Emigration: the movement of people out of an area across a national boundary.

Endangered: when the numbers of a species are so low or it is facing such severe threats it may become extinct.

Environmental crises: severe difficulties caused by natural disasters.

Environmental refugees: people displaced by environmental disasters caused by climate change.

Equal rights legislation: laws made to ensure that all people have an equal chance to participate in all forms of activity.

Ethnic group: a group with a distinct culture that can be traced through history to a specific location.

Eugenics: the study of ways to improve human inheritance.

Extended family: a nuclear family, with other relatives, for example, grandparents or cousins living in the same house or close by.

Extinct: the total disappearance of a particular type of living organism.

Extraordinary rendition: the sending of suspects to countries outside US for interrogation or imprisonment, specifically to aviod US laws protecting prisoners rights.

Extrinsic satisfaction: where the most important thing is the wage rather than the work task involved. The money compensates for the dull and boring work by providing for satisfaction outside of work in leisure.

F

Fair trade: sustainable trade and improved working conditions for producers in LEDCs.

Fairtrade Foundation: organisation that gives companies the right to use the fairtrade logo, and checks up on them.

Family: a group of people connected by marriage or blood relationships.

Family size: the average number of children a woman has.

Feral child: a human child who has lived away from human contact or brought up with little experience or very poor care.

Force: trying to resolve a conflict using some form of violence.

Formal economy: people in full or part-time paid employment.

Fossil fuel: fuel formed from the remains of ancient plants and animals.

Free trade: trade without government tariffs and subsidies. Prices and products determined by supply and demand.

G

G8: group of the world's eight most powerful countries that meet annually to discuss world issues.

Gang: a group of people who join together and often get involved in some form of conflict.

Gender identity: all of the attributes and characteristics that are associated with belonging to one or the other of the sexes.

Gender roles: the tasks and expectations assigned to males and females in a society.

Gene: the basic unit of heredity.

Genetic inheritance: the result of a transfer of genes from parent to offspring.

Genocide: (geno = people, race; cide = murder) the destruction of a large number of people (racial, social, political, cultural or religious group).

Geothermal energy: energy obtained from rock heated by the earth's core.

Global branding: a set of values used to promote a product around the world.

Global citizen: thinks about their effect on the world by preserving the environment and keeping natural resources for others to use in the future.

Global interdependence: the countries of the world rely on each other for trade, resources and jobs.

Global responsibility: individuals and businesses making choices that affect the world in a positive way.

Global warming: a warming of the climate in recent decades, due to human influences.

Globalisation: where activities in one part of the world have consequences for people in other parts of the world.

Government action: laws or incentives introduced by a government to reduce global warming.

Government organisations: in the UK the DFID (Department For International Development) that manages aid to the World Bank and UN.

Government policy: trade and agricultural policies such as tariffs and subsidies that protect their own industries against foreign imports.

Greenhouse gases: gases such as carbon dioxide that trap heat in the earth's atmosphere.

Gross National Product (GNP): total Income in US $ from goods and services in a country for one year, including income from overseas.

Gypsy: the common name in the UK for the Sinti and Roma people who live all over Europe.

H

Habitat: the natural environment of animal or plant.

Heavily Indebted Poor Countries (HIPC): countries eligible for a debt relief scheme run by the World Bank and the IMF.

HIV/AIDS: Human Immunodeficiency Virus / Acquired Immunodeficiency Syndrome.

Holocaust: the persecution of millions of people, mainly Jews, by the Nazis.

Honey pot: an area of attractive scenery or historic interest visited by large numbers of tourists.

Household: the people who live in the same accommodation.

Househusband: the male parent who stays at home and looks after the children and the house while the female goes out to work.

Human right: a legal or moral entitlement to do something or to be protected from something, for example, the right to freedom of expression or the right not to be tortured.

Humanitarian aid: resources sent to save lives or reduce suffering after a crisis.

Hydro-electric power (HEP): energy generated by water spinning a turbine.

I

Identity-giving: an act or process that defines part of a person's identity.

Immigration: the movement of people into an area across a national boundary.

Imperialism: the act of creating an empire by invading other countries.

Indoctrination: when someone attempts to make you accept certain facts and ideas without question.

Industrial sabotage: an attempt to disrupt production or interfere with the quality of goods produced, for example, putting a bolt put in a sealed section means the object mysteriously rattles or putting the wrong message in a stick of rock.

Industrialisation: the change from a farming society to a society based around production of goods in factories.

Infant mortality rate: the number of children who die before their first birthday per 1,000 born.

Informal economy: unofficial employment, which may be paid or unpaid.

Information technology: a term that encompasses all forms of technology used to create, store, exchange and use information in its various forms (data, voice conversations, still images, motion pictures, multimedia and other forms including those not yet conceived).

Insider group: people who hold most power and influence in a society.

Institutional discrimination: existence of prejudice in the way an organisation works and delivers its services.

Insurgents: groups of people who buy weapons and fight for a specific cause.

Integration: when two cultures combine and live alongside each other in harmony.

International agreements: agreements between two or more countries.

International Monetary Fund (IMF): is a global financial organisation set up in 1945 to stabilise currencies and lend money in crises.

Inter-racial: between different races.

Intolerance: the lack of willingness to respect differences among people.

Intrinsic satisfaction: where the most important feature of work is the amount of fulfilment and satisfaction that it provides.

IQ tests: a means of measuring intelligence.

Islamic fundamentalism: the belief that Shari'ah law should be used over and above any laws made by elected politicians.

Issue: something about which people have different views.

J

Job sharing: when two or more people fill one full-time post.

L

Leisure: having free time to do whatever you want, subject to finance and ability.

Less economically developed country (LEDC): with a low standard of living, for example, Ethiopia, Bangladesh.

Life expectancy: the average length of time a person is expected to live.

Literacy rate: the percentage of adults who can read and write simple sentences.

Lobbying: individuals or groups attempt to influence the opinion of MPs to vote a certain way on a specific subject.

Lone (single)-parent family: one parent (mother or father) living with their children often after divorce, separation of death of a parent.

Long-term cause: cause which takes many years to develop.

M

Marriage: the legal partnership between man and woman.

Marriage rate: the number of marriages per 1,000 people.

Media: methods of communication including newspapers, radio, TV and internet.

Migration: the movement from one place to another on a permanent or semi-permanent basis.

Millennium Development goals (MDGs): eight goals agreed by world leaders to reduce world poverty by 2015.

Minerals: any rock which is mined, drilled or quarried, e.g. coal, gold.

Monogamy: marriage to one partner at a time.

Morals: provide guidance on what is right and wrong.

More economically developed country: with a high standard of living, for example UK, US.

Multicultural: a society which consists of the culture of several different races.

Multilateral aid: money given by donor countries give money to the World Bank or UN who then distribute aid.

Multinational: a multinational company has its activities spread over a number of different countries.

Multinational company (MNC): a business that manages production or delivers services in at least two countries.

Multiple identities: when a person has a number of identities in different parts of their life.

N

National Health Service (NHS): provides nursing care for elderly people in addition to health services for the rest of the population.

National park: reserve of land, usually declared by national government to be protected from human development and pollution.

Nationalism: the belief that one's country is superior to other countries.

Natural resources: raw materials found within or on the earth, which can be used by humans.

Negotiation: the process of achieving an agreement by discussion.

Non-governmental organisation (NGO): an organisation that is not run by, or associated with, any particular government. It may operate at local, national or international level, for example, Amnesty International, Oxfam.

Non-renewable resources: can only be used once and can never be replaced.

Norms: unwritten rules defining the appropriate pattern of behaviour.

Nuclear family: a mother, father and their children.

Nuclear power: producing energy from uranium atoms.

Nurture: the effect of personal experiences from the womb to adulthood. It is how you have been brought up.

O

Occupation: jobs people do, measured by the percentage of population working in agriculture.

Official statistics: statistics collected and published by government agencies and departments of government.

OPEC: Organisation of the Petroleum Exporting Countries.

Outsider groups: people whose culture is new or different to those who hold most power in society.

P

Pacifism: the opposition to violence as a means of settling conflict.

Parental responsibility: parents are to ensure they protect, provide a house, education, medical treatment, and discipline their children.

Peer group: people of the same age who associate regularly.

People per doctor: the total population divided by the number of qualified doctors.

Perspective: a viewpoint that a person or group has about an issue.

Pester power: the power children have over parents to make them buy something.

Poaching: catching or killing animals illegally.

Pollution: something that poisons or damages air, water or land.

Polygamy: marriage to more than one partner at the same time.

Poverty cycle: set of factors such as low income and poor diet that cause poverty to continue.

Power station: place where electricity is generated.

Practices: the way a culture, beliefs, values and so on are put into action, for example a person with religious beliefs may regularly go to a place of worship.

Prejudice: a negative opinion formed against a person or group based on a stereotype.

Pressure groups: organised groups that attempt to influence policy or business decisions on a particular issue.

Primary product: a natural resource that can be used as a raw material in other industries.

Primary sector: the part of the economy of a country makes use of the raw materials of the land and sea.

Primitive tribe: one with a simple culture that has survived for a very long time. It is likely to be characterised by a hunting/gathering existence.

Prisoner of conscience: someone who is imprisoned for expressing their political views.

Propaganda: information which is used to influence others' opinions. It may 'bend' the facts or not tell the whole story.

Protocol: written record of an agreement between two or more countries.

Q

Quaternary sector: the suggested term to describe the information technology services part of a country's economy.

R

Racial prejudice: a belief that one race or ethnic group is superior to another.

Reconstituted family: a family where at least one child is not common to both adults, for example, when parents divorce and one remarries to form a new family that may include step-brothers/sisters or half brothers/sisters.

Recycling: turning used products into new products in order to prevent waste, reduce pollution and lower greenhouse gases.

Relative poverty: an individual living on less than half the average income of the society they live in.

Religion: a system of beliefs about life and death and the mysteries of the physical and spiritual worlds, usually involving the idea of a supreme being.

Renewable energy: energy from natural resources that are infinite or can be re-used, for example, hydro-electric.

Renewable resources: will not run out, or can be replaced, provided they are not over-used.

Reproductive function: families produce the next generation by having children.

Residential care: for people who can not stay in their own homes. Meals and personal care, which are provided. Staff are usually available 24 hours a day.

Resocialisation: the way people meet new situations and have to adapt to them as they age.

Responsibility: a duty which binds you to a course of action demanded by a human right.

Ridicule: words or actions which make fun of people to hurt their feelings.

Rites of passage: a ceremony or event that marks an important stage in a person's life.

Ritual: an event that expresses some religious meaning.

Role model: someone whom you use as a reference point for your behaviour. You want to be like them.

S

Sanctions: economic restrictions imposed by countries to put pressure on another country to force it to change.

Scapegoating: blaming a person or group for things they did not necessarily do.

Secondary sector: the part of the economy of a country that turns raw materials into products that the country needs.

Serial monogamy: a series of relationships including a pattern of marriage, divorce and then remarriage.

Sexual function: adults in families have stable sexual relationships.

Shari'ah: Islamic law based directly on the Qur'an and Sunnah.

Short-term cause: immediate cause which triggers an incident.

Significant other: a person who is of great importance to you in your life.

Silicon chip: an electronic device made from a piece of silicon that holds millions of microscopically small electrical components.

Single-parent family: one parent (mother or father) living with their children often after divorce, separation or death of a parent. Also called a lone-parent family.

Single-person household: a person living on their own, by choice, through relationship breakdown or death of a partner.

Social control mechanisms: the means of ensuring conformity and order in a society. Some mechanisms, such as those in socialisation, are informal but there are also formal mechanisms such as the law.

Social construct: an idea, such as the age of childhood, which is decided by society.

Social identity: when a person is identified or labelled as a specific type of person.

Social Services: provides help for people in their own homes and help fund some residential care.

Socialisation: the process by which a child learns the ways of its culture. It can be seen as a process of stages.

Socialisation function: the process by which parents teach acceptable behaviour to children.

Solar power: energy generated from sunlight.

Stereotype: a fixed, general view of a whole group of people which does not recognise individual differences. Stereotypes are usually negative.

Stewardship: looking after something so it can be passed on to the next generation.

Student household: a group of non-related students sharing accommodation, eating arrangements and bills.

Subculture: a culture that exists within the dominant culture and has many similarities to the dominant culture, but also significant differences.

Subsidy: money paid to a business or farmers to make their goods cheaper than foreign imports.

Surrogate mother: a woman who becomes pregnant with a child, usually for a couple who are unable to have their own children.

Sustainable: methods that preserve and maintain, rather than destroy.

Sustainable development: economic and social development that meets the needs of current and future generations.

Sustainable tourism: has a low impact on the environment and local culture and contributes to biodiversity.

Systematic persecution: the deliberate and organised harassment and murder of people.

T

Tariff: a tax on foreign goods when they are imported into a country.

Teenage mums: girls who have children under the age of 20.

Tertiary sector: the part of the economy of a country that covers all the services received.

Third party: a person who attempts to find a resolution between those involved in a conflict but is not involved in the conflict itself.

Tidal power: energy generated as the tide goes in or out of a coastal area or estuary.

Tourism: a trip made for pleasure, usually including at least one night away.

Trade union: an organisation of workers created to protect and advance the interests of its members.

Traditions: the handing down from generation to generation of customs and beliefs.

Tribalism: the existence of people who share a strong group identity.

Tweenager: a fashion conscious 8–12 year old.

U

UN Rights of the Child: 54 rights that all children in the world should be entitled to, according to the United Nations.

Unemployment: when you have no employment and register with the Department of Work and Pensions as available for work.

Unfair terms of trade: policies that favour one trading partner, usually MEDCs.

Unilateral aid: aid given by one country or organisation, whether the recipient country agrees or not.

Urbanisation: the movement of people from the countryside, to live in towns and cities.

V

Values: what a person feels to be important to them. Values are usually shared among members of a culture.

Victim: someone who is attacked by an aggressor.

Violation: an act which disregards someone's rights.

Violence: an act of aggression which is intended to cause pain.

Voluntary euthanasia: where someone is helped to die with their consent.

W

Wave power: energy generated by waves in the sea.

Weapons of mass destruction (WMD): weapons that are intended to cause huge loss of life and/or property (nuclear, chemical and biological weapons).

Wind power: energy generated from wind.

Work: the production of goods and services that usually earns a wage or salary though some work is unpaid.

World Bank: set up in 1945 to lend money to countries to pay for development projects.

World Trade Organisation (WTO): set up in 1995 to promote free and fair trade.

Acknowledgements

Photo Acknowledgements

1.1 A; David R. Frazier Photolibrary, Inc./Alamy, 1.1 B; North Wind Picture Archives/Alamy, 1.1 D1; Istockphoto, 1.1 D2;Istockphoto, 1.1 D3; Reuters/Corbis, 1.1 D4; Istockphoto, 1.1 F; Istockphoto, 1.1 G;North Wind Picture Archives/Alamy, 1.1 J; Istockphoto, 1.1 K; Istockphoto, 1.1 N; Istockphoto, 1.1 N; Corbis, 1.1 O; Julio Donoso/CORBIS SYGMA, 1.1 P; Fotolia, 1.1 R and 1.1 T; Glasgow Evening Times, 1.2 A; Fotolia, 1.2 B; Blue Lantern Studio/Corbis, 1.2 C; Tom Grill/Corbis, 1.2 D; Getty, 1.2 E; Hulton-Deutsch Collection/Corbis1.2 K; Bettmann/Corbis, 1.2 L; Hulton-Deutsch Collection/Corbis, 1.2 O; Ben Radford/Corbis, 1.2 P1; Fotolia, 1.2 P2; Fotolia, 1.2 P3; Getty, 1.2 Q1; Istockphoto, 1.2 Q2; Istockphoto, 1.2 T; Fotolia, 1.2 U; Cartoonstock.com, 1.2 W; BRUCE,GILBERT/LANDOV/PA Photos, 1.2 X; Dimitri Iundt/TempSport/Corbis, 1.3 A; Istockphoto, 1.3 B; Bettmann/Corbis, 1.3 C; Bettmann/Corbis, 1.3 D; Istockphoto, 1.3 E; Istockphoto, 1.3 F; Istockphoto, 1.3 G; Getty, 1.3 H; Jean du Boisberranger/Hemis/Corbis, 1.3 J; Hulton-Deutsch Collection/Corbis, 1.3 K; Rex Features, 1.3 O; Gary Trotter; Eye Ubiquitous/Corbis, 1.3 Q; Reuters/Corbis, 1.3 S; Stefano Bianchetti/Corbis, 1.3 T; Bettmann/Corbis, 1.3 U; Underwood & Underwood/Corbis, 1.4 B; Shepard Sherbell, 1.4 D; Corbis, 1.4I; Rex Features, 1.5 A; Robert Harding Picture Library Ltd/ Alamy, 2.1 D; Peter Jordan/Alamy, 2.1 F; Anthony West/Corbis, 2.1 G; Realimage/Alamy, 2.1 H; Worldwide Picture Library/Alamy, 2.1 I; Evan Bowen-Jones, 2.1 J; Mark Conlin/Alamy, 2.1 K; Neil McAllister/Alamy, 2.2 B; Roy Garner/Alamy, 2.2 F; Ashley Cooper/Corbis, 2.2 G; Frank Lane Picture Agency/Corbis, 2.2 H; Oxford Scientific (OSF)/Photolibrary, 2.3 A, , Reuters/Corbis, 2.3 F; RUSSELL BOYCE/Reuters/Corbis, 2.4 D; PA Photos, 2.4 F; Galen Rowell/Corbis, 2.5 B; Modern Landscapes/Istockphoto, 3.3 M; Bettmann/Corbis, 3.3 N; PA Photos, 3.4 B; PA Photos, 3.4 C; Reuters/Corbis, 3.4 D; PA Photos, 3.4 E; Fotolia, 3.4 H; PA Photos, 3.4 G; Fotolia, 3.4 I; PA Photos, 4.1 E; Istockphoto, 4.1.G1; Geoff Manasse/Photolibrary, 4.1.G2; Photos India/Photolibrary, 4.1.G3; Istockphoto, 4.2 B1; Imagestate RM/Photolibrary, 4.2 B2; Bettmann/Corbis, 4.2 B3; Istockphoto, 4.2 F1; Getty, 4.2 F2; PA Photos, 4.2 F3; PA Photos, 4.2 K; PA Photos, 4.3 B; TopFoto, 4.3 C1; US Holocaust Memorial Museum, 4.3 C2; US Holocaust Memorial Museum, 4.3 F; Polish National Archive, 4.4 A1; Michael St. Maur Sheil/Corbis, 4.4 C; PA Photos, 4.4 D; Matthew Ashton/AMA/Corbis, 4.4 E1; Kick It Out, 4.4 E2; Najlah Feanny/Corbis, 4.4 E3; Reuters/Corbis, 4.4 E4; Kick It Out, 4.4 F1; Paul Thompson Images/Alamy, 4.4 F2; Vassil Donev/epa/Corbis, 4.4 F3; Art Directors, 4.4 H; Cristina Fumi / Alamy, 4.4 I; Valerie Kuypers/epa/Corbis, 4.5 A; Corbis, 4.5 A2; Bettmann/Corbis, 5.1 A1; Frans Lemmens/zeta/Corbis, 5.1A2; Alistair Heap/Alamy, 5.1 A3; Istockphoto, 5.1 A4; Jenny Matthews/Alamy, 5.2 C; Henri Bureau/Sygma/Corbis, 5.2 D; Les Stone/Sygma/Corbis, 5.2 E; Construction Photography/Corbis, 5.2 H; Grant Neuenburg/Reuters/Corbis, 5.2 J; PA Photos, 5.3 A; Istockphoto, 5.3 C; Istockphoto, 5.3 D; Andrew Holbrooke/Corbis, 5.4 B; Neil Cooper/Alamy, 5.4 D; PA Photos, 5.4 E; Mark Boulton/Alamy, 5.4 F; Ariadne Van Zandbergen, 6.1 A1; Istockphoto, 6.1 A2; Hill Street Studios/Corbis, 6.1 A3; Fotolia, 6.1 A4; Istockphoto, 6.1 C; LOOK Die Bildagentur der Fotografen GmbH/Alamy, 6.1 D, , Israel images/Alamy, 6.2 B; Albrecht G. Schaefer/Corbis, 6.2 D; Istockphoto, 6.3 D; Bob Krist/Corbis, 6.3 E; PA Photos, 6.3 F; Istockphoto, 6.3 I; Alina Novopashina/UPPA/Photoshot, 6.4 B; Rex Features, 6.4 F; PA Photos, 6.4 G; Istockphoto, 6.4 H1; Danita Delimont/Alamy, 6.4 H2; The Print Collector/Photolibrary, 6.4 H3; Fotolia, 7.1 A; Sébastien Cailleux/Sygma/Corbis, 7.1 F1; Fotolia, 7.1 F2; Fotolia, 7.1 I1; Istockphoto, 7.1 I2; Istockphoto, 7.1 P; Fotolia, 7.1 P; Fotolia, 7.2 A; The London Art Archive/Alamy, 7.2 C; Bob Thomason/Getty, 7.2 D1; Hulton Archive/Getty, 7.2 D2; Hulton Archive/Getty, 7.2 D3; Michael Rosenfeld/Getty, 7.2 E; Brand X/Corbis, 7.2 F; Istockphoto, 7.3i, ii, iii; Fotolia, 7.3 B1; redsnapper / Alamy, 7.3B2; General Motors/Reuters/Corbis Sygma, 7.3 E; Hulton-Deutsch Collection/Corbis, 7.3 F; Selwyn Tait, 7.3 K; Richard Chapman/www.doubt.it, 7.4 C; Nicholson from The Australian www.nicholsoncartoons.com.au, 7.4 G; Patrick Chauvel/Sygma/Corbis, 7.4 K; Istockphoto, 7.5 A; Richard Chapman/www.doubt.it, 8.4 A; Solo Syndication, 8.4 B; Chris Madden, 8.4 C; Richard Chapman/www.doubt.it, 8.4 D; Cotton Farm Action Group, 8.4 E; Cotton Farm Action Group, 8.4 F; AQA, 8.4 G; Bernard Hoyle, 8.6B; Fotolia

Text Acknowledgements

1.1R and T; 2 extracts from Glasgow Evening Times, Gangs Supplement, 8 February, 2008. Reprinted with permission of the editorial/Evening Times, 1.2R; short quote by Professor Robert Plomin. Reprinted with kind permission, 1.2T;Use of figures by Thomas Bouchard 1979. Reprinted with kind permission of the author 1.3P; Short quote by Ruth Lea. Reprinted with kind permission, 1.3R, Life in the UK test (extracts), CROWN COPYRIGHT, Crown Copyright materials reproduced with the permission of the Controller, Office of Public Sector Information (OPSI), 2.3D; LOAF poster. Reprinted with permission of Christian Ecology, 2.5A; pie chart from figures taken from 'Analysis of household waste composition' by Dr. J. Parfitt, WRAP, 2002 Reprinted with permission of WRAP, 3.2F; short extract adapted from 'Seized on a bus : a baseball bat, six knives, and two screwdrivers' by Sean O'Neill, The Times, 20 May, 2008. Copyright © NI Syndications. Reprinted with permission, 3.3L; Courtesy of the Nelson Mandela Foundation, 3.5 A; Short extract adapted from 'Boy 14 is latest victim of gang violence' by David Brown, The Times, 9 April, 2007. © NI Syndications. Reprinted with permission, 4.1 ONS stats, , crown copyright, crown copyright, , , Crown Copyright materials reproduced with permission of the controller, Office of Public Sector Information, OPSI, 4.1D; Extracts adapted from an article by India Knight, The Times, 10 August, 2008. © NI Syndications. Reprinted with permission, 4.1F; Poster reproduced with kind permission of the Equality and Human Rights Commission, 4.1H; Short extract adapted from 'Gay claims force out Mugabe's Tv chief' by Chris McGreal, The Guardian, 4 April, 2002. copyright © Guardian News & Media Ltd 2002. Used with permission, 4.1, H; Short extract from The Times, 19 July 2008. © NI Syndications. Reprinted with permission, 4.2C; Short extract from 'A World of casual racism' exposed at BA' by Andy McSmith, The Independent, 2th April, 2008. Reprinted with permission, 4.2; Short extract from http://news.nationalgeographic.com/news/2001/02/0215_tuskegee.html by Lisa Krause/NG News. Reprinted with permssion of National Geographic Stock, 4.2D; Short extract adapted from article by Sean Rayment, Defence Correspondent, The Telegraph, 2 October, 2008. Reprinted with permission, 4.2, E; Short extract adapted from article by Sean Rayment, Defence Correspondent, The Telegraph, 2 October, 2008. Reprinted with permission, 4.2I; Short extract from SEIZE THE DAY by Tanni Grey-Thompson,Hodder. Reprinted with permission of Hodder & Stoughton Ltd, 4.3, Figures by permission of Refugees International 4.3H; Short extract from The Insider Story, TES Teacher, 19 March, 2008. Reprinted with permission, 4.3H; Short extract adapted from The Times, 24 July, 2008, © NI Syndications. Reprinted with permission, 4.4, Extract adapted from 'Kick It Out 2007' www.kickitout.org. Reprinted with permission, 5.1E; Figures (table and map) from HUMAN DEVELOPMENT REPORT 2007/2008 UNDP. Reprinted with permission of Palgrave Macmillan, 5.1C; Reprinted with permission of Palgrave Macmillan, 5.2,G; Short extracts from www.cafod.org.uk/trade/sugar-farmer. Reprinted with permission www.cafod.org.uk/trade/sugar-farmer, 5.4, DFID data, Adapted from DFID website, reproduced with permission, 5.4; Adapted from 'http://www.oxfam.org.uk/resources/ethiopia.html 11/3/09 with the permission of Oxfam GB, Oxfam House, John Smith Drive, Cowley, Oxford OX4 2JY UK www.oxfam.org.uk Oxfam GB does not necessarily endorse any text or activities that accompany the material, nor has it approved the adapted text, 5.4C; Adapted from 'http://www.oxfam.org.uk/coolplanet/kidsweb/world/ethiopia/ethoxf4.htm 11/3/09 with the permission of Oxfam GB, Oxfam House, John Smith Drive, Cowley, Oxford OX4 2JY UK www.oxfam.org.uk Oxfam GB does not necessarily endorse any text or activities that accompany, 5.4; short extract adapted from www.mangroveactionproject.org Reprinted with permission, 5.4G; Extract from 'The Millenium Development Goals' United Nations. Reprinted with permission, 6.1E; Short extract from THE KIBBUTZ: AWAKENING FROM UTOPIA by Daniel Gavron, 2000. Reprinted with permission of Rowman & Littlefield Publishers, Inc, 6.4; Confessions of a househusband' from The Daily Telegraph, 21 November, 2007. Reprinted with permission, 6.5, 7.1K, 7.3A, 7.3D, 7.4D, 7.4E, 7.4I, 7.4J, 8.5 A, B, D, 8.5C, 8.5E, 8.5F ; Crown Copyright materials are reproduced with permission of the controller, Office of Public Sector Information OPSI, 7.1 Figures adapted from HRM Guide website www.hrmguide.net. Reprinted with permission, 7.4B; Figures from Equal Opportunities Commission 2007. Reprinted with permission.

Index